Investing in Bonds

A Wiley Brand

Investing
in Bonds

Second Edition

by Russell Wild

Investing in Bonds For Dummies®, Second Edition

Published by: **John Wiley & Sons, Inc.**, 111 River Street, Hoboken, NJ 07030-5774, www.wiley.com

Copyright © 2023 by John Wiley & Sons, Inc., Hoboken, New Jersey

Published simultaneously in Canada

For general information on our other products and services, please contact our Customer Care Department within the U.S. at 877-762-2974, outside the U.S. at 317-572-3993, or fax 317-572-4002. For technical support, please visit https://hub.wiley.com/community/support/dummies.

Wiley publishes in a variety of print and electronic formats and by print-on-demand. Some material included with standard print versions of this book may not be included in e-books or in print-on-demand. If this book refers to media such as a CD or DVD that is not included in the version you purchased, you may download this material at http://booksupport.wiley.com. For more information about Wiley products, visit www.wiley.com.

Library of Congress Control Number: 2023939562

ISBN 978-1-394-20097-9 (pbk); ISBN 978-1-394-20099-3 (ebk); ISBN 978-1-394-20098-6 (ebk)

SKY10051366_071823

Contents at a Glance

Contents at a Glance

Table of Contents

Introduction

A bond is basically an IOU. You lend your money to Uncle Sam, to General Electric, to Microsoft, to the city in which you live — to whatever entity issues the bonds — and that entity promises to pay you a certain rate of return in exchange for borrowing your money. Bond investing is very different from stock investing, where you purchase shares in a company, become an alleged partial owner of that company, and then start to pray that the company turns a profit and the CEO doesn't pocket it all.

Stocks and bonds complement each other like peanut butter and jelly. Bonds are the peanut butter that can keep your jelly from dripping to the floor. They're the life rafts that can keep your portfolio afloat when the investment seas get choppy. And yes, bonds are handy as a source of steady income, but, contrary to popular myth, that shouldn't be their major role in most portfolios.

Bonds are the sweethearts that may have saved your grandparents from selling apples on the street during the hungry 1930s. (Note that I'm not talking about high-yield "junk" bonds here.) They're the babies that may have saved your 401(k) from devastation during the three growly bear-market years on Wall Street that started this century. In 2008, high-quality bonds were just about the only investment you could've made that wound up in the black at a time when world markets frighteningly resembled the Biblical Red Sea. And in February and March of 2020, when COVID-19 unleashed itself upon the world and the Dow dropped 37 percent over the course of several days? Yup, bonds were the place to be.

Bonds belong in nearly every portfolio. Whether they belong in *your* portfolio is a question that this book will help you answer.

About This Book

Allow the following pages to serve as your guide to understanding bonds, choosing the right bonds or bond funds, getting the best deals on your purchases, and achieving the best prices when you sell. You'll also find out how to work bonds into a powerful, well-diversified portfolio that serves your financial goals much better (I promise) than day-trading stock options or attempting to make a profit flipping real estate in your spare time.

I present to you, in easy-to-understand language, the sometimes complex, even mystical and magical world of bonds. I explain such concepts as bond maturity, duration, coupon rate, callability (yikes), and yield. And I show you the differences among the many kinds of bonds, such as Treasurys, agency bonds, corporates, munis, zeroes, convertibles, strips, and Treasury Inflation-Protected Securities (TIPS).

I also fill you in on some important goings-on in the bond world over the past decade. Notably, I cover the COVID crash of early 2020 and the "rush to safety" that made bonds, especially U.S. Treasury bonds, the belle of the ball. I also discuss less cheerful times for bonds, starting with the super-low interest rates of the past decade or so and culminating in early to mid-2022 with a sudden, steep rise in interest rates, bringing a serious sag in bond prices.

In this book, you discover the mistakes that many bond investors make, the traps that some wily bond brokers lay for the uninitiated, and the heartbreak that can befall those who buy certain bonds without first doing their homework. (Don't worry — I walk you through how to do your homework.) You find out how to mix and match your bonds with other kinds of assets — such as stocks and real estate — taking advantage of the latest in investment research to help you maximize your returns and minimize your risk.

If you've ever read one of these black-and-yellow *For Dummies* books before, you know what to expect. This isn't a book you need to read from front to back. Feel free to jump back and forth to glean whatever information you think will help you the most. No proctor with bifocals will pop out of the air, Harry Potter–style, to test you at the end. You needn't commit all the details to memory now — or ever. Keep this reference book for years to come as your little acorn of a bond portfolio grows into a mighty oak.

Most of the heavy technical matter is tucked neatly into the shaded sidebars. But if any technicalities make it into the main text, I give you a heads up with a Technical Stuff icon. That's where you can skip over or speed read — or choose to get dizzy. Your call!

Keep in mind that when this book was printed, some web addresses may have needed to break across two lines of text. Wherever that's the case, rest assured that this book uses no any extra characters (hyphens or other doohickeys) to indicate the break. So, when going to one of these web addresses, just type in exactly what you see in this book. Pretend that the line break doesn't exist.

Foolish Assumptions

If you feel you truly need to start from scratch in the world of investments, perhaps the best place is the latest edition of *Investing For Dummies* by Eric Tyson (Wiley). But the book you're holding in your hands is only a smidgen above that one in terms of assumptions about your investment savvy. I assume that you're intelligent, that you have a few bucks to invest, and that you have a basic education in math (and maybe a rudimentary knowledge of economics) — that's it.

In other words, even if your investing experience to date consists of opening a savings account, balancing a checkbook, and reading a few Suze Orman columns, you should still be able to follow along. Oh, and for those of you who are already buying and selling bonds and feel completely comfortable in the world of fixed income, I'm assuming that you, too, can learn something from this book.

Icons Used in This Book

The margins of this book are filled with little images. In the *Dummies* universe, these are known as *icons*, and they signal certain (I hope) exciting things going on in the accompanying text.

TIP

Although this is a how-to book, it also has plenty of whys and wherefores. Any paragraph accompanied by the Tip icon, however, is guaranteed to be at least 99.99 percent how-to.

REMEMBER

Read twice! The Remember icon indicates that something important is being said and is really worth committing to memory.

The world of bond investing — although generally not as risky as the world of stock investing — still offers pitfalls galore. Wherever you see the Warning icon, you know that danger of losing money lies ahead.

If you don't really care how to calculate the after-tax present value of a bond selling at 98, yielding 4.76 percent, maturing in nine months, and subject to the Alternate Minimum Tax (AMT), but instead you're just looking to gain a broad understanding of bond investing, feel free to skip or skim the denser paragraphs that are marked with this icon.

Where to Go from Here

Where would you *like* to go from here? If you want, start at the beginning of this book. If you're mostly interested in municipal bonds, hey, no one says you can't jump right to Chapter 3 — it's entirely your call. Maybe start by skimming the table of contents or the index.

1

Getting Started with Bond Investing

bonds are

- » Knowing why some bonds pay more than others
- » Meeting the major bond issuers
- » Considering individual bonds versus bond funds
- » Examining bonds' successes and failures
- » Recognizing the role bonds play in today's financial markets and beyond

Chapter **1**
Focusing on Bond Fundamentals

Long before I ever knew what a bond was, I agreed to lend $5 to Tommy Potts, a blond, goofy-looking kid in my seventh-grade class. This was the first time I'd ever lent money to anyone. I can't recall why Tommy needed the $5, but he did promise to repay me, and he was my pal.

Weeks went by, then months, and I couldn't get my money back from Tommy, no matter how much I bellyached. Finally, I decided to go to a higher authority, also known as Tommy's dad. I figured that Mr. Potts would give Tommy a stern lecture on the importance of maintaining his credit and good name. Then Mr. Potts would either make Tommy cough up my money, or he'd make restitution himself.

"Er, Mr. Potts," I said, "I lent Tommy five bucks, and —"

"You lent *him* money?" Mr. Potts interrupted, pointing his finger at his deadbeat 12-year-old son, who, if I recall correctly, at that point had turned over one of his pet turtles and was spinning it like a top.

"Um, yes, Mr. Potts — $5."

Mr. Potts neither lectured nor reached for his wallet. Instead, he erupted into boisterous laughter. "You lent *him* money!" he bellowed repeatedly, laughing, slapping his thighs, and pointing to his turtle-spinning son. "You lent *him* money! *Ha . . . ha . . . ha . . . .*"

And that, dear reader, was my very first experience as a creditor. I never saw a nickel from Tommy, in either interest or returned principal. Oh, yes, I've learned a lot since then.

Understanding What Makes a Bond a Bond

Now suppose that Tommy Potts, instead of being a goofy kid in the seventh grade, were the U.S. government. Or the city of Philadelphia. Or Procter & Gamble. Tommy, in his powerful new incarnation, needs to raise not $5 but $50 million. So, Tommy decides to issue a bond. A bond is really not much more than an IOU with a serial number. People in suits, to sound impressive, sometimes call bonds *debt securities* or *fixed-income securities.*

A bond is always issued with a specific *face amount,* also called the *principal* or *par value.* Most often, simply because it's convention, bonds are issued with face amounts of $1,000. So, to raise $50 million, Tommy would have to issue 50,000 bonds, each selling at $1,000 par. Of course, he would then have to go out and find investors to buy his bonds.

REMEMBER

Every bond pays a certain rate of interest, and typically that rate is fixed over the life of the bond (hence, *fixed-income* securities). The *life* of the bond is the period of time until maturity. *Maturity,* in the lingo of financial people, is the date that the principal is due to be paid back. (Oh, yeah, the bond world is full of jargon.) The *rate of interest* is a percentage of the face amount and is typically (again, simply because of convention) paid out twice a year.

So, if a corporation or government issues a $1,000 bond, paying 3.5 percent interest, that corporation or government promises to fork over to the bondholder $35 a year — or, in most cases, $17.50 twice a year. Then, when the bond matures — be it 1, 10, or 20 years down the road — the corporation or government repays the $1,000 to the bondholder.

In some cases, you can buy a bond directly from the issuer and sell it back directly to the issuer. But you're more likely to buy a bond through a brokerage house or bank. You can also buy a basket of bonds through a company that packages bonds into bond funds, mutual funds, or exchange-traded funds (ETFs). These brokerage houses and fund companies will most certainly take a piece of the pie — and sometimes a quite sizable piece.

So far, so good?

In short, dealing in bonds isn't really all that different from the deal I worked out with Tommy Potts. It's just a bit more formal. Plus, the entire business is regulated by the Securities and Exchange Commission (SEC), among other regulatory authorities, and most bondholders — unlike me in the seventh grade — wind up getting paid back!

Choosing your time frame

REMEMBER

Almost all bonds these days are issued with life spans, or maturities, of up to 30 years. Few people are interested in lending their money for longer than that, and people young enough to think more than 30 years ahead rarely have enough money to lend. In bond lingo, bonds with a maturity of less than five years are typically referred to as *short-term bonds,* bonds with maturities of 5 to 12 years are called *intermediate-term bonds,* and bonds with maturities of 12 years or longer are called *long-term bonds.* With specific reference to Treasury securities, zero- to one-year maturities are bills, one- to ten-year maturities are notes, and ten years and longer are bonds.

In general (sorry, but you're going to read those words a lot in this book; bond investing comes with few hard-and-fast rules), the longer the maturity, the greater the interest rate paid. That's because bond buyers generally (there I go again) demand more compensation the longer they agree to tie up their money and assume whatever additional risk may come to bear over the years.

At the same time, bond issuers are willing to fork over more interest in return for the privilege of holding onto your money longer.

It's the same theory and practice with bank certificates of deposit (CDs): Typically, a two-year CD pays more than a one-year CD, which, in turn, pays more than a six-month CD.

The different rates that are paid on short-, intermediate-, and long-term bonds make up what's known as the *yield curve. Yield* refers to the annual payout on your investment. Because longer term bonds tend to pay more, the yield curve, when seen on a page, typically slopes up to the right. But sometimes the curve can be flat or, in rare instances, even slope downward (that's called *yield-curve inversion*). In Chapter 2, I provide an in-depth discussion of interest rates, bond maturity, and the all-important yield curve.

Picking who you trust to hold your money

Let's consider again the analogy between bonds and bank CDs. Both tend to pay higher rates of interest if you're willing to tie up your money for a longer period of time. But that's where the similarity ends.

When you give your money to a savings bank to plunk into a CD, that money — your principal — is almost certainly guaranteed (up to $250,000 per account, per person, per ownership registration) by the Federal Deposit Insurance Corporation (FDIC). You can choose your bank because it's close to your house or because it gives lollipops to your kids, but if solid economics are your guide, your best bet is to open your CD where you're going to get FDIC insurance (almost all banks carry it) and the highest rate of interest. End of story. *Per person, per ownership registration,* in case you're wondering, means that a joint account would be insured up to $500,000.

REMEMBER

Things aren't so simple in the world of bonds, where the FDIC does *not* insure your investment. In this world — and I can't emphasize this enough — a higher rate of interest isn't always the best deal. When you fork over your money to buy a bond, your principal, in most cases, is guaranteed only by the issuer of the bond. That "guarantee" is only as solid as the issuer itself. (Remember my seventh-grade experience?) That's why

U.S. Treasury bonds (guaranteed by the U.S. government) pay one interest rate, Microsoft bonds pay another rate, and Carnival Corp. bonds pay yet another rate. Can you guess where you'll get the highest rate of interest?

You'd expect the highest rate of interest to be paid by Carnival Corp. (Currently, in large part thanks to COVID-19, it's a somewhat shaky company.) Why? Because lending your money to the cruise line involves the risk that your money may sail off into oblivion. In other words, if the company sinks, you may lose a good chunk of your principal. That risk requires any shaky company to pay a relatively high rate of interest. Without being paid some kind of risk premium, you'd be unlikely to lend your money to a company that may not be able to pay you back. Conversely, the U.S. government, which has the power to levy taxes and print money, isn't going bankrupt anytime soon. Therefore, U.S. Treasury bonds, which are said to carry only an infinitely small risk of default, tend to pay the most modest interest rates. Often, the interest rate paid on Treasury bonds is referred to as the *risk-free rate*.

If Tommy Potts were to come to me for a loan today, needless to say, I wouldn't lend him money. Or if I did, I'd require a huge risk premium, along with some kind of collateral (more than his pet turtles). Bonds issued by the likes of Tommy Potts or Carnival Corp. — bonds that carry a relatively high risk of default — are commonly called *high-yield* or *junk bonds*. Bonds issued by solid companies and governments that carry little risk of default are commonly referred to as *investment-grade bonds*.

There are many, many shades of gray in determining the quality and nature of a bond. It's not unlike wine tasting in that regard. In Chapters 2 and 11, I give specific tips for "tasting" bonds and choosing the finest vintages for your portfolio.

Distinguishing bonds, stocks, and cryptocurrencies

Aside from the maturity and the quality of a bond, other factors can weigh heavily in how well a bond purchase treats you. In this book, I introduce you to such bond characteristics as *callability*, *duration*, and *correlation*, and I explain how the winds of the economy — and even the whims of the bond-buying public — can affect the returns on your bond portfolio.

REMEMBER

For the moment, I simply want to point out that, by and large, bonds' most salient characteristic — and the one thing that most bonds share — is a certain stability and predictability, well above and beyond that of most other investments. Because you are, in most cases, receiving a steady stream of income, and because you expect to get your principal back in one piece, bonds tend to be more conservative investments than, say, stocks, commodities, cryptocurrencies, and collectibles. In a typical year, the value of investment-grade bonds may rise or fall no more than the stock market will on an average day (or some cryptocurrencies will in an average hour!).

Is conservative a good thing? Sometimes. Sometimes not. It's true that many people (men more often than women, according to solid research) invest their money too aggressively, just as many people (regardless of gender) invest their money too conservatively. The appropriate portfolio formula depends on what your individual investment goals are and your personal taste for risk. I help you figure these out in Chapter 10.

Why Hold Bonds? (Spoiler Alert: It Isn't to Make You Rich)

In the real world, plenty of people own bonds — but often the wrong bonds in the wrong amounts and for the wrong reasons. Some people have too many bonds, making their portfolios too conservative; others have too few bonds, making their stock-heavy portfolios too volatile. Some have taxable bonds where they'd be better off with tax-free bonds, and vice versa. Others are so far out on a limb with shaky bonds that they may as well be lending their money to Tommy Potts.

The first step in building a bond portfolio — or any portfolio, for that matter — is to have clear investment objectives. ("I want to make money" — something I hear from clients all the time — is *not* a clear investment objective!) I help you develop clear objectives in Chapter 8. In the meantime, I want you to consider some of the typical reasons — both good and bad — why people buy and hold bonds.

Identifying the best reason to buy bonds: Diversification

Most people buy bonds because they perceive a need for steady income, and they think of bonds as the best way to get income without risking principal. This is one of the most common mistakes investors make: compartmentalization. They think of principal and interest as two separate and distinct money pools. They're not.

Let me clarify: Joe Typical buys a bond for $1,000. At the end of six months, he collects an interest payment —income — of, say, $25. He spends the $25, figuring that his principal (the $1,000) is left intact to continue earning money. At the same time, Joe buys a stock for $1,000. At the end of six months, the price of his stock and, therefore, the value of his investment has grown to, say, $1,025. Does he spend the $25? No way. Joe reckons that spending any part of the $1,025 is spending principal and will reduce the amount of money he has left working for him.

In truth, whether Joe spends his interest or his principal, whether he spends his income or generates cash flow from the sale of stock, he's left with the *very same* $1,000 in his portfolio.

REMEMBER

Thinking of bonds, or bond funds, as the best — or only — source of cash flow or income can be a mistake. Bonds are a better source of steady income than stocks because bonds, in theory (and usually in practice), always pay interest; stocks may or may not pay dividends and may or may not appreciate in price. Bonds also may be a logical choice for people who need a certain sum of money at a certain point in the future — such as college tuition or cash for a new home — and can't risk a loss.

But unless you absolutely need a steady source of income, or a certain sum on a certain date, bonds may not be such a hot investment. Over the long haul, they have tended to return much less than stocks. I revisit this issue, and talk much more about the differences between stocks and bonds, in Chapter 10.

REMEMBER

For now, the point I want to make is that the far better reason to own bonds, for most people, is to *diversify* a portfolio. Simply put, bonds tend to zig when stocks zag, and vice versa. The key to truly successful investing is to have at least several different *asset classes* — different investment animals with different characteristics — all of which can be expected to yield positive long-term returns but that do not all move up and down together.

There are very few assets classes — if any! — that serve as valiantly as bonds where it comes to diversifying a portfolio of stocks. History proves this, and you don't need to go back very far. In 2008, when the S&P 500 lost nearly 37 percent, U.S. Treasurys rose by 20 percent.

Going for the cash

Bonds aren't very popular with the get-rich-quick crowd — for good reason. The only people who get rich off bonds are generally the insiders who trade huge amounts and can clip the little guy. Nonetheless, certain categories of bonds — high-yield corporate (junk) bonds, for example — have been known to produce impressive gains.

WARNING

High-yield bonds may have a role — a limited one — in your portfolio. But know up front that high-yield bonds don't offer the potential long-term returns of stocks, and neither do they offer the portfolio protection of investment-grade bonds. Instead of zigging when the stock market is zagging, many high-yield bonds tend to zag right along with your stock portfolio. Be careful!

Some high-yield bonds are better than others — and they're held by relatively few people. I recommend those in Chapter 3.

REMEMBER

Even high-quality, investment-grade bonds are often purchased with the wrong intentions. A U.S. Treasury bond, though generally thought to be the safest bond of all, *doesn't guarantee your return of principal unless you hold it to maturity.* If you buy a 20-year bond and you want to know for sure that you're going to get your principal back, you'd better plan to hold it for 20 years. If you sell it before it matures, you may lose a bundle. Bond prices, especially on long-term bonds — yes, even Uncle Sam's bonds — can fluctuate greatly. I discuss the reasons for this fluctuation in Chapter 2.

I also discuss the complicated and often misunderstood concept of bond returns. You may buy a 20-year U.S. Treasury bond yielding 3 percent, and you may hold it for 20 years, to full maturity. Yes, you'll get your principal back, but you may actually earn more or less than 3 percent interest on your initial investment. It's complicated, but I explain this variation in a way you can understand — I promise! — in Chapter 2.

Introducing the Major Players in the Bond Market

Every year, millions — yes, literally millions — of bonds are issued by thousands of different governments, government agencies, municipalities, financial institutions, and corporations. They all pay interest. In many cases, the interest rates aren't all that much different from each other. In most cases, the risk that the issuer will *default* — fail to pay back your principal — is minute. So, why, as a lender of money, would you want to choose one type of issuer over another? Glad you asked!

Following are some important considerations about each of the major kinds of bonds, categorized by who issues them. I'm just going to scratch the surface right now. For a more in-depth discussion, see Chapter 3.

Supporting your Uncle Sam with Treasury bonds

Politicians like raising money by selling bonds, as opposed to raising taxes, because voters hate taxes. Of course, when the government issues bonds, it promises to repay the bond buyers over time. The more bonds the government issues, the greater its debt.

At the time of writing, the debt of the United States government is slightly more than $30 trillion: almost $91,000 for every U.S. citizen. (Yikes!) The interest payments on that debt currently total more than $560 billion a year.

Some economists argue that the national debt will lead us to ruin. Others argue that because the government can print money, the only real danger of running too long in the red is inflation, and until there's runaway inflation, we needn't worry about it. We're not going to solve this debate here. Our focus is on the role that Treasury bonds may play in your portfolio.

In Chapter 3, I describe all the many kinds of Treasury bonds — from EE bonds to I bonds and T-bills to Treasury Inflation-Protected Securities (TIPS) — and the unique characteristics of each. For the moment, I merely want to point out that all of them are backed by the "full faith and credit" of the federal government.

Despite its huge debt, the United States of America isn't going bankrupt anytime soon. And for that reason, Treasury bonds have traditionally been referred to as "risk-free." Careful, though: The prices of Treasury bonds still fluctuate.

REMEMBER

When bond experts speak of Treasury bonds as having no risk, or almost no risk, what they mean is that the bonds have no *credit* risk. But Treasury bonds are very much subject to the other kinds of risk that beset most other bonds: interest-rate risk, inflation risk, and reinvestment risk. I discuss these types of risk in Chapter 9.

Collecting corporate debt

Bonds issued by for-profit companies are riskier than government bonds but tend to compensate for that added risk by paying higher rates of interest. (If they didn't, why would you or anyone else want to take the extra risk?) For the past few decades, corporate bonds in the aggregate have tended to pay about a percentage point higher than Treasurys of similar maturity. Since 2008, this spread has broadened, with ten-year corporate bonds paying about a percentage point and a half more than their governmental counterparts.

TIP

As you'll discover, I'm a big fan of diversification. It's especially important to diversify when dealing with any kind of investment that comes with default risk. For that reason, I don't like to see people plunk too great a percentage of their portfolios into any individual corporate bond. Wealthier investors — those with portfolios of $1 million or more — can diversify by buying a collection of bonds. Savvy investors can temper their risks by familiarizing themselves with bond ratings and researching the issuing companies' bottom lines. But I generally advocate bond ownership — especially when it comes to corporate bonds — in bond funds. I discuss these funds at the end of this chapter and again, in greater depth, in Chapter 5.

WARNING

Oh, one more little thing about corporate bonds for the moment: They tend to get *called* a lot. That means that the corporation changes its incorporated mind about wanting your money and suddenly throws it back at you, redeeming the bond. Bond calls tend to happen when rates have fallen, and that's no fun. They add a dose of unpredictability to what should be a predictable investment.

Demystifying government and government-like agencies

Federal agencies, such as the Government National Mortgage Association (Ginnie Mae), and government-sponsored enterprises (GSEs), such as the Federal Home Loan Banks, issue a good chunk of the bonds on the market. Even though these bonds can differ quite a bit, they're collectively referred to as *agency bonds.* What we call agencies are sometimes part of the actual government, and sometimes a cross between government and private industry. In the case of the Federal National Mortgage Association (Fannie Mae) and the Federal Home Loan Mortgage Corporation (Freddie Mac), they have been, following the mortgage crisis of 2008, somewhat in limbo.

To varying degrees, Congress and the Treasury would serve as protective big brothers if one of these agencies or GSEs were to take a financial beating and couldn't pay off its debt obligations.

In general, agency bonds are considered the next-safest thing to Treasury bonds. As such, the interest paid on these bonds is typically just a smidgen higher than the interest rate you would get on Treasurys of similar maturity, although in recent times, you can get a smidgen-plus. At the time of this writing, agency bonds maturing in 2032 were yielding about 4.16 percent versus 2.96 percent for Treasurys.

REMEMBER

By convention when financial people (I qualify) write about "Ginnie Mae bonds" or "Treasurys," and there's no specific mention of maturity, you can assume that the writer is referring to bonds with a ten-year maturity. That's just the customary default. It's like when a recipe calls for "sugar" without stipulating what kind of sugar. You just instinctively reach for white sugar.

I discuss agency bonds — the traditional kind of bonds these agencies offer — in Chapter 3. But many bonds that the federal agencies issue or guarantee are distinctly nontraditional in that they represent an ownership interest in pools of mortgages. These bonds, called *mortgage-backed securities*, are more complicated than traditional bonds. And I'm sorry to say that many people who invest in them haven't the foggiest idea what they're investing in — although some found out the hard way in late 2007 and 2008, when some of their mortgage-backed securities took a serious hit. Find out more about these babies in Chapter 3 as well.

Going cosmopolitan with municipal bonds

The bond market, unlike the stock market, is overwhelmingly institutional. In other words, most bonds are held by governments, insurance companies, money/asset managers, pension funds, and endowment funds. The only exception — the only kind of bond more popular with individual investors than institutions — is the municipal bond.

Municipal bonds (*munis* for short) are issued by cities, states, and counties. They're used to raise money for either the general day-to-day needs of the citizenry (schools, roads, sewer systems) or for specific projects (a new bridge, a sports stadium).

Munis' popularity with individual investors may be due in small part to the warm and fuzzy feelings to be had by investing in local infrastructure. But truth be told, their popularity stems much more from their special tax status.

REMEMBER

Interest on most municipal bonds is exempt from federal income tax. Interest on municipal bonds issued by your own city or state may be exempt from both federal *and* local taxes. Traditionally, the interest rates paid have been modest, but many individual investors — especially those in the higher tax brackets — often get a better after-tax return on municipal bonds than on comparable taxable bonds. In recent years, munis have tended to yield slightly more than Treasurys — even on a before-tax basis.

Like corporate bonds, but unlike Treasurys, municipal bonds are often subject to being called. You may *think* you're buying a ten-year investment, but you may be forced to relinquish the bond in two years instead. (Bond brokers must, per regulations, reveal this "defect," and they usually do, but they certainly don't highlight it.)

REMEMBER

Municipal bonds tend to be less risky than corporate bonds but not as safe as Treasury and agency bonds. Just as corporate bonds are given ratings, so are municipal bonds. It's important to know before investing whether the local government issuing a bond has the wherewithal to pay back your principal. Cities don't go bankrupt often, but it does happen. And some pundits have expressed fears that, in the future, more municipalities than ever may declare bankruptcy. (That fear is part of what's driven up the yield on these bonds.) I reveal more on munis in Chapter 3.

Buying Solo or Buying in Bulk

One of the big questions about bond investing that I help you answer later in this book is whether to invest in individual bonds or bond funds.

REMEMBER

I generally advocate bond funds — both bond mutual funds and ETFs. Mutual funds and ETFs represent baskets of securities (usually stocks or bonds, or sometimes both) and allow for instant and easy portfolio diversification. You do, however, need to be careful about which funds you choose. Not all are created equal — far, far from it.

I outline the pros and cons of owning individual bonds versus bond funds in Chapter 11. Here, I give you a quick sneak preview of that discussion.

Picking and choosing individual bonds

Individual bonds offer investors the opportunity to really fine-tune a fixed-income portfolio. With individual bonds, you can choose exactly what you want in terms of bond quality, maturity, and taxability.

For larger investors — especially those who do their homework — individual bonds may also be more economical than your average bond fund. But that's only true for investors who are up on the latest advances in bond buying and selling.

Once upon a time, any buyers or sellers of individual bonds had to take a giant leap of faith that their bond broker wasn't trimming too much meat off the bone. No more. In Chapter 4, I show you how to find out exactly how much your bond broker is making off you — or trying to make off you. I show you how to compare comparable bonds to get the best deals. And I discuss some popular bond strategies, including the most popular and potent one — *laddering* your bonds, which means staggering the maturities of the bonds you buy.

Going with a bond fund or funds

Investors now have a choice of hundreds of bond mutual funds and ETFs. Most have the same basic drawbacks: management expenses and a certain degree of unpredictability above and beyond individual bonds. But even so, many make for good investments.

Where to begin your fund search? I promise to help you weed out the losers and pick the best. As you'll discover (or as you know already if you've read my book *Exchange-Traded Funds For Dummies* [Wiley]), I'm a strong proponent of buying *index funds* — mutual funds or ETFs that seek to provide exposure to an entire asset class (such as bonds or stocks) with little trading and low expenses. Especially now with interest rates so low, keeping your expenses rock-bottom is crucial. Index funds are the way to go for most investors to get the bond exposure they need. I suggest some good bond index funds, as well as other bond funds, in Chapter 5.

TIP

If you'd like to know more about funds in general, pick up copies of the latest editions of *Exchange-Traded Funds For Dummies* and Eric Tyson's *Mutual Funds For Dummies* (Wiley).

The Triumphs and Failures of Fixed-Income Investing

Picture yourself in the year 1926. Calvin Coolidge occupies the White House. Ford's Model T can be bought for $200. Charles Lindbergh is gearing up to fly across the Atlantic. And you, having just arrived from your journey back in time, brush the time-travel dust off your shoulders and reach into your pocket. You figure that if you invest $100, you can then return to the present, cash in on your investment, and live like a corrupt king. So, you plunk down the $100 into some long-term government bonds.

Fast-forward to the present, and you discover that your original investment of $100 is now worth $16,180. It grew at an average annual compound rate of return of about 5.5 percent. (In fact, that's just what happened in the real world.) Even though you aren't rich, $16,180 doesn't sound too shabby. But you need to look at the whole picture.

Beating inflation, but not by very much

Yes, you enjoyed a return of 5.5 percent a year, but while your bonds were making money, inflation was eating it away — at a rate of about 2.9 percent a year. What that means is that your

$16,180 is really worth only about $1,070 in 1926 dollars. Your investment, your $100, in *real* terms (inflation-adjusted dollars) actually grew about 10.7 times.

To put that another way, your real (after-inflation) yearly rate of return for long-term government bonds was about 2.53 percent. In about half of the 95 years, your bond investment either didn't grow at all in real-dollar terms or actually lost money.

Compare that scenario to an investment in stocks. Had you invested the very same $100 in 1926 in the S&P 500 (500 of the largest U.S. company stocks), your investment would've grown to $855,668 in *nominal* (preinflation) dollars. In 1926 dollars, that would be $56,200. The average nominal return was 10 percent, and the average real annual rate of return for the bundle of stocks was 6.9 percent. Your investment in real dollars grew not 10.7 times (the case with bonds), but about 562 times. (Those rates ignore both income taxes and the fact that you can't invest directly in an index, but they're still valid for comparison purposes.)

So, which would you rather have invested in: stocks or bonds? Obviously, stocks were the way to go. In comparison, bonds seem to have failed to provide adequate return.

Providing help in times of distress

But hold on. There's another side to the story. Yes, stocks clobbered bonds over the course of the past nine or ten decades. But who makes an investment and leaves it untouched for that long? Rip Van Winkle maybe. But outside of fairy-tale characters, no one does. Real people in the real world usually invest for much shorter periods. And there have been some shorter periods over the past nine or ten decades when stocks have taken some stomach-wrenching falls.

The worst of all falls, of course, was during the Great Depression that began with the stock market crash of 1929. Any money that your grandparents or great-grandparents may have had in the stock market in 1929 was worth not even half as much four years later. Over the next decade, stock prices would go up and down, but Grandma and Grandpa wouldn't see their $100 back until about 1943. Had they planned to retire in that period, well, they may have had to sell a few apples on the street just to make ends meet.

A bond portfolio, however, would've helped enormously. Had Grandma and Grandpa had a diversified portfolio of, say, 70 percent stocks and 30 percent long-term government bonds, they would've been pinched by the Great Depression but not destroyed. Although $70 of stock in 1929 was worth only $33 four years later, $30 in long-term government bonds would've been worth $47. All told, instead of having a $100 all-stock portfolio fall to $46, their 70/30 diversified portfolio would've fallen only to $80. Big difference!

Closer to our present time, a $10,000 investment in the S&P 500 at the beginning of 2000 was worth only $5,800 after three years of a growly bear market. But during those same three years, long-term U.S. government bonds soared. A $10,000 70/30 (stock/bond) portfolio during those three years would've been worth $8,210 at the end. Another big difference!

In 2008, as you're well aware, stocks took another big nosedive. The S&P 500 tumbled 37 percent in that dismal calendar year. And long-term U.S. government bonds? Once again, our fixed-income friends came to the rescue, rising nearly 26 percent. In fact, nearly every investment imaginable, including all the traditional stock-market hedges, from real estate to commodities to foreign equities, fell hard that year. Treasury bonds, however, continued to stand tall.

And closest to home, when it became clear that the world was facing a COVID-19 pandemic, from February through the end of March 2020, the S&P declined over the course of a month by 34 percent. Over that same period, the iShares 7–10 Year Treasury Bond ETF (IEF) increased in value by roughly 6 percent.

REMEMBER

Clearly, long-term government bonds can, and often do, rise to the challenge during times of economic turmoil. Why are bad times often good for many bonds? I explain the reasons for this phenomenon in Chapters 2 and 3. For now, know that bonds have historically been a best friend to investors when investors have most needed a friend. Given that bonds have saved numerous stock investors from impoverishment, bond investing in the past eight to nine decades may be seen not as a miserable failure but as a huge success.

Realizing How Crucial Bonds Are Today

I could talk about the importance of corporate debt to the growth of the economy, the way in which municipal bonds help to repair roads and build bridges, and how Ginnie Mae and Fannie Mae bonds help to provide housing to the masses, but I think I'll just let this one sentence suffice. This is, after all, not a book on macroeconomics and social policy but a book on personal investing. So, allow me to address the crucial role that bonds play in the lives of individual investors — people like you and me.

With roughly 25 percent of their portfolios invested in fixed income, U.S. households' economic welfare is closely tied to the fortunes of the bond market.

REMEMBER

I would argue that with the demise of the traditional pension over the past decades, bond investing became more important than ever. Back when you knew your company would take care of you in old age, you may have played footloose and fancy-free with your portfolio without having to worry that a scrambled nest egg might mean you couldn't afford to buy eggs. Today, a well-tuned portfolio — that almost certainly includes a good helping of bonds — can make the difference between living on Easy Street and living *on* the street.

Keep in mind that most of the money in the bond market today is institutional money. If you have a life insurance policy, chances are that your life insurance company has most of your future payoff invested in bonds. If you have money in your state's prepaid college tuition program, chances are that your money is similarly indirectly invested in bonds. If you're one of the fortunate people whose employer still offers a pension, chances are that your employer has your future pension payout invested in bonds.

In total, about $124 trillion is invested in bonds worldwide at the time of this writing, and the amount is growing year by year. Many economists speculate that as the baby boomer generation continues to move into retirement, the demand for income-generating investments like bonds will only grow. If you live and work in a developed nation, your economic well-being is much more closely tied to the bond markets than you think.

Viewing Recent Developments, Largely for the Better

As the prices of everything from groceries and gas to college tuition and medical care continue to climb, it's nice to know that at least two things on this planet have gotten cheaper in the past few years: computers and bond trades. And as any seasoned bond investor will tell you, saving money on trades isn't the only exciting development of late. Here are some others worth noting:

>> **New and better bond funds:** According to Morningstar Direct, you have almost 2,500 bond funds in which you can invest at the time of this writing. (If I were to include various "classes" of these funds, such as many mutual-fund companies offer, basically for small investors and large investors, the number would be well over 7,000.) Of these, roughly 400 are *bond index funds* — funds that seek to capture the returns of an entire swath of the bond market — which, from my vantage point, tend to be the best options for most bond investors. These funds carry an average yearly expense ratio of 26 basis points (26/100 of 1 percent), which is way, way less than most bond funds. (The average for nonindex bond mutual funds is 85 basis points.)

TIP

The newest kid on the block, ETFs — somewhat similar to mutual funds — are the greatest thing to happen to bond investing in a very long time. ETFs allow small investors to invest like the big boys, with extremely low expenses and no minimum investment requirements. As of this printing, more than 500 bond ETFs exist. Some of them carry annual expense ratios so low as to be laughable. (How often is it that you get to laugh all the way to the bank?)

I discuss both ETFs and mutual funds in Chapter 5.

>> **Greater access to information:** One of the advantages of all index funds, but especially ETFs over traditional actively managed mutual funds, is their relative *transparency*. That means that when you invest in an ETF, you know exactly what you're buying. Traditional mutual funds aren't required to reveal their specific investments; you may think you're buying one thing and end up with another.

When it comes to buying and selling individual bonds, it's as if a muddy pond has been transformed into a glass aquarium. Not long ago, a bond broker would give you a price for a bond, and you'd have absolutely no idea how fair a deal you were getting. Nowadays, you can search online and usually get a very good idea of how fair a deal you're getting, how much the broker is making, and whether better deals can be had. I give you a complete tour of the aquarium in Chapter 4.

>> **The expansion of Uncle Sam's treasury chest:** If you're going to invest in individual bonds, U.S. Treasury bonds may make the most sense. The Treasury now has a website (www.treasurydirect.gov) where you can buy its bonds directly and not have to deal with any brokers whatsoever, nor will you need to fork over any kind of markup. I walk you through the process in Chapter 3.

TIP

One special kind of Treasury bond — TIPS — has been in existence since the mid-1990s. An exciting development in the world of bonds, TIPS offer only modest interest rates, but the principal is readjusted twice annually to keep up with inflation. TIPS represent an entirely new *asset class* (kind of investment), and I advocate that most of my clients hold at least one-quarter of their bond allocation in TIPS. They can be important portfolio diversifiers. Read all about them in Chapter 3.

>> **Internationalization of the bond market:** The U.S. government isn't the only government to issue bonds. U.S. corporations aren't the only corporations to issue bonds either. For added portfolio diversification, and possibly a higher yield, you may want to look abroad. Until recently, international diversification in fixed income was difficult. Now it's as easy as (but not as American as) apple pie. As with U.S. bonds, you have your pick of short-term or long-term bonds, safe-and-simple bonds, or risky-with-high-return potential bonds. You can invest in the relatively calm waters of the United Kingdom, Japan, or Germany. Or you can travel to countries such as Mexico, Brazil, and Russia, where the bond markets are choppy and exciting. Join me on the voyage abroad in Chapter 3.

NEED A HOBBY? TRY SCRIPOPHILY

The term *scripophily* (pronounced *scrip awful lee*) derives from a contest held by the *Financial Times* newspaper in 1978 to come up with an appropriate name for collecting antique stocks and bonds. Bob Kerstein, CEO of Scripophily.com, estimates that the hobby boasts 20,000 to 30,000 enthusiasts in the United States alone.

Kerstein's website (www.scripophily.com) features more than 17,000 old certificates from various nations, industries, and eras. Many of them are works of art, some even featuring paintings from famous artists of their day. But the majority of the old stocks and bonds have one thing in common, says Kerstein: "They may be valuable as collector items, but they are usually worthless as redeemable securities." He says he's seen scams whereby con artists try to sell old corporate bonds (both domestic and international) as redeemable securities, even though they have no market value, other than as collectibles. "Those old bonds may look like they're still redeemable, but they are not," he warns.

Liberty Bonds, sold during World War I, are *very* popular among collectors — much more popular than when they were first issued. (The lack of consumer enthusiasm for them proved to be a bit of an embarrassment to the U.S. Treasury; unlike World War II, which rallied tremendous public support, World War I wasn't very popular among Americans.) Kerstein advises, "If you happen to have a Liberty Bond, don't cash it in with the government — a collector might pay you many times as much as the government."

Chapter **2**

Investigating Interest

I n the city of Uruk, in the month of Ululu, on the 11th day of the 9th year of Nebuchadnezzar (that would be 595 BC), a man named Nabu-usabsi lent a half-mina, or about ½ pound, of silver to Nabu-sar-ashesu. They signed an agreement witnessed by a holy priest and four countrymen. The agreement stated that within one year, Nabu-sar-ashesu would return to Nabu-usabsi his half-mina of silver plus another ten shekels, each shekel equal to about $\frac{1}{60}$ of a pound of silver. If you do the math, that equates to a yearly rate of interest of 33⅓ percent.

That story from an ancient Babylonian text was retold, nearly 2,600 years later, in *A History of Interest Rates*, a 700-page textbook by Sidney Homer and Richard Sylla, first published in 1963. (Wiley published a fourth edition in 2005.) The book is an amazing collection of research into credit and interest rates going back not only to the 9th year of Nebuchadnezzar, but to possibly prehistoric times.

And why, pray tell, am I bringing this up in a book on bond investing in the computer age? Because most of today's credit is tied up in bonds, and the most salient feature of any bond is the interest rate paid. Interestingly (pardon the pun), many of the same forces that drove interest rates 2,600 years ago are *still* driving interest rates today, as you find out in this chapter.

In this chapter, I examine what forces affect interest rates and the demand for credit. I introduce the many and sometimes *purposely* confusing ways in which bond returns are measured and reported. And I give you the tools you need to determine whether Mr. Nabu-usabsi was getting a fair return on his investment, as well as what you, as a thoroughly modern bond investor, should expect in return for *your* bond investments.

Calculating Rates of Return: A Tricky Business

Bond investing can be tricky business, indeed — way trickier than stock investing. To help me explain why, I'm going to call upon our Babylonian friends, Nabu-usabsi and Nabu-sar-ashesu. And I'm going to introduce two new characters, Lila-Ir-lender and Kudur-broker. The two Nabus are real characters from a bygone era. Lila-Ir-lender (said to be a distant cousin of Hammurabi) is fictional. Kudur-broker is also fictional.

Lila-Ir-lender, like Nabu-sar-usabsi, is a moneylender. Kudur-broker is, appropriately enough, a broker. Instead of dealing only in minas and shekels and agreements written on parchment, let's assume the existence of bonds. With lenders, borrowers, and a broker, we have a complete bond market.

Okay, are you ready now to see why this bond business can be so tricky? Good. Let's return to ancient Babylonia!

Cutting deals

Instead of merely signing an agreement, suppose that Nabu-usabsi, in return for lending his half-mina of silver to Nabu-sar-ashesu, gets a bond. Nabu-sar-ashesu's bond clearly states that Nabu-usabsi will get his investment back in one year, plus 33⅓ percent interest. In the parlance of the bond world, the bond is issued with a *face value* of a half-mina of silver, a *coupon rate* (or interest rate) of 33⅓ percent, and a *maturity* (or expiration date) of one year. I talk about these terms in more detail later.

For now, I want to impress upon you that measuring bond returns isn't always an easy matter. Why not? After all, the agreement calls for 33⅓ percent interest. Simple enough, eh? Not really.

Suppose that Nabu-usabsi wants to get his 33⅓ percent interest not as a lump sum at the end of the year but in two installments, as most bonds work: 16⅔ percent after six months, and another 16⅔ percent after another six months. That's obviously a better deal for Nabu-usabsi because he gets the 16⅔ percent sooner and can, if he wants, reinvest that money for another six months. Let's suppose that, in fact, he's able to reinvest that money for a very high interest rate. By the end of the year, Nabu-usabsi will actually earn more than 33⅓ percent on his original investment. But how is his *real* rate of return calculated?

Changing hands

To complicate matters further, suppose that Nabu-sar-ashesu, our bond issuer, has agreed that his bond can be sold and that he will continue to pay 33⅓ percent interest to whoever buys the bond. In walks Lila-Ir-lender, who wants to buy the bond from Nabu-usabsi but uses Kudur-broker, the bond broker, to make the deal. Kudur-broker pays Nabu-usabsi ½ pound of silver to obtain the bond. He turns around and sells it to Lila-Ir-lender for ⁶⁄₁₀ pound of silver and pockets the difference for himself.

Lila-Ir-lender is now the proud owner of a bond that's paying 33⅓ percent on the *original face value* (½ pound of silver). She, however, paid more for the bond, thanks to the bond broker's markup. So, even though she's holding a bond that's paying 33⅓ percent, she isn't really getting 33⅓ percent on her money; she's getting less.

Now how much is the true rate of return on the bond? Is it 33⅓ percent, or is it 27¾ percent, which (rounding off a bit) is the actual percentage return that Lila-Ir-lender would be getting on the money she laid out?

Embracing the complexity

You see why this bond business can be so confusing? (Yes, it would be just as confusing if the names were Mike and Sue instead of Nabu-usabsi and Nabu-sar-ashesu!)

I need to warn you that this chapter is the most technical one in the book. You're about to read some things that confuse even many financial professionals. I do my best to present the information clearly, and I promise to give you an intermission halfway through the chapter so you can catch your breath. (You must bring your own popcorn, though.) But you're probably right now wondering the following: Do you really need to know all this? Can you skim this chapter, or should you really know how to calculate yield to maturity, yield to call, and things like that? Well, it depends.

REMEMBER

If you're okay investing in bond mutual funds, especially the bond index funds that I recommend in Chapter 5, and if you're going to buy and hold your investment, then a cursory knowledge of what makes bonds tick is probably just fine. (Knowing how they fit into a well-diversified portfolio, as outlined in Chapter 10, is probably more important.) If you're intent, however, on dealing in individual bonds or trying to flip bonds to make a profit (good luck!), you'd better either know this stuff cold or find a bond broker you can really trust.

Understanding what follows is easier than finding a bond broker you can really trust. Trust me.

Conducting Research to Judge the Desirability of a Bond

Determining the true value of a bond investment and how much you're really going to get out of it in the end requires three levels of research. It's like buying a home. Shopping for a home, here are the three levels of research you conduct:

>> **Level one:** You notice the curb appeal. You take note of the size of the home and whether you find it attractive. You also, of course, note the offering price.

>> **Level two:** You look at the property taxes, the age of the plumbing, the cost of utilities, and the condition of the roof.

>> **Level three:** You expand your view to look critically at the surroundings. How are the schools? Are area homes appreciating? Do the neighbors park their pickup trucks on the front lawn?

With a bond, you need to go through similar levels of research:

>> **Level one:** You notice the curb appeal of the bond. What's the face value, coupon rate, and sales price? What's your money going to be used for?

>> **Level two:** You dig deeper into the qualities of the bond. What are its ratings, duration, and maturity, and is it callable?

>> **Level three:** You look at broader economic factors (the bond's "neighborhood"), which can greatly influence the value of your bond investment: the prevailing interest rates, inflation rate, state of the economy, and forces of supply and demand in the fixed-income market.

I know that you may not be familiar with all the terms I'm using here, such as *duration* and *callable*. You soon will be. I introduce all of them in the following sections.

Level one: Getting the basic information

Here are the first things you want to know about a bond:

>> What's its face value?

>> What's the coupon rate?

>> How much are you being asked to pay for the bond?

>> What does the bond issuer intend to do with your money?

You can ascertain all these answers quite readily, either by looking at the bond offer itself or by having a conversation with the broker.

Face value

Also known as *par value* or the *principal*, the *face value* is the original dollar amount of the bond. This is the amount that the bond issuer promises to pay the bond buyer at maturity. The face value of the majority of bonds in today's market is $1,000. But note that a $1,000 par value bond doesn't necessarily have to sell for $1,000. After the bond is on the open market, it may sell for an amount above or below par. If it sells above par, it's known as a *premium bond*. If it sells below par, it's known as a *discount bond*.

WARNING

Heads up: Discount bonds are discounted for a reason — or, perhaps, two or three reasons. Most commonly, the discounted bond isn't paying a very high rate of interest compared to other similar bonds. Or the issuer of the bond is showing some signs of financial weakness that could potentially lead to a default. Don't think you're necessarily getting a bargain by paying less than face value for a bond. Chances are, you aren't.

Coupon rate

The *coupon rate* is the interest rate the bond issuer (the debtor) has agreed to pay the bondholder (the creditor), given as a percent of the face value. The term *coupon rate* refers to the fact that in the old days, bonds had actual coupons attached that you would rip off at regular intervals to redeem for cash. Bonds no longer have such coupons; in fact, they aren't printed on paper anymore. Nearly all bonds are electronic now, but the term remains.

With rare exceptions (so-called "floating-rate" securities), a bond's coupon rate never changes. That's the reason that bonds, like certificates of deposit (CDs), are called *fixed-income* investments, even though, as you'll see shortly, the term is a bit of a misnomer. A 5 percent bond always pays 5 percent of the face value, which is usually $50 a year on a $1,000 bond, typically paid as $25 every six months. As I mention in the previous section, the bond doesn't have to be bought or sold at par. But the selling price of a bond never affects the coupon rate.

TIP

The coupon rate, set in stone, tells you how much cash you'll get from your bond each year. Simply take the coupon rate (which will be a percentage) and multiply it by the face value of the bond. Divide that amount in half. That's how much cash you'll typically receive twice a year. A $1,000 bond with a coupon rate of 4 percent gives you $20 cash twice a year.

Sale price

In general, a bond sells at a *premium*, or above face value, when prevailing interest rates have dropped since the time that bond was issued. If you think about it, that makes sense. Say your bond is paying 5 percent, and interest rates across the board have dropped to 3 percent. The bond in your hand, which is paying considerably more than new bonds being issued, becomes a valuable commodity. On the other hand, when general interest rates rise, existing bonds tend to move to *discount* status, selling below face value. Who wants them when new bonds are paying higher rates?

REMEMBER

Don't ask why, but bond people quote the price of a bond on a scale of 100. If a bond is selling at *par*, or face value, it will typically be quoted as selling at 100. But that doesn't mean you can buy the bond for $100. It means you can buy it at par. On a $1,000 par bond, that means you can buy the bond for $1,000. If the same bond is selling at 95, that means you're looking at a discount bond, selling for $950. And if that bond is selling for 105, it's a premium bond; you need to fork over $1,050.

REMEMBER

Most investors put too much weight on whether a bond is a discount bond or a premium bond. Although it matters somewhat, especially with regard to a bond's volatility (discussed later in this chapter), it doesn't necessarily affect a bond's total return. *Total return* refers to the sum of your principal and income, capital gains on your original investment, *plus* any income or capital gains on money you've earned on your original investment and have been able to reinvest. Total return is, very simply, the entire amount of money you end up with after a certain investment period, minus what you began with. More on that later in this chapter.

Purpose

It won't matter to every investor, but it matters a lot to me: What's the nature of the company or the municipality asking to borrow your money, and what do they intend to do with that money? Will your money be used by a known polluter to build a plant that will pump more carbon dioxide into the atmosphere? Will you be financing the manufacture of lethal weapons destined for sale to foreign dictators, or the production of products such as tobacco that are known to cause cancer? Will you be lending money to a company that runs factories filled with child laborers? Or will your money be used to build schools, develop clean energy sources, feed the hungry, and make the world a better place for our children?

If these things matter to you, there are ways to gauge the social and environmental ripples of a bond, and these will be discussed in later chapters.

Level two: Finding out intimate details

After you know the face value, coupon rate, and sale price (discount or premium), and after you've questioned whether you want to lend money to a particular bond issuer, you're ready to start a little deeper digging. Here's what you want to know next about the bond:

>> Is the bond issuer capable of repaying you your money? Or could the issuer go belly-up and *default* on, or fail to repay, all or part of your loan?

>> When will you see your principal returned?

>> Is there a chance that the bond will be called?

Ratings: Separating quality from junk

Not all bonds pay the same coupon rates. In fact, some bonds pay way more than others. One of the major determinants of a bond's coupon rate is the financial standing of the issuer.

The U.S. Treasury, a major issuer of bonds, pays modest rates of return on its bonds — generally a full percentage point less than similar bonds issued by corporations. The reason? Uncle Sam doesn't have to pay more. People assume that the U.S. government isn't going to renege on its debts, so they're willing to lend the government money without demanding a high return. Shakier entities, such as a new company, a city in financial trouble, or the Russian government (which has a history of defaulting) would have to offer higher rates of return to find any creditors. So they must, and so they do.

An entire industry of bond-rating companies, such as Moody's, S&P Global Ratings, and Fitch Ratings, exists to help bond investors figure their odds of getting paid back from a company or municipality to which they lend money. These firms dig into a bond issuer's financial books to see how solvent the entity is. Theoretically, the higher the rating, the safer your investment; the lower the rating, the more risk you take. In addition, other resources can tell you how much extra interest you should expect for taking on the added risk of lending to a shaky company. (Much more on ratings in Chapter 3.)

REMEMBER

Ratings are very helpful — it's hard to imagine markets working without them — but neither the ratings nor the raters are infallible. In the case of Enron, the major ratings firms S&P and Moody's had the company's bonds rated as *investment grade* until four days prior to the company declaring bankruptcy. Investment grade means that the risk of loss is very low and the odds of getting repaid very high. Weren't Enron bondholders surprised!

That was 2002. Six years later came the subprime mortgage crisis, in which investors in certain mortgage bonds lost a bundle. Just about the time that everyone thought the ratings agencies had learned something since the Enron debacle and reestablished the public's trust, they once again failed investors quite miserably. They apparently failed to see — or perhaps they did see but failed to report — the impending collapse of these mortgage bonds. As Michael Lewis writes in his 2010 book *The Big Short* (W. W. Norton & Company), a colorful exposé of the subprime scandal, "The rating agencies, who were paid fat fees by Goldman Sachs and other Wall Street firms for each deal they rated, pronounced 80 percent of the new tower of debt triple-A."

But there are plenty of times the raters get it right. The majority of bond issuances that wind up in default received low credit ratings well in advance of going bust.

Insurance

Some bonds come insured and are advertised as such. This is most common in the municipal bond market, although less common than it was years ago. Even though default rates are very low among municipalities, cities know that people buy their bonds expecting safety. So, they sometimes insure. If a municipality goes to the trouble of having an insurance company back its bonds, you know that you're getting a safer investment, but you shouldn't expect an especially high rate of interest. (No, you can't decline the insurance on an insured bond. It doesn't work like auto-rental insurance.)

TIP

Some proponents of holding individual bonds say that you should delve not only into the financial health of the bond issuer but also, in the case of an insured bond, into the financial health of the insurance company standing behind the issuer. That's a fair amount of work, which is one reason I tend to favor bond funds for most middle-class family portfolios.

Maturity

Generally, the longer the maturity of the bond, the greater the interest rate paid. The reason is simple enough: Borrowers generally want your money for longer periods of time and are willing to pay accordingly. Lenders generally don't want their money tied up for long periods and require extra incentive to make such a commitment. Finally, the longer you invest your money in a bond, the greater the risk you're taking — both that the issuer could default and that interest rates could pop, lessening the value of your bond. Paradoxically, holders of long-term bonds face risk from falling interest rates as well. This risk is called *reinvestment risk.*

REMEMBER

I don't care who the issuer is, when you buy a 20-year bond, you're taking a risk. Anything can happen in 20 years. Companies that were once shining examples of profitability and managerial excellence have gone bankrupt, leaving bondholders holding the bag. Think Lehman Brothers, General Motors, Chrysler, Enron, and Delta Airlines. Investors who bought bonds in these companies might've thought they were as secure in their investments as, well, people today buying bonds from Microsoft, Apple, or Amazon.

Callability

When you walk out of a store with a pair of shoes, you can pretty much rest assured that you're not going to get a call from the store the next day demanding that you return the shoes. When you buy a bond that's callable, that's exactly what happens.

A bond that's *callable* is one that can be retired by the company or municipality on a certain date prior to the bond's maturity. Because bonds tend to be retired when interest rates fall, you don't want your bond to be retired; you generally aren't going to be able to replace it with anything paying as much. Because of the added risk, callable bonds tend to carry higher coupon rates to compensate bond buyers.

WARNING

Be careful when buying any individual callable bond. Much of the real pain I've seen in the bond market has occurred over calls. I've seen cases in which a bond buyer will pay a broker a hefty sum to buy a bond callable in, say, six months. The bond, sure enough, gets called, and the bondholder suddenly realizes that they paid the broker a fat fee and made nothing — perhaps got a *negative* return — on their investment. Of course, the broker never bothered to point out this potentially ugly scenario. (Reading this book, especially Chapter 4, will ensure that *you* never meet with a similar fate!)

Taxes

Back in the early days of the bond market in the United States, the federal government made a deal with the cities and states: You don't tax our bonds, and we won't tax yours. And, so far, all parties have kept their word. When you invest in Treasury bonds, you pay no state or local tax on the interest. And when you invest in municipal bonds, you pay no federal tax on the interest. Accordingly, muni bonds pay a lower rate of interest than equivalent corporate bonds. But you may still wind up ahead on an after-tax basis.

Whether or not the tax-free status of municipal bonds makes them appropriate for your portfolio is covered in Chapter 3. I'll warn you in advance that the simple taxable versus tax-free calculators you find online don't always steer you in the best direction.

(Okay, I promised earlier that I'd give you a break about halfway through this chapter. Now's the time: INTERMISSION! Feel free to step away, get a snack, and come back when the glaze has cleared from your eyes.)

Welcome back. Ready to move onto that third level now? Remember, this chapter is all about estimating the value of a bond investment. As I show next, getting that estimate requires the use of a wide-angle lens.

Level three: Examining the neighborhood

Your home, no matter how well you maintain it or whether you renovate the kitchen, tends to rise or fall in value along with the value of all other houses in your neighborhood. Many things outside your control — the quality of the schools, employment opportunities, crime rates, and earthquake tremors — can greatly influence the value of homes in your area, including yours. Similarly, a bond, no matter its quality or maturity, tends to rise and fall in value with the general conditions of the markets and of the economy.

Prevailing interest rates

REMEMBER

Nothing affects the value of bonds (at least in the short to intermediate run) like prevailing interest rates. When interest rates climb, bond prices fall, usually in lockstep. And when interest rates fall, bond prices climb. The relationship is straightforward and logical enough. If you're holding a bond paying yesterday's interest rate, and today's interest rate is lower, you're holding something that's going to be in hot demand, and people will pay you dearly for it. If you're holding a bond paying yesterday's interest rate, and today's rate is higher, you're holding mud.

Okay, that part is simple. Interest rates drive bond prices. But what drives interest rates?

Interest rates come in many different flavors. At any point in time, there are prevailing interest rates for home mortgages, credit card payments, bank loans, short-term bonds, and long-term bonds, but to a great extent they move up and down together. The forces that drive interest rates are numerous, entwined, and largely unpredictable — even though many people claim to be fortune tellers.

TECHNICAL STUFF

In the short run — from hour to hour, day to day — the Federal Reserve, which controls monetary policy in the United States, has great power to manipulate interest rates across the board. The Federal Reserve's job is to help smooth the economy by tinkering with interest rates to help curb inflation and boost growth. Low interest rates make borrowing easy, both for businesses and consumers. That helps to heat up the economy, but it can also result in inflation. High interest rates discourage borrowing and tend to slow economic growth, but they also help to rein in inflation. So when inflation is running too high in the eyes of the Fed, it moves to raise interest rates. And when the economy is growing too slowly, the Fed tends to lower interest rates. Obviously, it's a balancing act, and perfect balance is hard to achieve.

In the longer run — month to month, year to year — interest rates tend to rise and fall with inflation and with the anticipated rate of future inflation.

TIP

Rising interest rates are, in the short run, a bondholder's worst enemy. The possibility that interest rates will rise — and bond prices will, therefore, fall — is what makes long-term bonds somewhat risky. If you want to avoid the risk of price volatility, go with short-term bonds, but be willing to accept less cash flow from your bond holdings.

HOW DOES THE FED MOVE INTEREST RATES?

The U.S. Federal Reserve has three "magic" powers with which to expand or contract the money supply, or move interest rates:

- **Open market operations:** This term means nothing more than the buying and selling of Treasury and federal agency bonds. When bonds are sold and the public's money is funneled into government hands, the money supply is tightened, inflation tends to slow, and interest rates tend to rise. When bonds are purchased back and the public's money is returned, the economy is given a boost and interest rates tend to fall. This purchasing, especially when the Treasury is scooping up longer-term bonds, is often referred to in news reports as *quantitative easing* (QE).

- **The discount rate:** This term refers to the interest rate that commercial banks must pay for government loans. The more the banks have to pay, the more they tend to charge their customers, and interest rates tend to rise.

- **Reserve requirements:** The *reserve* is the amount of money that banks must hold on hand as a percentage of their outstanding loans. The higher the reserve requirements, the tougher it is for banks to lend money, and interest rates tend to rise as a result.

The rate of inflation

The *inflation rate* signals the degree to which you have to cough up more money to buy the same basket of goods; it indicates your loss of purchasing power. In the long run, the inflation rate has great bearing on returns enjoyed by bondholders. The ties between the inflation rate and the bond market are numerous.

In economic theory, bondholders are rational beings with rational desires and motivations. (In reality, individual investors often act irrationally, but as a group, the markets seem to work rather rationally.) A rational buyer of bonds demands a certain *inflation-risk premium.* That is, the higher the rate of inflation or the expected rate of inflation, the higher an interest rate bondholders demand. If inflation is running at 3 percent, bond buyers know that they need returns of at least 3 percent just to break even. If the inflation rate jumps to 6 percent, the inflation-risk premium doubles; bond buyers won't invest their money (or won't invest it happily) unless they get double what they were getting before.

Inflation is also a pretty good indicator of how hot the economy is. When prices are rising, it usually reflects full employment and companies expanding. When companies are expanding, they need capital. The need for capital raises the demand for borrowing. An increased demand for borrowing raises prevailing interest rates, which lowers the price of bonds.

TIP

As a bondholder, you can get stung by inflation. Badly. That's why I recommend that a certain portion of your bonds — around one-quarter, or more if you're shunning stocks — be held in inflation-adjusted bonds, such as Treasury Inflation-Protected Securities (TIPS). It's also why a 100 percent bond portfolio rarely, if ever, makes sense. Stocks have a much better track record of keeping ahead of inflation. Real estate and commodities can do a pretty good job, too.

Forces of supply and demand

The public is fickle, and that fickleness is perhaps nowhere better seen than in the stock market. Although the bond market tends to be less affected by the public's whims, it does happen. At times, the public feels pessimistic, and when the public feels pessimistic, it usually favors the stability of government bonds. When the public is feeling optimistic, it tends to favor the higher return potential of corporate bonds. When the public feels that taxes are going to rise, it tends to favor tax-free municipal bonds. As in any other market — shoes, automobiles, lettuce — high consumer demand can raise prices, and low demand tends to lower prices.

Understanding (and Misunderstanding) Yield

Okay, time to hold onto your hat. After you know something about researching the particulars of a bond offering and the climate of the bond market, it's time to talk *yield*. Yield is what you want in a bond. It's income, and it contributes to return. But yield is also confusion. People — including overly eager bond salespeople — often misuse the term or use it inappropriately to gain an advantage in the bond market.

Don't be a yield sucker. Understand what kind of yield is being promised on a bond or bond fund, and know what it really means.

Coupon yield

REMEMBER

This one is easy. The *coupon yield*, or the coupon rate, is part of the bond offering. A $1,000 bond with a coupon yield of 4 percent will pay $40 a year. A $1,000 bond with a coupon yield of 6 percent will pay $60 a year. Usually, the $40 or $60 or whatever is split in half and paid out twice a year on an individual bond.

Bond funds don't really have coupon yields, although they have an average coupon yield for all the bonds in the pool. That average tells you something, for sure, but you need to remember that a bond fund may start the year and end the year with a completely different set of bonds — and a completely different average coupon yield.

Current yield

Like coupon yield, current yield is easy to understand, at least on a superficial level. But a deeper level exists, and because of that, current yield is the most often misused kind of yield. In short, *current yield* is derived by taking the bond's coupon yield and dividing it by the bond's price.

Suppose you had a $1,000 face value bond with a coupon rate of 5 percent, which would equate to $50 a year in your pocket. If the bond sells today for 98 (in other words, it's selling at a discount for $980), the current yield is $50 ÷ $980 = 0.0510, or 5.10 percent. If that same bond rises in price to a premium of 103 (selling for $1,030), the current yield is $50 ÷ $1,030 = 0.0485, or 4.85 percent.

The current yield is a sort of snapshot that gives you a rough (and possibly entirely inaccurate) estimate of the return you can expect on that bond over the coming months. If you take the current yield for just one day, translated into nickels and dimes, and multiply that amount by 30, you'd think that would give you a good estimate of how much income your bond will generate in the next month, but that's not the case. The current yield changes too quickly for that kind of prediction to hold true. The equivalent would be taking a measure of today's rainfall, multiplying it by 30, and using that number to estimate rainfall for the month. (Well, the current yield would be a *bit* more accurate, but you get my point.)

Yield to maturity

A much more accurate measure of return, although still far from perfect, is the *yield to maturity*. It's a considerably more complicated deal than figuring out current yield. Yield to maturity factors in not only the coupon rate and the price you paid for the bond, but also how far you have to go to get your principal back and how much that principal will be.

Yield-to-maturity calculations make a big assumption that may or may not prove true: They assume that as you collect your interest payments every six months, you reinvest them at the same interest rate you're getting on the bond. With this (often faulty) assumption in mind, here's the formula for calculating yield to maturity:

> Um, I don't know.

I can't remember it. Like most other financial planners, I'd have to look it up. It's a terribly long formula with all kinds of horrible Greek symbols and lots of multiplication and division, and I think there's a muffler and an ice tray thrown in. But, thank goodness, I don't need to know the formula.

TIP

Thanks to the miracle of modern technology, I can punch a few numbers into my financial calculator, or I can go to any number of online calculators. (Try putting "yield-to-maturity calculator" in your favorite search engine.) I like the calculator on www. moneychimp.com, which is a great financial website that features all sorts of cool calculators.

After you find a yield-to-maturity calculator, you'll be asked to put in the par, or face value, of the bond (almost always $1,000); the price you're considering paying for the bond; the number of years to maturity; and the coupon rate. If, for example, I were to purchase a $1,000 par bond for $980, if that bond was paying 5 percent, and if it matured in ten years, the yield to maturity would be 5.262 percent.

A few paragraphs ago, I calculated the current yield for such a bond to be 5.10 percent. The yield to maturity on a *discounted bond* (a bond selling for below par) is always higher than the current yield. Why? Because when you eventually get your principal back at maturity, you'll be, in essence, making a profit. You paid only $980, but you'll see a check for $1,000. That extra $20 adds to your yield to maturity. The reverse is true of bonds purchased at a *premium*, or at a price higher than par value. In those cases, the yield to maturity is lower than the current yield.

WARNING

Unscrupulous bond brokers have been known to tout current yield, and only current yield, when selling especially premium-priced bonds. The current yield may look great, but you take a hit when the bond matures by collecting less in principal than you paid for the bond. Your yield to maturity, which matters more than current yield, may, in fact, stink.

Yield to call

If you buy a *callable bond*, the company or municipality that issues your bond can ask for it back, at a specific price, long before the bond matures. Premium bonds, because they carry higher-than-average coupon yields, are often called. What that means is that your yield to maturity is pretty much a moot point. What you're likely to see in the way of yield is *yield to call*. This amount is figured out the same way that you figure out yield to maturity (use www. moneychimp.com if you don't have a financial calculator), but the end result — your actual return — may be considerably lower.

Keep in mind that bonds are generally called when market interest rates have fallen. In that case, not only is your yield on the bond you're holding diminished, but your opportunity to invest your money in anything paying as high an interest rate has passed. From a bondholder's perspective, calls aren't pretty, which is why callable bonds must pay higher rates of interest to find any buyers. (From the issuing company's or municipality's perspective, callable bonds are just peachy; after the call, the company or municipality can, if it wants, issue a new bond that pays a lower interest rate.)

WARNING

Certain hungry bond brokers may "forget" to mention yield to call and instead quote you only current-yield or yield-to-maturity numbers. In such cases, you may pay the broker a big cut to get the bond, hold it for a short period, and then have to render it to the bond issuer, actually earning yourself a *negative* total return. Ouch. Fortunately, regulatory authorities have gotten somewhat tougher, and such forgetfulness on the part of brokers is less common, but it still happens.

Worst-case basis yield

Usually a callable bond has not just one possible call date, but several. *Worst-case basis yield* (or *yield to worst call*) looks at all possible yields and tells you what your yield would be if the company or municipality decides to call your bond at the worst possible time.

REMEMBER

Callable bonds involve considerably more risk than noncallable bonds. If interest rates drop, your bond will likely be called. Your yield on the existing bond just dropped from what you expected, and you won't be able to reinvest your money for a like rate of return. If interest rates have risen, the company probably won't call your bond, but you're stuck with an asset, if you should try to sell it, that has lost principal value. (Bond prices always drop when interest rates rise.)

The 30-day SEC yield

Because you have so many ways of measuring yield, and because bond mutual funds were once notorious for manipulating yield figures, the U.S. Securities and Exchange Commission (SEC) requires that all bond funds report yield in the same manner. The 30-day SEC yield, which attempts to consolidate the yield to maturity of all the bonds in the portfolio, exists so the mutual fund bond shopper can have some measure with which to comparison shop. This measure isn't perfect, in large part because the bonds in your bond fund today may not be the same bonds in your bond fund three weeks from now. Nonetheless, the 30-day SEC yield can be helpful in choosing the right funds. (More on fund shopping in Chapter 5.)

Appreciating Total Return (This Is What Matters Most!)

Even though bonds are called *fixed-income investments*, and even though bond returns are easier to predict than stock returns, ultimately you can't know the exact total return of any bond investment until the investment period has come and gone. That's true for bond funds, and it's true for most individual bonds (although many die-hard investors in individual bonds refuse to admit it). *Total return* is the entire pot of money you wind up with after the investment period has come and gone. In the case of bonds or bond funds, that amount involves not only your original principal and your interest, but also any changes in the value of your original principal. Ignoring for the moment the risk of default (and potentially losing all your principal), here are other ways in which your principal can shrink or grow.

Figuring in capital gains and losses

In the case of a bond fund, your principal is represented by a certain number of shares in the fund multiplied by the share price of the fund. As bond prices go up and down (due to a number of factors, but primarily in response to prevailing interest rates), so, too, does the share price of the bond fund. As I discuss later in this chapter when I get to bond volatility, the share price of a bond fund may rise and fall quite a bit, especially if the bond fund is holding long-term bonds, and doubly especially if those long-term bonds are of questionable quality, or *junk bonds*.

In the case of individual bonds, unless you buy a bond selling at a premium, your principal comes back to you whole — but only if you hold the bond to maturity or if the bond is called. If, on the other hand, you choose to sell the bond before maturity, you wind up with whatever market price you can get for the bond at that point. If the market price has appreciated (the bond sells at a premium), you can count your capital gains as part of your total return. If the market price has fallen (the bond sells at a discount), the capital losses offset any interest you've made on the bond.

Factoring in reinvestment rates of return

Total return of a bond can come from three sources:

>> Interest on the bond

>> Any possible capital gains or losses

>> Whatever rate of return you get, if any, when you reinvest the money coming to you every six months

REMEMBER

Believe it or not, on a very long-term bond, the last factor — your so-called *reinvestment rate* — is probably the most important of the three. That's because of the amazing power of compound interest.

The only kind of bond where the reinvestment rate isn't a factor is one where your only interest payment comes at the end when the bond matures. These kinds of bonds are called *zero-coupon bonds*. In the case of zero-coupon bonds, no compounding occurs. The coupon rate of the bond is your actual rate of return, not accounting for inflation or taxes.

Here's an example: Suppose you buy a 30-year, $1,000 bond that pays 6 percent on a semiannual basis. If you spend the $30 you collect twice a year, you get $1,000 back for your bond at the end of 30 years, and your total annual rate of return, ignoring taxes and inflation, is 6 percent simple interest. But now suppose that each and every time you collect those $30 payments, you immediately reinvest them at the same coupon rate. Over the course of 30 years, that pile of reinvested money grows at an annual rate of 6 percent *compounded*.

In this scenario, at the end of six months, your investment is worth $1,030. At the end of one year, your investment is worth $1,060.90. (The extra 90¢ represents a half-year's interest on the $30.) The following six months, you earn 6 percent on the new amount, and so on, for 30 more years. Instead of winding up with $1,000 after 30 years, as you would if you spent the semiannual bond payments, you instead wind up with $5,891.60 — almost six times as much!

Allowing for inflation adjustments

Of course, that $5,891.60 due to 6 percent compound interest probably won't be worth $5,891.60 in 30 years. Your truest total rate of return needs to account for inflation. If *inflation* — the rise in the general level of prices — were 3 percent a year for the next 30 years (roughly what it's been in the past decade), your $5,891.60 will be worth only $2,366.24 in today's dollars — a real compound return of 2.91 percent.

To account for inflation when determining the real rate of return on an investment, you can simply take the nominal rate of return

(6 percent in this example) and subtract the annual rate of inflation (3 percent in this example). That gives you a rough estimate of your real total return.

TECHNICAL STUFF

But if you want a more exact figure, here's the formula to use:

1 + Nominal rate of return ÷ 1 + Inflation rate – 1 × 100 = Real rate of return

Assuming a 6 percent nominal rate of return and 3 percent inflation:

1.06 ÷ 1.03 – 1 × 100 = 2.91

Why the more complicated calculation? You can't just subtract 3 from 6 because inflation is eating away at both your principal *and* your gains throughout the year.

Weighing pretax versus posttax

Of course, we can't finish this discussion without mentioning taxes. Taxes almost always eat into your bond returns. Here are two exceptions:

>> Tax-free municipal bonds where you experience neither a capital gain nor a capital loss, nor is the bondholder subject to any alternative minimum tax. (More on taxes and munis in Chapter 3.)

>> Bonds held in a tax-advantaged account, such as a Roth individual retirement account (IRA) or a 529 college savings plan.

For most bonds, the interest payments are taxed as regular income, and any rise in the value of the principal, if the bond is sold (and sometimes even if the bond isn't sold), is taxed as capital gain.

For most people these days, long-term capital gains (more than one year) on bond principal are taxed at 15 percent. Any appreciated fixed-income asset bought and sold within a year is taxed at your normal income-tax rate, whatever that is. (If you make more than $40,526, your federal tax bracket is at least 22 percent.)

Measuring the Volatility of Your Bonds

When investment pros talk about *volatility*, they're talking about risk. And when they talk about risk, they're talking about volatility. Volatility in an investment means that what's worth $1,000 today may be worth $900 — or $800 — tomorrow. Bonds are typically way less risky than stocks, which is why we love bonds so much, but bonds *can* fall in value. Some bonds are much more volatile than others, and before you invest in any bond, you should have a good idea what kind of volatility, or risk, you're looking at.

Time frame matters

The more time until the bond matures, the greater the bond's volatility. In other words, with long-term bonds, there's a greater chance that the principal value of the bond can rise or fall dramatically. Short-term bonds sway much less. On the other hand — and here's a somewhat funny contradiction — the further off your need to tap into the bond's principal, the less that volatility should matter to you.

As I explain earlier in this chapter, nothing affects the value of your bond holdings as much as prevailing interest rates. If you're holding a bond that pays 5 percent, and prevailing interest rates are 6 percent, your bond isn't worth nearly as much as it would be if prevailing interest rates were 5 percent (or, better yet, 4 percent). But just how sensitive is the price of a bond to the ups and downs of interest rates? It depends, mostly on the maturity of the bond.

Suppose you're holding a fresh 30-year bond with a coupon rate of 5 percent, and suddenly prevailing interest rates move from 5 percent to 6 percent. You're now looking at potentially 30 years of holding a bond that's paying less than the prevailing interest rate. So, how attractive does that bond look to you, or anyone else? Answer: It looks like used oil dripping from the bottom of an old car.

But suppose you're holding either a very short-term bond or an old 30-year bond that matures next month. In either case, you'll see your principal very soon. Does it matter much that prevailing interest rates have risen? No, not really. The price of your bond isn't going to be much affected.

Quality counts

High-quality, investment-grade bonds, issued by solid govern-ments or corporations, tend to be less volatile than junk bonds. This has nothing to do with interest rates but, rather, with the risk of default. When the economy is looking shaky and investor optimism fades, few people want to be holding the debt of entities that may fail. In times of recession and depression, high-quality bonds may rise in value and junk bonds may fall, as people clamor for safety.

Overall, the junk bonds bounce in price much more than the investment-grade bonds. And, generally speaking, junk bonds tend to move in the same direction as stocks, while U.S. Treasurys often move in the opposite direction, making them more powerful diversifiers.

The coupon rate matters, too

Returning to the effect of interest rates on bond prices, not all bonds of like maturity have the same sensitivity to changes in prevailing rates. Aside from the maturity, you also need to con-sider the coupon rate. Bonds with the highest coupon rates on the market — bonds currently selling at a premium — tend to have the least volatility. Can you guess why that might be?

Imagine that you're considering the purchase of two $1,000 bonds: One matures in three years and is paying a 10 percent interest rate ($100 a year); the other also matures in three years and is paying a 5 percent interest rate ($50 a year). Obviously, the market price of the 10 percent bond will be much higher. (It will sell at a premium vis-à-vis the 5 percent bond.) It will also be less sensitive to interest rates because you are, in effect, getting your money back sooner.

With the 5 percent bond, your investment won't pay off until the bond matures and you get your $1,000 face value (probably much more than you paid for the bond). And who knows where inter-est rates will be then? With the 10 percent bond, you get your investment paid back much sooner, and you're free to reinvest that money. You have much less *reinvestment risk* — the risk that you'll be able to reinvest your money only at pitifully low rates.

The most volatile of bonds — those most sensitive to fluxes in interest rates — are zero-coupon bonds that pay all their interest at maturity.

Fortunately, a mathematical whiz named Frederick Macaulay gave us a formula back in the 1930s for calculating the sensitivity of a bond to prevailing interest rates. The formula works regardless of whether the bond is a zero-coupon bond or is paying regular coupons. The formula allows us to compare and contrast various bonds of various kinds to estimate their future volatility.

The wickedly complex formula measures something called *duration*. Duration (sometimes referred to as *Macauley Duration*, after its creator), tells you how much a bond will move in price if interest rates change by 1 percent.

Figuring out the duration of a bond is pretty much impossible without either a PhD in mathematics from MIT or a computer. If you don't have the PhD, use the computer — just search the web for "bond duration calculator" — or ask the broker who wants to sell you the bond to do it for you. If you're considering purchasing a bond mutual fund, you'll find the fund's average duration, which is sometimes called *average effective duration*, in the prospectus or other fund literature. You'll also find it on www. morningstar.com, your brokerage firm's website, or a number of sources where bond funds are contrasted and compared.

The duration formula considers a bond's par value, coupon rate, yield to maturity, and the number of years until the bond matures. It then spits out a single number. Here's what that number means: The principal value of a bond or bond fund with a duration of, say, 6, can be expected to change 6 percent with every 1 percent change in interest rates. If prevailing interest rates go up 1 percent, the bond or bond fund should drop in value 6 percent. If interest rates fall by 1 percent, the bond or bond fund should rise 6 percent.

Of course, if you're holding an individual bond to maturity, or if you have no intention of selling your bond fund any time in the near future, such fluctuations in price are less important than if you plan to collect your money and run any time soon.

Foreign bonds, added risk

In Chapter 3, I talk about bonds issued outside the borders of the United States. Many of these bonds are denominated not in dollars, but in yen, pounds, euros, or other currencies. When a bond is denominated in another currency, you can make out like a bandit if that currency appreciates against the dollar while you're holding the bond. Ah, but that gate can swing both ways: If you're holding a bond denominated in a currency that depreciates against the dollar, you may walk away from your investment with much less than you'd planned.

WARNING

The coupon rate on international bonds can sometimes be very attractive — but beware: Currency exchange rates are highly unpredictable. (Currency flux can be hedged away, but hedging is pricey.) Many international bond funds also ask too much in management fees, but that's another story that I cover in Chapter 3.

Revisiting the Bonds of Babylonia

I'd like to return for a moment to the beginning of this chapter and to ancient Babylonia. Here's my question: Was Mr. Nabu-usabsi's $16\frac{2}{3}$ percent return a good or bad investment?

Part of the answer lies in the ability of Mr. Nabu-sar-ashesu (the guy who got the silver) to repay the loan. History doesn't tell us if he was a good credit risk or if, in fact, the loan was ever repaid. The other part of the answer is whether that interest rate was fair for the time. Was it in line with other similar loans? We don't quite know that either.

What we do know is that lending money at a certain fixed interest rate (such as you do when you buy a bond) is often a good idea if prevailing interest rates are falling and a bad idea if interest rates are rising. At least that's true in the short run, such as a one-year period. Mr. Nabu-usabsi was probably gleeful if interest rates fell throughout the ninth year of Nebuchadnezzar.

In the longer run, it isn't clear that falling interest rates are a bond buyer's best friend. Buying bonds at a time of rising interest rates isn't necessarily a mistake. I explain in Chapters 4, 5, and 11 how to strategize your bond buys and sells to make money in just about any kind of economy and any interest-rate environment.

REMEMBER

Historical records make it clear that interest rates have fluctuated all across the board over the millennia. But lending your money (as you do when you buy a bond), if done wisely, is a time-honored way of making your money work for you. Throughout the rest of this book, I show you exactly how to do that.

Chapter 3

Surveying Types of Bonds

This chapter gives you a good picture of the major categories of bonds, including Treasurys, corporate bonds, agencies, and municipal bonds (or munis). If none of the major categories suit you, I provide a thumbnail sketch of some of the more unusual, sometimes quirky kinds of bond offerings available, such as church bonds and sustainability-linked bonds.

In each section, you discover the nuances that make each bond category unique. I show you why certain kinds of bonds pay higher rates of interest than others and, at the same time, may carry more risk. You can start to zero in on the kinds of bonds that make the most sense for you — the kinds of bonds that will make your portfolio shine.

Investing with Uncle Sam

Umpteen different kinds of debt securities are issued by the U.S. Treasury. *Savings bonds*, which you can purchase for small amounts and, until a decade ago, came in certificate form (making for nice, if not slightly deceptive, bar mitzvah and birthday gifts), are but one kind. In fact, when investment people speak of *Treasurys*, they're usually not talking about savings bonds but about larger-denomination bonds known formally as *Treasury bills, Treasury notes,* and *Treasury bonds.* All of these are now issued only in electronic, or *book-entry*, form.

REMEMBER

That's right. As of the start of 2012, those glorious U.S. savings bonds have been available in electronic form only. Aside from their cyber commonality, all U.S. Treasury debt securities, whether a $50 savings bond or a $1,000 Treasury note, have four other important things in common:

>> Every bond, an IOU of sorts from Uncle Sam, is backed by the "full faith and credit" of the U.S. government and, therefore, is considered by many investors — Americans and Chinese and Japanese alike — to be one of the safest bets around.

>> Because it's assumed that any principal you invest is safe from default, Treasury bonds, of whatever kind, tend to pay relatively modest rates of interest — lower than other comparable bonds, such as corporate bonds, that may put your principal at some risk.

>> True, the U.S. government isn't likely to go bankrupt anytime soon, but Treasury bonds are nonetheless still subject to other risks inherent in the bond market. Prices on Treasury bonds, especially those with long-term maturities, can swoop up and down like hungry hawks in response to such things as prevailing interest rates and investor confidence in the economy.

>> All interest on U.S. government bonds is off-limits to state and local tax authorities, just as the interest on most munis is off-limits to the Internal Revenue Service (IRS). However, except in rare cases, you're required to pay federal tax.

Beyond these similarities, the differences among U.S. government debt securities are many and, in some cases, like night and day. One huge difference: Some Treasury issues are marketable and others are not. (The nonmarketable bonds can only be bought directly from the Treasury and sold back to the Treasury.)

Savings bonds

Until a bit over a decade ago, U.S. savings bonds had been popular as gifts in part because they were sold as nicely designed certificates. On January 1, 2012, however, they became electronic entities, just like other Treasury securities. They have lost much of their appeal as gifts in this less attractive, less personal format.

You may now buy your electronic savings bonds straight from the official Treasury website (www.treasurydirect.gov). If your purchase is intended as a gift, the website allows you to print a gift certificate, which may be presented in lieu of the once keepsake-quality, elaborately designed bond.

Of course, savings bonds can be more than just gifts. You can buy one for yourself. People do so, despite their awfully low interest rates of late. Savings bonds start as low as $25. Beyond that, you don't need to pick a specific denomination. If you want to invest, say, $43.45, go for it, or if you want to invest $312.56, that's fine too. Any amount over $25 but under $10,000 (per individual, per year) is accepted.

Note that these "denomination-free" bonds are available only through the Treasury website and only for savings bonds. The other Treasury securities (bills, notes, or bonds) can also be purchased through the website, and elsewhere, but only in specific increments.

REMEMBER

Aside from the ability to invest a small amount, savings bonds are unique among Treasury debt securities in that they're strictly nonmarketable. When you buy a U.S. savings bond, you put either your own name and Social Security number on the bond or the name and Social Security number of the giftee. The only person entitled to receive interest is the one whose name appears on the bond. The bond itself, just like an airline ticket, can't be sold to another buyer — in stark contrast to Treasury bills and bonds that can, and often do, pass hands more often than poker chips.

EE bonds

EE bonds are the most traditional kind of savings bond. Series EE bonds carry a face value of twice their purchase price. They're *accrual bonds*, which means they earn interest as the years roll on even though you aren't seeing any cash. You can pay taxes on that interest as it accrues, but in most cases it makes more sense to defer paying the taxes until you decide to redeem the bond. Uncle Sam allows you to do that.

Series EE bonds issued prior to May 2005 pay various rates of interest depending on the date of the bond. Most of these rates are based on fairly complicated formulas and fluctuate over time. If you own a pre–May 2005 savings bond and you aren't sure what kind of interest the bond is paying, the best thing to do is to look it up on the Treasury website (www.treasurydirect.gov). EE bonds issued during May 2005 or afterward pay a fixed interest rate, but that rate can change every six months.

EE bonds are nonredeemable for the first year you own them, and if you hold them for fewer than five years, you surrender three months of interest. Any individual can buy up to $10,000 in EE savings bonds a year. Interest compounds twice a year for 30 years.

TIP

Historically, savings bonds have paid a rate of interest that has barely kept up with inflation. If you hold them for 17 years, you'll do better, but 17 years is a long time. Therefore, you don't want to make them a major part of your investment scheme. If you already have old savings bonds, you may want to consider swapping them for a higher-yielding investment. If you want to keep them, consider opening an account at www.treasurydirect.gov and turning your paper bonds into electronic securities. That way, you won't need to worry about them being lost or destroyed.

I bonds

These babies are built to buttress inflation. The I series bonds offer a fixed rate of return, plus an adjustment for rising prices. Every six months, on May 1 and November 1, the Treasury announces both the fixed rate for all new I bonds and the inflation adjustment for all new and existing I bonds.

After you buy an I bond, the fixed rate is yours for the life of the bond. The inflation rate, as I said, adjusts every six months. You collect all your interest only after cashing in the bond. (That is called *accrual interest.*)

The rules and parameters for I bonds are pretty much the same as they are for EEs: You have to hold them a year, and if you sell within five years, you pay a penalty. There's a limit to how many I bonds you can invest in ($10,000 a year, per person). And in certain circumstances, the proceeds may become tax-free if used for education expenses.

Because the rate of inflation can vary dramatically from one six-month period to another, at times I bonds make for fabulous short-term investments. In November 2005, for example, following a spike in the price of oil after Hurricane Katrina, the official inflation rate shot up, and I bonds were paying an impressive 6.73 percent. At that point, I was recommending that anyone who had cash to invest might want to consider them very seriously. But by the following May, with inflation having cooled, the yield on I bonds dropped rather precipitously to 2.43 percent. They were no longer such a hot investment; you could have done much better with a bank CD.

TIP

If you plan to hold I bonds as a long-term investment — longer than a year or two — you should be more concerned with the fixed rate (which will be in effect throughout the life of the bond) than the inflation adjustment (which will vary). Remember that if you cash out before five years, you'll pay a penalty of three months' interest. You can purchase I bonds at the Treasury website (www. treasurydirect.gov).

Treasury bills, notes, and bonds

The total amount of Treasury debt is about $30 trillion. About $7 trillion of this is made up of nonmarketable debt obligations, such as savings bonds. The other $23 trillion of the approximately $30 trillion in outstanding Treasury debt is made up of *marketable* (tradable) securities known as bills, notes, and bonds. This "bills, notes, and bonds" stuff can be a little confusing because technically they're all bonds that are backed by the full faith and credit of the U.S. government. They're all issued electronically and can be purchased directly from the Treasury, which holds weekly auctions; through the "secondary market" (after the security has been issued) via a broker; or in fund form. And they can trade like hotcakes. And they do — roughly $700 billion of marketable Treasurys exchange hands every day.

The major difference among these marketable Treasurys is the time you need to wait to collect your principal:

>> Treasury bills have maturities of a year or less.

>> Treasury notes are issued with maturities from two to ten years.

>> Treasury bonds are long-term investments that have maturities of 10 to 30 years from their issue date.

The bills carry denominations of $100 but are sold on the open market at a discount from their face value. You get the full amount when the bill matures. The notes and bonds, on the other hand, are sold at their face value, have a fixed interest rate, and kick off interest payments once every six months. The minimum denomination for notes and bonds is $100.

The main difference among various Treasury offerings is the maturity. Generally, but not always, the longer the term, the higher the rate of interest. Therefore, the longer you can tie up your money, the greater your investment returns are likely to be. So, one of the first questions you need to ask yourself before investing in Treasurys — or most other bonds, for that matter — is the following: When might I need to cash this baby out?

Keep in mind that you don't have to hold any of these securities (bills, notes, or bonds) until maturity. You can, in fact, cash out at any point. (You'll need to do that through a broker, and the broker will charge a commission.) The more time remaining before your bond is fully matured, the more its price can fluctuate and the more you risk losing money.

Treasury inflation-protected securities

Like I bonds, Treasury Inflation-Protected Securities (TIPS), introduced in 1997, receive both interest and a twice-yearly kickup of principal for inflation. As with interest on other Treasury securities, interest on TIPS is free from state and local income taxes. Federal income tax, however, must be coughed up each year on both the interest payments and the growth in principal.

TIPS, unlike I bonds, are transferable. You can buy TIPS directly from the Treasury, through a broker, or in fund form. (More detailed purchasing instructions are coming later in this chapter.)

They're currently being issued with terms of 5, 10, and 30 years, although plenty of 20-year term TIPS are in circulation. The minimum investment to buy an individual Treasury Inflation-Protected Security is $100.

One of the sweet things about TIPS is that if inflation goes on a rampage, your principal moves north right along with it. If *deflation*, a lowering of prices, occurs — though it hasn't since the 1930s — you won't get an inflation adjustment, but you won't get a deflation adjustment, either. You'll get back at least the face value of the bond.

REMEMBER

TIPS sound great, and in many ways they are. Be aware, though, that the coupon rate on TIPS varies with market conditions and tends to be minimal. If inflation is calmer than expected moving into the future, you'll almost certainly do better with traditional Treasurys. If inflation turns out to be higher than expected, your TIPS will be the stars of your fixed-income portfolio.

Also remember that TIPS with longer maturities can be quite volatile, even more so than other bonds. TIPS are designed to keep you even with inflation, and they may do just that, but there's no guarantee. We may, for example, experience an inflation rate of 5 percent over the course of the next year. In that case, your $1,000 invested in TIPS will get you $50 from Uncle Sam. On that score, you have your guarantee. But if investor sentiment turns away from TIPS, your principal may potentially drop by $50 or even more. So, as you can see, TIPS are not manna from heaven.

TIP

Over the very long haul, I would fully expect the return on TIPS to be roughly the same as that on other similar-maturity Treasurys. But on a year-to-year basis, the two kinds of bonds will flip-flop. Flip-flopping — another word for diversification — is a good thing. I generally recommend to clients that about one-quarter of their bond portfolio be devoted to inflation-protected securities. I would recommend less than that to anyone who has a portfolio with lots of stocks (and, perhaps, commodities and real estate), because these have a good track record keeping up with inflation. I might recommend something slightly more than one-quarter of the fixed-income allocation for someone with an all-bond or close to an all-bond portfolio. Because TIPS are federally taxable, and the tax is on the full inflation adjustment, even if you don't see it as cash, TIPS are best kept, if at all possible, in a tax-advantaged account, such as an individual retirement account (IRA).

Getting Down to Business: Corporate Bonds

REMEMBER

To put it bluntly, corporate bonds can be something of a pain in the pants, especially when compared to Treasury bonds, covered earlier in this chapter. Here's what you need to worry about when investing in corporate bonds:

>> **The solidity of the company issuing the bond:** If the company falls to pieces like the Jenga game you played with your kid or grandkid last weekend, you may lose some or all of your money. Even if the company doesn't collapse but merely teeters, you can lose money.

>> **Callability:** There's a chance that the issuing company may call in your bond and spit your money back in your face at some terribly inopportune moment, such as when prevailing interest rates have just taken a tumble.

>> **Liquidity:** Will someone be there to offer you a fair price if and when you need to sell? Will selling the bond require paying some broker a big, fat markup?

>> **Economic upheaval:** In tough economic times, when many companies are closing their doors and the stocks in your portfolio are plummeting, your bonds may decide to join in the unhappy nosedive, en masse. There go your hopes for an easy, sleep-in-late retirement.

So, why even mess with corporate bonds? Some experts argue that corporate bonds are indeed worth all the hassle and doubt because the higher rates of interest they pay make them preferable to Treasurys. Others argue that the difference in interest rates between corporate bonds and Treasurys (known as the *spread*) isn't worth the potential trouble of holding corporates.

Comparing corporate bonds to Treasurys

When it comes to adding stability to a portfolio — the number one reason that bonds belong in your portfolio if you ask me — Treasurys and investment-grade (high-quality) corporate bonds are your two best choices. They may have saved your grandparents from destitution during the Great Depression. They may have spared your 401(k) when most stocks hit the skids in 2000–2002 or when your savings again took a nosedive in 2008.

Generally, corporate bonds tend to outperform Treasurys when the economy is good and underperform when the economy lags.

Over the long run, corporate bonds outdistance Treasurys by a solid margin. According to data from the Stern School of Business at NYU, $100 invested in Treasurys in 1928 would today be worth about $8,600. That same $100 invested in corporate bonds would be worth about $54,300. (And that same $100 invested in stocks would be about $762,000.)

In recent times, with bonds having taken a very serious hit in 2021 and in the first half of 2022, the ten-year annual return on intermediate Treasurys is roughly 1 percent, while the ten-year return on intermediate corporate bonds is approximately 3 percent (versus 13 percent for the U.S. stock market).

You could — you *should* — include both Treasurys *and* corporate bonds in your portfolio. That's what I do with my own money and for most of my clients. That way, you get the best of both worlds.

The crucial credit ratings

Appropriately weighing potential risk and return is what good investing is all about, really. As for the risk and return on corporate bonds, the potential return (always something of a guessing game) is quoted in terms of yield, and there are many kinds. If you haven't yet read Chapter 2, now may be a good time to do so; I detail the various kinds of yield there.

Spreads between corporate bonds and Treasurys can widen and narrow greatly, and sometimes with great rapidity, depending on market sentiment. When people feel good about the economy, they're more likely to trust in corporations, and the corporations don't need to offer the higher interest rates that they do when people are feeling pessimistic.

Regardless of market sentiment, corporate bonds almost always produce higher yield of some sort. Is the extra juice worth the added risk of owning a corporate bond? Only you can decide what suits you best. Whether you decide to invest your money with corporate bond purveyors, and to what degree, will depend on your individual risk tolerance, your need for return, and your trust in the economy. I help you make determinations like these throughout this book, especially in Chapter 9.

Just as risk-return trade-off exists between corporate bonds and Treasurys, there's a big risk-return trade-off among corporate bonds. The largest determinant of the risk and return you take on a bond is the fiscal muscle of the company behind the bond. That fiscal muscle is measured in theory, and often but not always in practice, by a company's credit ratings.

An entire industry is devoted to rating companies by their financial strength. The most common ratings come from Moody's, S&P Global Ratings, and Fitch Ratings, but other rating services exist, such as Dominion and AM Best. Your broker, I assure you, subscribes to at least two of these services and will be happy to share the ratings with you.

The highest ratings — Moody's Aaa and S&P's AAA — are the safest of the safe among corporate bonds, and those ratings are given to few corporations. If you lend money to one of these stellar companies, you should expect in return a rate of interest only modestly higher than Treasurys (even though S&P in 2011 downgraded Treasurys to a "mere" AA rating). As you progress from these five-star companies down the ladder, you can expect higher rates of interest to compensate you for your added risk. Table 3-1 shows how Moody's, S&P, and Fitch define bond credit quality ratings.

TABLE 3-1 Bond Credit Quality Ratings

Credit Risk	Moody's	S&P	Fitch
Investment grade			
Tip-top quality	Aaa	AAA	AAA
Premium quality	Aa	AA	AA
Near-premium quality	A	A	A
Take-home-to-Mom quality	Baa	BBB	BBB
Not investment grade			
Borderline ugly	Ba	BB	BB
Ugly	B	B	B
Definitely don't-take-home-to-Mom quality	Caa	CCC	CCC

Credit Risk	Moody's	S&P	Fitch
You'll be extremely lucky to get your money back	Ca	CC	CC
Interest payments have halted or bankruptcy is in process	C	D	C
Already in default	C	D	D

If you're going to invest in individual bonds, diversification through owning multiple bonds becomes more important as you go lower on the quality ladder. The risk of default is much greater down there, so you'd be awfully foolish to have all your eggs in a basket rated Caa or CCC. (*Default* in bond-talk means that you bid adieu to your principal — or at least a good chunk of it.)

Keep in mind that one risk inherent to corporate bonds is that they may be downgraded, even if they never default. Say a bond is rated A by Moody's. If Moody's gets moody and later rates that bond Baa, the market will respond unfavorably. Chances are, in such a case, that the value of your bond will drop. Of course, the opposite is true, as well. If you buy a Baa bond and it suddenly becomes an A bond, you'll be sitting pretty. If you want to hold your bond to maturity, such downgrades and upgrades aren't going to matter much. But should you decide to sell your bond, they can matter a lot.

TIP

Diversifying your bonds not only by company but also by industry is a good idea. If, say, the utility industry experiences a major upheaval, the rate of both downgrades and defaults is sure to rise. In such a case, you would be better off not having all utility bonds.

How often do defaults occur? According to data from S&P covering the years 1981 to 2020, *no* corporate bonds rated AAA defaulted during that period, and among AA bonds, only a very small handful did. Of all corporate bonds, only a select few are given those gloriously high ratings.

But a company given an AAA or AA rating might not remain super strong forever. The more troubled a company, the lower the odds it can pay back its debt. Moving down the ladder, as you would expect, the default numbers grow. Bonds rated A, in a typical year, will see no defaults, but when the economy hits the ropes, a few A bonds might sink.

Special considerations for investing in corporate debt

Just as maturity is a major consideration when choosing a Treasury (covered earlier in this chapter), it should be a big consideration when choosing corporate bonds. In general, the longer the bond's maturity, the higher its interest rate will be because your money will potentially be tied up longer. And the longer the maturity, the greater the volatility of the price of the bond, especially important if you want to cash out at any point prior to the bond's maturity.

Calculating callability

One consideration that pertains to corporate bonds but not to Treasurys is the nasty issue of callability. Treasurys aren't called. (Once upon a time they were, but no longer.) Corporate bonds, as well as municipal bonds, often are. And that can make a huge difference in the profitability of your investment.

If you own a callable bond, chances are that it will be called at the worst moment — just as interest rates are falling and the value of your bond is on the rise. At that moment, the company that issued the bond, if it has the right to issue a call, no doubt will. And why not? Interest rates have fallen. The firm can pay you off and find someone else to borrow money from at a lower rate. Because calls aren't fun, callable bonds must pay higher rates of interest.

TIP

If you're inclined to go for the extra juice that comes with a callable bond, I say fine. But you should always do so with the assumption that your callable bond will be called. With that in mind, ask the broker to tell you how much (after taking their markup into consideration) your yield will be between today and the call date. Consider that a worst-case yield. (It's often referred to as *yield to worst*, sometimes abbreviated YTW.) Consider it the yield you'll get, and compare it to the yield you'll be getting on other comparable bonds. If you choose the callable bond and it winds up not being called, hey, that's gravy.

WARNING

Some squirrelly bond brokers, to encourage you to place your order to buy, will assure you that a certain callable bond is unlikely to be called. They may be right in some cases, but you should never bank on such promises.

Coveting convertibility

Another wrinkle in corporate bonds is a particular kind of issue called a *convertible bond*. Some corporate bond issuers sell bonds that can be converted into a fixed number of shares of common stock. With a convertible bond, a lender (bondholder) can become a part owner (stockholder) of the company by converting the bond into company stock. Having this option is desirable (options are always desirable, no?), so convertible bonds generally pay lower interest rates than do similar bonds that aren't convertible.

If the stock performs poorly, no conversion happens; you're stuck with your bond's lower return (lower than what a nonconvertible corporate bond would get). If the stock performs well, a conversion happens, so you win (so to speak).

REMEMBER

Convertible bonds, which are fairly common among corporate bonds, introduce a certain measure of unpredictability into a portfolio. As I explain in Chapter 10, perhaps the most important investment decision you can make is how to divide your portfolio between stocks and bonds. With convertibles, whatever careful allotment you come up with can be changed overnight. Your bonds suddenly become stocks. You're rewarded for making a good investment, but just as soon as you receive that reward, your portfolio becomes riskier. It's the old trade-off in action.

I'm not saying that convertible bonds are horrible investments, but I'm not sure they deserve a sizable allotment in most individuals' portfolios.

Reversing convertibility — imagine that

One relative newcomer to the world of corporate bonds is the *reverse convertible* security, sometimes referred to as a *revertible* or a *revertible note*. I'm really not too thrilled with this product.

WARNING

A reverse convertible converts to a stock automatically if a certain company stock tumbles below a certain point by a certain date. Why would anyone want such a thing? You guessed it: The bond pays a thrillingly high interest rate (perhaps 2 or 3 or more percentage points above and beyond even the high rates paid on junk bonds), but only for a year or so. That's the hook. The catch is that the company paying the high interest rate is often in dire trouble. If it goes under, you could lose a bundle. Is that really the kind of risk you want to take with a fixed-income investment?

Appreciating high yield for what it is

Bonds don't exactly jump from investment-grade to high-yield bonds, sometimes known as *junk bonds*. There are, of course, shades of investment-grade and shades of junk. But generally, if a bond receives a rating less than a Baa from Moody's or a BBB from S&P, the market considers it high yield or junk.

High-yield bonds offer greater excitement for the masses. The old adage that risk equals return is clear as day in the world of bonds. High-yield bonds offer greater yield than investment-grade bonds, and they're more volatile. But they're also one other thing: much more correlated to the stock market. In fact, during a recession, as well as in times of swiftly rising inflation, stocks and junk bonds will move in the same direction most of the time. Treasurys and investment-grade corporate bonds are much, much less correlated — during all kinds of market conditions. And during recessions and depressions, when stocks really take it on the chin, Treasurys especially usually shine. So, if bonds are going to serve as ballast for our portfolios, which is what they do best, why would anyone want high-yield bonds?

Many people misunderstand them. If they understood them better, they probably wouldn't invest. They certainly wouldn't opt to give high-yield bonds a major allocation on the fixed-income side of the portfolio.

Powerful and a Tad Mysterious: Agency Bonds

Some agency bonds are like Treasury bonds, backed by the so-called full faith and credit of the U.S. government. You're going to get your principal back even if Congress has to do the unthinkable and tax the rich.

REMEMBER

Most agency bonds, however, are not backed by the *full* faith and credit, but perhaps by *nine-tenths* of the faith and credit of the U.S. government. The language used is that the federal government has assumed a *moral obligation* or an *implied guarantee* to stand behind these bonds. No one I've ever met seems to know what an implied guarantee really means. I can tell you, however, that no one ever lost their principal investing in agency bonds due to a default.

Some agency bonds are traditional in the sense that they pay a steady rate of interest and usually, like most bonds, issue payments twice a year. Others are more free-floating. But roughly three-quarters of agency bonds are entirely different animals. These odd ducks are called *mortgage-backed securities*; they pay interest *and* principal, usually monthly, with the amount potentially varying greatly from payment to payment.

Identifying the bond issuers

Who or what issues agency bonds? The answer to that question is more complex than you may imagine. Here are just some of the many agencies that issue bonds:

>> Federal Farm Credit Banks (FFCB)

>> Federal Home Loan Banks (FHLB)

>> Federal Home Loan Mortgage Corporation (FHLMC)

>> Federal National Mortgage Association (FNMA)

>> Financial Assistance Corporation (FAC)

>> General Services Administration (GSA)

>> Government National Mortgage Association (GNMA)

>> Government Trust Certificates (GTC)

>> Private Export Funding Corporation (PEFCO)

>> Resolution Funding Corporation (REFCORP)

>> Small Business Administration (SBA)

>> Tennessee Valley Authority (TVA)

>> U.S. Agency for International Development (USAID)

The first thing to know about these various government agencies is that they fit under two large umbrellas — well, maybe three umbrellas at the moment. Some of the agencies that issue bonds really are U.S. federal agencies; they're an actual part of the government just as Congress, the jet engines on Air Force One, and the fancy silverware at the White House are. Such official agencies include the GSA, the SBA, and USAID.

Most of the so-called agencies, however, aren't quite parts of the government. Technically speaking, they're *government-sponsored enterprises* (GSEs): corporations created by Congress to work for the common good but then set out more or less on their own.

Many of these faux agencies are publicly held, issuing stock on the major exchanges. Such pseudo-agencies include the Federal Home Loan Mortgage Corporation (known colloquially as *Freddie Mac*), the Federal National Mortgage Association (known as *Fannie Mae*), and the Federal Home Loan Banks. You notice, of course, that these nongovernmental enterprises start with the word *federal*. Confusing, isn't it?

REMEMBER

What's the difference between federal agencies and government-sponsored enterprises, especially with regard to their bonds? The official-government group issues bonds that carry the full faith and credit of the U.S. government. The second group, well, their bonds carry that mysterious implicit guarantee or moral obligation. Because this second group is much larger than the first both in terms of the number of agencies and the value of the bonds they issue, when investment experts speak of *agency bonds*, they're almost always talking about the bonds of the GSEs.

Now, if matters weren't complicated enough, you'll recall that I mention the recent appearance of a third umbrella. Ready? After finding themselves in hot water during the subprime mortgage crisis, the two largest of the GSEs — Freddie Mac and Fannie Mae — are currently in *receivership*. In other words, for well over a decade now, they've been legal wards of the federal government. So, for the moment, they are, in effect, more like real federal agencies than they are GSEs. At least as far as bondholders are concerned, the bonds of these two agencies for the time being no longer carry the *implicit* government guarantee of your investments. Instead, they now carry the *explicit* guarantee. The future remains uncertain.

Sizing up the government's actual commitment

No GSE yet has defaulted on its bonds, whether traditional bonds or mortgage-backed securities. Because of the very small risk of default inherent in agency bonds, the greater risk of price volatility due to public sentiment, and lesser liquidity and less certain tax considerations, agency bonds — at least those that are not mortgage-backed — tend to pay slightly higher rates of interest than Treasury bonds. The spread between Treasurys and the agency bonds is almost never beyond half a percentage point.

The mortgage-backed securities that agencies issue tend to yield higher returns than other agency bonds, not because of the risk of default but because of their greater volatility given the ups and downs of the mortgage market to which the interest payments are tied.

Eyeing default risks, yields, markups, and more

The honest-and-true federal agencies, such as the SBA, are said to have no risk of default; therefore, their bonds pay more or less what Treasurys do. You may get a smidgen more interest — maybe 5 basis points, or 5/100 of 1 percent — to compensate you for the lesser *liquidity* of such agency bonds because they're harder to sell in a flash.

Other agency bonds are issued by GSEs, and the risk of default, although real, is probably next to nothing. But you get a higher rate of interest on these bonds than you do with Treasurys to compensate you for the fact that the risk of default does exist.

REMEMBER

With all agency bonds, you pay a markup when you buy and sell, which you don't with Treasurys if you buy them directly from the government. If you're dealing in individual bonds and you're not careful, that markup could easily eat up your first several months of earnings. It also could make the difference between agency bonds and Treasury bonds a wash.

Most agency bonds pay a fixed rate of interest twice a year. About 25 percent of them are *callable*, meaning that the agencies issuing the bonds have the right to redeem the bond and return your principal. The other 75 percent are noncallable bonds, which are sometimes referred to as *bullet bonds*. Callable bonds tend to pay somewhat higher rates of interest, but your investment takes on a certain degree of uncertainty.

TIP

When choosing among different agencies, you want to carefully compare yield to maturity, which Chapter 2 covers, and make sure that you know full well whether you're buying a traditional bond or a mortgage-backed security. They're completely different animals.

Weighing taxation matters

REMEMBER

The taxes you pay on agency bonds vary. Interest from bonds issued by Freddie Mac and Fannie Mae is fully taxable. The interest on most other agency bonds — including the king of agency bonds, the Federal Home Loan Banks — is exempt from state and local tax.

Treasury bonds, which most resemble agency bonds, are always exempt from state and local tax. And munis are almost always free from federal tax. Needless to say, your personal tax bracket will make some bonds look better than others.

Banking Your Money on Other People's Mortgages

Far more complicated even than floaters are the mortgage-backed securities issued by federal agencies such as the Government National Mortgage Association (known colloquially as *Ginnie Mae*) and by some GSEs, such as Fannie Mae and Freddie Mac. As I point out earlier in this chapter, most bonds referred to as *agency bonds* are mortgage-backed securities. And they're a huge part of the U.S. bond market — about 28 percent of the Bloomberg U.S. Aggregate Bond Index, to which many "total bond market" funds are linked.

Mortgage-backed securities— the majority of which are issued by agencies — are very different from most other bonds. They don't offer as consistent and predictable a stream of interest income as do most bonds.

Bathing in the mortgage pool

When you purchase a mortgage-backed security from, say, Ginnie Mae (minimum investment $25,000), your money goes into a pool of mortgages. Whereas most bonds pay you a set rate of interest, usually twice a year, mortgage-backed securities pay you a certain rate of interest plus the steady or not-so-steady return of your principal. (You don't get a big lump sum when the bond matures.) Most mortgage-backed securities issue monthly payments.

The amount of principal you get back on a monthly basis is determined largely by the rate at which mortgage-holders pay off their debt. If interest rates drop and thousands of the mortgage holders decide suddenly to prepay their existing mortgages so they can refinance, you may get back your principal much faster than you'd anticipated. In a sense, a mortgage-backed security has the same "back-atcha" risk as a callable bond.

Deciding whether to invest in the housing market

You don't need to invest the $25,000 minimum required by Ginnie Mae to invest in mortgage-backed securities. You can get a Freddie Mac for as little as $1,000. But should you?

No, I don't think so. Neither does David Lambert, founding partner of Collins Lambert Integrated Wealth Management based in Lebanon, New Jersey. Lambert was formerly the head trader at the agency-bond desk for a major Wall Street firm. This guy knows a *lot* about agency bonds. "If I were a retail investor, unless I had a really huge amount of money and felt that I really knew what I was doing, I wouldn't invest directly in mortgage-backed securities," Lambert says. "The complexity of them makes them inappropriate for the average investor."

TIP

Instead, says Lambert, if you want to invest in mortgage-backed securities, do so by investing in, perhaps, a good mortgage-backed security fund. "There are plenty of good ones out there — both mutual funds and exchange-traded funds. I'd look to a solid company like Vanguard, Fidelity, iShares, or PIMCO," he says. I discuss bond funds, and fund companies such as these (which I also tend to like), in depth in Chapter 5.

(Practically) Tax-Free: Municipal Bonds

If not for the fact that munis are exempt from federal income tax, their popularity over the years would've rivaled a pitcher of buttermilk at a college keg party. Historically, the returns on high-quality munis have been about 80 percent of what Treasurys have paid. But a strange thing has happened lately. In the past couple of years, munis, as a bond category, have paid out at just about the same rate as Treasurys — at times, even more. Keep in mind, of course, that Treasurys aren't exactly world-famous for their high returns. They never were, and they especially aren't these days. However, although munis are generally safe investments, they aren't as safe as Treasurys.

Sizing up the muni market

In 2021, thousands of issuers across the United States issued $358 billion in municipal bonds. That's small potatoes compared to the size of the Treasury market. But, unlike Treasurys, which are held by both individual and government investors all over the world, munis are purchased almost entirely by U.S. households. Munis, due to their tantalizing tax advantage, are the only major kind of bond more popular with individual investors than with institutions.

The issuers of municipal bonds include, of course, municipalities (duh), such as cities and towns. But they also include states, U.S. territories, counties, public universities, certain private universities, airports, not-for-profit hospitals, public power plants, water and sewer administrations, various and sundry nonprofit organizations, bridge and tunnel authorities, housing authorities, and an occasional research foundation.

Any government, local agency, nonprofit, or what-have-you that is deemed to serve the public good, with a blessing from the IRS and sometimes voters, may have the honor of issuing a municipal bond.

Comparing and contrasting munis with other bonds

The tax-exempt status of munis is unquestionably their most notable and easily recognizable characteristic. Like most bonds, munis come with differing maturities. Some mature in a year or less, others in 20 or 30 years, and a select few have even longer maturities. Unlike most bonds, munis tend to be issued in minimal denominations of $5,000 and multiples of $5,000 (not a minimum of $1,000 and multiples of $1,000, like corporate bonds and most Treasurys).

Unlike Treasurys, both corporate bonds and munis are often *callable*, meaning the issuer can kick back your money and sever your relationship before the bond matures. Like other bonds, munis generally have a fixed interest rate, but the price of the bond can go up and down; unless you hold your bond to maturity, you may or may not get your principal returned in full. (And even if you get your principal back in full, it may have been seriously eaten away by inflation after several decades in hiding.) If the maturity of the bond is many years off, the price of the bond can go up and down considerably — usually in inverse relation to interest rates, as Chapter 2 discusses.

Delighting in diversification

The tax-exempt status of munis isn't the only reason they may belong in your portfolio. Municipal bonds also offer a fair degree of diversification, even from other bonds.

Because they're the only kind of bond more popular with households than with institutions, the muni market may, at times, be swayed more by public demand than other bond markets. For example, when the stock market tanks and individual investors get butterflies in their stomachs, they tend to sell out of their stock holdings (often a mistake) and load up on what they see as less risky investments — bonds of all sorts, including munis.

REMEMBER

When the demand for munis goes up, just as when the demand for, say, gold or oil goes up, it tends to drive prices higher. Popular demand or lack of demand can have a huge effect on muni pricing — more so than individual-investor caprices influence the values of corporate bonds and Treasurys. Those taxable bonds, in contrast, tend to be more interest-rate sensitive. As I discuss in Chapter 2, when interest rates rise, bond prices generally fall; when interest rates drop, bond prices tend to move up.

The differences among the many kinds of bonds indicate it's likely a good idea to hold at least several varieties in your portfolio. As an example of the kind of diversification I'm talking about, consider that in 2010, investment-grade (high-quality) corporate bonds returned nearly 18 percent. (Interest rates were falling, which is good for bonds, and corporations were starting to look stronger after the pummeling of 2008.) But that same year, munis returned a mere 2 percent. The following year, in 2011, munis made a phenomenal comeback; it was their turn to shine. They earned, in the aggregate, a tax-free 10 percent. Meanwhile, corporate bonds began to slow, earning about 7.5 percent for the year.

More recently, in 2021, as interest rates rose and the COVID-19 pandemic raged on, munis more than held their own, as taxable bonds slipped. By the end of the year, the S&P U.S. Aggregate Bond Index, measuring both Treasurys and corporate bonds, fell by –1.4 percent, while the S&P Municipal Bond Index rose 1.77 percent. If we look at ten-year returns for the two indexes, as of the end of 2021, the S&P U.S. Aggregate Bond index clocked in at 2.86 percent, while the S&P Municipal Bond Index rose by 3.22 percent. It was an extremely good decade for munis.

Choosing from a vast array of possibilities

You want munis that are rated, whether or not they're prerefunded, insured, or general obligation bonds. Quite a few municipal offerings aren't rated. An unrated bond may be perfectly fine, with the issuer on firm financial footing, but perhaps a small concern that didn't feel like paying for the ratings. (Oh, yes, bond issuers need to pay to be rated.) But you'll need to do a lot of digging to confirm that the issuer is able to repay the loan. And remember that small-fry bond issues, even if the issuer is fiscally sound, may still be very *illiquid*, meaning you may not be able to sell the bonds when you want, if at all. I suggest, if you're an average investor, going mostly with the top-rated munis: Moody's Aa or higher.

WARNING

The lower-rated munis may give you a bit extra yield, but they probably aren't worth the added risk, except perhaps for a limited portion of your portfolio. Keep in mind that a lower-rated bond can be more volatile than a higher-rated one. Default isn't the only risk. If you suddenly need to cash out the muni part of your portfolio, and high-yield munis are in the tank, you may not have access to much of your cash.

TIP

As long as a muni has a high rating and is a general obligation muni (not a revenue muni), consider going without the insurance or pre-refunding for that possible drop of extra juice. General obligation bonds generally don't default. On average, we've seen only one such default each decade. That's not to say it can't happen to you tomorrow, but if you choose a top-rated general obligation bond, your odds of losing money to a default are about on a par with the odds that my dog, Zoey, will run for public office.

You also want to choose a municipal bond that carries a maturity you can live with. (Most pre-refunded bonds have short maturities.) If the bond is callable, well, is that something you can live with and still be happy about? Callable bonds pay slightly higher coupon rates but are less predictable than noncallable bonds.

REMEMBER

When choosing munis, their tax benefits are of great importance — and those benefits can vary. Do you want a muni that's merely free from federal income tax, or do you want a muni that's double- or triple-tax-free? Here's the scoop:

>> *National munis* are exempt from federal tax but aren't necessarily exempt from state income tax. (Some states tax bond coupon payments, and others don't.)

>> *State munis,* if purchased by residents of the same state, are typically exempt from state tax, if there is one. Some state munis are also exempt from all local taxes.

>> Munis that are exempt from both federal and state tax are called *double-tax-free* bonds. Some locally issued bonds may be exempt from federal, state, *and* local tax; these are often referred to as *triple-tax-free* bonds.

You need to do a bit of math to determine which kind is better for you: national or state, double- or triple-tax-free. Consult your tax advisor before laying out any big money on munis. The tax rules are complicated and forever changing. Some states impose taxes if you invest in states other than your own, but others may even tax you on munis issued by your own state. Bonds issued in Puerto Rico and other U.S. territories carry their own tax peculiarities. It's a jungle out there!

International Bonds and Other Seemingly Exotic Offerings

Very few American investors own foreign bonds directly. Those who have any exposure whatsoever tend to get that exposure through funds, whether mutual funds or exchange-traded funds (ETFs). But even in the fund world, international bonds are afterthoughts. Given the gargantuan size of the foreign bond market, you may find that last sentence a bit surprising — especially because foreign bonds sometimes make very sensible investments. And although it was once difficult to invest in this arena, it's easy today. Most of the 240 funds that allow for exposure to either international or global bonds have been around for several years. (*Global* refers to a mix of U.S. and non-U.S.)

When most investment professionals look at the world of global fixed income, they see two large categories of bonds: developed-world bonds and emerging-market bonds.

Developed-world bonds

Just as the U.S. government and corporations issue bonds, so, too, do the governments and corporations of Australia, Canada, England, France, Germany, Italy, Japan, Sweden, and many other countries, large and small, hot and cold, rich and not-so-rich. Foreign bonds, just like domestic bonds, come with varying maturities, risk levels, and peculiar characteristics. Some are callable; others not. Some are inflation-adjusted; others not. Some are fixed-rate; others have floating rates. Some, like U.S. bonds, tend to pay interest semiannually. Others, such as most European bonds, pay interest annually. Needless to say, not all foreign bonds yield the same return.

Whether they're issued by corporations or by governments, foreign bonds may be dollar-denominated; these are often called *Yankee bonds*. But most are denominated in the currency of their home countries, be it euros, pounds, yen, or krona.

Over the long run, you can expect that bonds of similar credit quality and duration, bearing similar risk, should yield roughly equal returns, no matter in which country they're issued or sold. After all, if British bonds consistently paid higher rates of interest than U.S. bonds, investment money would start to float eastward across the big pond. U.S. bond issuers, such as the Treasury, the state of California, and Microsoft, would eventually either have to up their coupon rates or raise capital another way, such as with bake sales or bingo games.

In the short run, however, interest rates can vary among bond markets, and more importantly, exchange rates can fluctuate wildly. U.S. investors putting their money into foreign fixed income are generally looking at fairly volatile investments compared to U.S. bonds — although that volatility can be greatly tempered by hedging the currency, as many foreign-bond fund mangers do. On the flip side, foreign bonds, especially without currency hedging, tend to have limited correlation to U.S. bonds (meaning their value is independent of U.S. bonds), so owning some foreign fixed income can be a sensible diversifier.

Investing in individual bonds is tricky. Investing in individual foreign bonds is trickier — kinda like buying a villa in Venice as opposed to a condo in Connecticut. To tap into the foreign fixed-income market, you're better off looking at investing through a mutual fund or ETF. Most foreign-bond funds are pricier than their U.S. cousins. Years ago, the difference was enormous, but nowadays, the difference is fairly slight. According to Morningstar Direct, the average domestic fixed-income fund has a management fee of 0.73 percent. The average global fixed-income fund is 0.85 percent for developed markets and 0.99 percent for emerging markets.

TIP

In Chapter 5, I provide the names of various mutual funds and ETFs that offer exposure to foreign developed-world bonds at a relatively reasonable price. Some of these funds offer pure unhedged exposure. Some are dollar-hedged. When a fund is *dollar-hedged*, it means the manager is using sophisticated financial tools (usually currency forwards) to offset any currency flux. These hedged funds (not to be confused with hedge funds) are less volatile than the currency unhedged funds, but you lose a lot of the diversification power.

The bonds of emerging-market nations

Emerging markets is something of a euphemism for nations we *hope* are emerging, otherwise known as the poorer countries of the world. Those who invest in these nations *hope* that they're emerging, but no one can say with any certainty. In any case, if you want to buy bonds issued in Argentina, Brazil, Indonesia, Mexico, Turkey, or Venezuela, the opportunities are out there. The interest rates can be considerably higher than the interest rates you find in the developed world; the trade-off is that the volatility can be enough to make your stomach contents start emerging.

The majority of emerging-market bonds are so-called *sovereign bonds*. That title sounds like it may have something to do with kings and queens, but all *sovereign* means is that these bonds are issued by national governments. U.S. Treasury bonds are sovereign bonds.

Unlike the bonds issued by developed nations, such as Germany, Japan, and Norway, most emerging-market bonds are denominated in U.S. dollars, although that's slowly changing. Still, given the poverty, tsetse flies carrying disease, and other problems of these nations, the governments' abilities to repay loans can be shaky. And then there's "geopolitical" risk. As I'm writing these words, the price of Russian bonds has tumbled as Vladimir Putin wages war on Ukraine, the civilized nations of the world enact strict economic penalties on Russia, the Russian economy verges on collapse, and the risk of Russia defaulting on its bonds rises with each passing day. Perhaps needless to say, Ukrainian bonds have fallen even harder.

There's been lots of talk lately about how the ratio of debt to gross domestic product (GDP) has reached higher levels in many developed-world nations than in many emerging-market nations. At present, the government-debt-to-GDP ratio is higher in France, Japan, and the United States than it is in Indonesia, Mexico, or Turkey. This is a turnaround from historical norms. But the government-debt-to-GDP ratio isn't the only determinant of a nation's default risk. And the ratings firms know this. Emerging-market nations — because of unstable governments, economies that are often reliant on commodity prices, lack of infrastructure, and geopolitical turmoil — are riskier places in which to invest and likely will remain such. Emerging-market bonds, therefore, must offer higher interest rates to remain attractive to investors.

I like emerging-market bonds, and I think they can belong (in modest amounts) in most portfolios of any fair size. If you're going to have high-yield bonds in your portfolio, emerging-market bonds make sense. When recession hits the United States and the Dow and S&P have a rough year, U.S. high-yield (junk) bonds usually tank. That makes sense. As companies hit hard times, marginal companies are most likely to default. Emerging-market bonds, however, have somewhat limited correlation to the U.S. stock market despite their synced tumble in 2008. That's why I advocate a small allocation — perhaps 6 percent to 8 percent — of a well-diversified bond portfolio in emerging-market bonds.

TIP

But, given the volatility of these bonds and the potentially high returns, I look at them more like stock investments than bond investments; in fashioning portfolios, I put emerging-market bonds on the equity side of the pie. There's only one practical way to invest in emerging-market bonds, and that's through a fund. I suggest some good fund options — both mutual funds and ETFs — in Chapter 5.

Bond Investing with a Conscience

Whatever your religion, whatever your personal values, you may find a bond or bond fund out there waiting for you to express your beliefs. No one ever said that making money has to be all about making money.

Having faith in church bonds

Churches in the United States have issued bonds for more than a century now. The bonds are most often secured by a deed of trust on church real estate or other property. Traditionally, most of these bonds have been sold as private offerings to bona fide members of the church congregation only. But in the past decades, a market has grown for church bonds offered to the general public.

Church bonds look and feel something like corporate bonds, but they have a certain advantage in that they're almost always backed by the issuer's real property. For that reason, when property held stable value, as it did for many years, church bonds rarely defaulted. But that situation changed when the real estate market tumbled in 2007–2008, and a number of churches missed payments on their bonds. Since then, the waters have been rather calm.

Charles Major is the president of Share Financial Services of Dallas, one of three broker-dealers in the United States that specialize in church bonds. He says that the historical default rate on church bonds is between 2 percent and 3 percent, but *default* means failing to make just one payment. In part because the bonds are backed by a hard asset, more serious defaults are relatively unknown. And that's the big advantage to church bonds, says Major. "You're going to get interest similar to what you'd get on a corporate BBB bond, but with risk comparable to what you'd get buying an AA bond."

The downside is that these bonds are fairly *illiquid*, meaning they're tough to sell without taking a significant hit. If you buy one — normally available in increments of $250, with a $1,000 minimum — you should plan on holding till maturity (the bond's, not yours). The other downside is that given the size of the issuances, the ratings agencies don't evaluate church bonds. You're entirely on your own to do your *due diligence* (homework in financial-speak). Oh, one other downside: Nearly all church bonds are callable, meaning that the church may give you your money back and retire the bond before it matures.

Church bonds are viable alternatives to corporate bonds, especially if you care where your money is going and reap emotional reward from knowing that you're helping to fund the growth of a church. But the offerings are limited, and most of the bonds can only be purchased by residents of certain states.

TIP

If you shop for church bonds, don't do it on a prayer; shop as you would for any other bond. As of 2009, church bonds have been given International Standard Book Numbers (ISBNs) and listed on the Trade Reporting and Compliance Engine (TRACE) system that allows you to see recent buys and sells and yields. Make sure you read the prospectus and understand the risks involved. Note especially the collateral offered on the bond. Then get competitive offers, and be sure that you're not paying an unreasonable markup to the broker. Chapter 4 provides a list of holy commandments for dealing in individual bonds of any faith.

These three broker-dealers specialize in church bonds and may be able to provide guidance above and beyond what you'd get from other brokers:

>> **CND Financial LTD:** www.cndfinancial.com or 800-810-3355

>> **Share Financial Services:** https://sharefinancial.com or 800-331-9152

>> **Stifel:** https://stifelinstitutional.com or 210-321-3039

Adhering to Islamic law: Introducing sukuk

According to Islamic principles, paying or charging interest is a definite no-no. You'd think, therefore, that bond investing would be sinful. Well, the sinfulness depends on the nature of the bond you purchase. Some special bonds, called *sukuk* (pronounced *soo-cook*), actually allow for virtuous investing, at least according to some followers of Islam. Other followers see the sukuk as smoke and mirrors. But although the controversy continues, there's about $711 billion in sukuk floating around the world, according to Fitch Ratings. In fact, you can even track sukuk performance with the Dow Jones Sukuk Index.

Most of these bonds are being issued in Islamic countries — Indonesia, Malaysia, and Saudi Arabia foremost — and sold to Middle Eastern and European investors. And though they may not be selling like hotcakes, sukuk bonds in the United States are on the market.

Traditional bonds pay you a fixed interest amount over the life of the bond, and then you get your principal back upon maturity. Sukuk may also pay you a fixed rate, but it isn't called interest, and the money is said to come not from the lending itself but rather from the sale or leasing of certain tangible assets, such as property, oil profits, or aircraft assets. A sukuk in full compliance with Islamic law also can't guarantee your principal; the return of your initial investment, as with your share of profits, may depend on whatever returns are garnered from the assets backing the bond.

Note that Islamic law, like the law of many other religions and governments, is often subject to interpretation. Just ask the bankers at Goldman Sachs who announced a $2 billion sukuk deal in late 2011 that wound up being hotly debated, with some Islamic scholars blessing the proposed deal and others objecting to it.

The central tenet of Islamic law is that money can't have any real value in and of itself, explains Eric Meyer, chairman and CEO of Shariah Capital, a Connecticut-based financial product development firm specializing in Islamic offerings. "Returns from an investment must stem from a hard asset that is both real and substantial," he says.

Like a traditional bond, a sukuk has a maturity date and a certain rate of return, but that rate of return may be either fixed or floating and is always backed by some hard ("real and substantial," as Meyer says) asset.

So far, the sukuk market in the United States is pretty small. But keep your eyes and ears open; more will likely be coming. I have no direct experience with sukuk, so all I can say is to do a lot of research before investing. (*Islamic Finance For Dummies*, by Dr. Faleel Jamaldeen [Wiley], is a good place to start.) If you're Muslim, you may want to check with your mullah to ascertain whether a particular offering meets your religious needs.

There's one, and only one, mutual fund sold in the United States that offers sukuk bonds, and that's the Amana Participation Fund (AMAPX), which has been around since 2015. The fund offers a mix of investment-grade and high-yield (junk) bonds. Amana charges 0.82 percent, fairly high in this low-interest-rate environment, but not outrageous. Most of the bond issuers are from emerging-market nations. See www.saturna.com for more information.

Sustainability-linked bonds

Let me clarify off the bat that I'm *not* talking in this section about ESG bonds. ESG stands for *environmental, social, and governance,* the criteria being used by many who want to invest for the good of humanity and the planet. ESG bonds once upon a time may have warranted discussion in a chapter on "exotic" offerings, but ESG is now decidedly mainstream.

What *is* exotic is something called *sustainability-linked bonds.* These bonds, unlike the majority of bonds, don't pay a fixed interest rate. Instead, they pay a certain rate of interest with *coupon step-ups* (added interest) if certain ESG goals aren't met. In 2019, the Italian energy group Enel SpA launched the first sustainability-linked bonds, worth $1.5 billion, with a five-year maturity. Investors get 2.65 percent interest if the company reaches its target of 55 percent renewable energy. If the company fails to do so, the interest rate increases by a quarter of a percentage point each year until the bond matures.

Since that time, numerous other companies have followed suit — more on the European side of the Atlantic than on this side, although it seems to be building some kind of traction here, especially among energy companies. NRG Energy, Solaris Midstream Holdings, and Enbridge, Inc., have all offered sustainability-linked bonds. Enbridge, an Alberta-based energy delivery firm, recently issued $1 billion (U.S. dollars) for a 12-year note paying 2.5 percent. If the company doesn't meet certain ESG goals involving greenhouse gas emissions, diversity in its workforce, and at least 40 percent women on the board by 2025, investors should see incremental bumps in their coupon payments to as high as 3.05 percent.

WARNING

Keep your eye open for more sustainability-linked bond offerings, but treat them with a tad of skepticism. Note that the company issuing the bond generally sets its own ESG goals. Depending on what those goals are, and depending on how competitively the interest rate compared to similar bonds, sustainability linkage could be either a good thing or a gimmicky thing.

Exploring the Bond Marketplace

IN THIS PART . . .

Pick individual bonds to invest in and know how to navigate the individual bond market.

Choose bond funds by slicing through the hyperbole and focusing on what matters.

Slake your thirst for cold, hard cash by expanding your idea of fixed income and exploring the concept of rebalancing.

Retire in comfort and security by getting familiar with optimal bond allocation and permissible rates of withdrawal.

Chapter **4**

Diving (Carefully!) into Individual Bonds

B y the time you read these words, this very chapter may well seem antiquated. That's how rapidly the world of individual bond trading is changing.

In this chapter, I do my best to get you up to current speed. And should the tales I tell become faded by time, fear not: I give you a few online resources so that with the tap of some keys and the click of a mouse, you can access the most modern methods — the most efficient, friendly, and profitable methods — for buying and selling individual bonds.

Navigating Today's Individual Bond Market

Typically, someone called a broker (an individual wearing a fancy suit) trades your bonds. A broker buys a bond at one price and sells it at a higher price. The difference, known as the *bid/ask spread*, is what the broker brings home. We're sometimes talking *lots* of bacon here. The bid/ask spreads on bonds can be big enough to make the commissions sometimes paid on stocks look like greyhound fat.

Once upon a time, and for many decades, commissions on stocks were as fat as spreads on bonds, sometimes fatter. In 1975, the Securities and Exchange Commission (SEC) deregulated the stock markets, allowing for open competition and discount brokerage houses. The competition brought down prices somewhat. Internet trading, which allowed the brokerage houses to economize, brought down prices even more. Within a few years, the money that most people spent to make a stock trade was reduced to a fraction of what it had been. In the 1970s, a typical stock trade cost $100 (more than $400 in today's dollars). Today, a stock trade may cost as little as $5, if it even costs that. Many brokerages charge you zilch.

And how has bond trading changed since 1975? It has changed, but like *men's* fashions change, not women's. You have to look harder to notice the differences.

Getting some transparency

Bond trading today is, in a sense, about where stock trading was in, oh, maybe the 1990s. You can find discount brokers (like Fidelity, Schwab, and Vanguard) who'll let you trade bonds online for as little as $1 a bond. Or you can spend $15 or $20 per bond or way more — up to several hundred dollars on the cost of a single trade. Even though, in 2018, the SEC passed a ruling that bond traders must reveal their take, bond traders can get around this ruling, and even when complying, the earnings of the broker and the cuts of various dealers with whom the broker works are often hidden in fine print.

TIP

Smart investors can — and should — ask brokers exactly what they're paying. Or, better yet, they can go to a system called the *Trade Reporting and Compliance Engine*. The Engine, otherwise known as TRACE, has made bond trading a bit more like stock trading, but considerably more complicated. TRACE is a system run by the Financial Industry Regulatory Authority (FINRA) that you can access through many financial websites, such as www.finra.org. This system ensures that every corporate bond trade in the United States is reported, and the details appear on the web.

TRACE ensures that trading costs are no longer hidden, bond yields (greatly affected by the bid/ask spreads) are easy to find, and good information is available. Among investment people, access to information is generally referred to as *transparency*. TRACE provides some pretty amazing transparency.

Unfortunately, not everyone knows about the TRACE system. Often, people don't realize that they can find out — for free — the price a broker paid, or at least a good estimate of what a broker paid for a bond. The world today is divided more or less evenly, I'd say, between those who know about TRACE and how to use it and those who don't. Those who don't know about TRACE pay a heavy price. Those who do, well, you're about to become one of those lucky people!

Ushering in a new beginning

The transparency that exists today, first ushered into practice between 2002 and 2005, has removed much of the mystery from bond trading. You can now go online and quickly get a pretty good idea of how much dealers and individuals are buying and selling a single bond for. You can also see how far a broker — *your* broker — is trying to mark up a bond and exactly what yield you'll get after the broker and all the broker's cousins have taken their cuts.

Unfortunately, the cuts taken on bond trades still tend to be too high, and you can't (except in rare circumstances) bypass the broker. But with some smart navigating on your part, you won't make the broker terribly rich at your expense either.

Dealing with Brokers and Other Financial Professionals

As I explain more fully in Chapter 11, you're probably better off investing primarily in bond funds than individual bonds unless you have a bond portfolio (not your total portfolio, but just the bond side of your portfolio) of perhaps $400,000. Building a diversified bond portfolio — diversified by type of bond, issuer, and maturity — is hard unless you have that amount to work with. Negotiating good prices on bonds is also hard when you're dealing with amounts that brokers tend to sneeze at.

Investing in individual bonds also requires substantially more work than investing in bond funds. With individual bonds, not only do you need to haggle, but you need to haggle again and again. After all, with individual bonds, you typically get interest payments every six months. Unless you spend the money right away, you need to concern yourself with constantly reinvesting those interest payments. Doing so can be a real job.

Then there's the risk of default. With Treasurys and agency bonds, you can presume that the risk of default is negligible, and with high-quality munis and top corporations, the risk is minimal. With most corporate bonds and some munis, however, the risk of the company or municipality losing its ability to pay you back is real. Even when issuers don't default, the major rating agencies may downgrade their bonds. A downgrade can mean a loss of money, too, if you decide you can't hold a bond till maturity. Don't start dabbling in individual corporate bonds or munis unless you're willing to put in some serious time and effort doing research.

With these caveats in mind, the first thing you need to be an investor in individual bonds is a *dealer* (someone or some institution to place the actual trades for you without robbing you blind or steering you astray).

Identifying the role of the dealer

Some bond dealers are very knowledgeable about fixed-income investing and can help walk you through the maze, making good suggestions for your portfolio. Some are very talented at finding the best buys in bonds and using certain sophisticated strategies to juice your fixed-income returns.

Unfortunately, the way dealers are paid creates a system where the traditional dealer's financial interests are somewhat in opposition to the interests of clients. The more the dealer makes, the less the client keeps. The more the client keeps, the less the dealer makes. The more the dealer can get you to *flip* (trade one bond for another), the more the dealer makes. Generally, the more you flip, the less likely you are to come out ahead.

I'm not saying that dealers are bad people or greedy people. I'm just saying that bond dealers are salespeople (some of them fabulously paid salespeople) and need to be seen as such.

Like those who sell cars, bond traders who act as *principals* (taking ownership of the bond) for many years weren't required to reveal what kind of markup they were making. That has changed, but only partially. They must reveal their markup, but not on all bonds. And they only have to reveal the markup after the trade. Also, you may have to ask. If you're a whiz at math, you can also figure out the markup, more or less, using TRACE (see the earlier section "Getting some transparency").

TIP

Some bond dealers today work as *agents* and charge you a flat fee, an hourly rate, a commission per trade (like a stock), or a percentage of assets under management. Like a good broker, a bond agent may know the ropes of bond trading well enough to help you make the best selections and get the best prices.

Agents have to reveal exactly what they're charging you. Alas, whereas agents are generally better to deal with than brokers because the financial conflict of interest doesn't exist, good agents are hard to find. And even if you do find one, agents often must work with dealers to perform trades.

Knowing whether you need a broker or agent at all

You don't need a broker or agent to buy Treasury bonds. You can do so easily and with no markup on www.treasurydirect.gov. And because you can buy Treasury bonds directly without a commission, some financial supermarkets will allow you to trade Treasury bonds without a commission — not even the $1-per-bond commission that you'd pay for a corporate or municipal bond trade. You'll still have to deal with a small spread when you buy and sell, though.

REMEMBER

Non-Treasury bonds trade in markets with intermediaries; you can't buy these securities directly from the issuers. Sure, you can loan your neighbor or brother-in-law $1,000 and demand the money back with interest (good luck!), and that's a bond, of sorts. But if you want to buy and sell marketable fixed-income securities, you must go through a recognized agent.

Going through a financial supermarket, such as Fidelity, T. Rowe Price, or Vanguard, is generally cheaper than going through a full-service, markup kind of broker. The supermarket's pricing, which is a *concession* or a fee (more or less), not a true markup, is perhaps more clear-cut. But the supermarket agents generally hold your hand only so much, and they won't make actual bond selections for you the way a full-service broker will.

Note: I've injected some qualifiers into the previous paragraph, such as *generally* and *perhaps.* I explain why in the upcoming section "Doing It Yourself Online," where I discuss online bond trading. The financial supermarkets, alas, sometimes make their way of trading sound easier, cheaper, and more transparent than it really is.

Selecting the right broker or agent

Whether you go with a full-service, markup kind of broker or with an agent, I'd ask you to do a few things:

TIP

>> **Find someone who truly specializes in bonds — preferably the kind you're looking to buy.** If you needed hand surgery, you wouldn't go to a gastroenterologist, would you? If your dealing in individual bonds is going to be any more profitable than, say, investing in a bond index fund, you need a broker or agent who truly knows and tracks the markets carefully — someone who can jump on a good deal. You don't want a broker who deals in bonds, stocks, gold coins, and collector art.

Start by asking people you know and respect for referrals. Make calls. Don't be shy. Ask lots of questions about a broker's background, including academic and professional history. Ask for client recommendations. Ask for numbers: What kind of return figures has this broker been able to garner for clients, and taking what kinds of risks?

If you want to make sure that the bond broker you hire isn't going to take your money and buy a one-way ticket to Rio the next morning, check the broker's background before you hand over the check. You can get information on the disciplinary record, professional background, and registration and license status of any properly registered broker or brokerage firm by using FINRA BrokerCheck, which is available at no charge to the public. You can access this service by going to https://brokercheck.finra.org or calling 800-289-9999.

WARNING

>> **Be on guard.** Always. Whenever you find a broker and agree to buy or sell individual bonds, be certain that you aren't paying an excessive markup. Although different people in the investment business have different concepts of what constitutes *excessive,* if you're asked to cough up the equivalent of more than three months' interest, that's excessive, in my humble opinion. Other financial types have their opinions. If you feel the costs are excessive, you may file a complaint using FINRA's online Complaint Center (www.finra.org/complaint).

>> **Know a dealer's limitations.** Most bond dealers I've known aren't the best people to build your entire portfolio. They often have limited knowledge of investments beyond bonds. (And that's probably a good thing; see the first bullet in this list.) If they deal in stocks at all, they often deal in pricy stock mutual funds that you don't want — the kinds that earn them a nice commission.

Checking the dealer's numbers

TIP

If you deal with a full-service broker, you won't have to know every detail about trading bonds online. But I'd still urge you, at a minimum, to become familiar with FINRA's website (www.finra.org). There, you can plug in information on any bond — either by the name of the issuer or the bond's CUSIP — and you'll experience the type of transparency I discuss earlier in this chapter. (If you don't know what a CUSIP is, see the nearby sidebar "What the heck is a CUSIP, anyway?")

On www.finra.org, click the For Investors link in the upper right of the home page, go to Tools and Calculators in the upper left, and then (no, they don't make this easy), scroll down to FINRA Market Data. You're there! Or if you know the CUSIP number of a bond you're interested in, it's quicker to go to https://finra-markets.morningstar.com/BondCenter/Default.jsp. If you're trading munis, as opposed to corporate bonds or Treasurys, the best place to go online is the website of the Municipal Securities Rulemaking Board (https://emma.msrb.org). You'll find what you need more easily on this site.

If a bond has recently been sold, these websites can provide you with lots of information: the bond's most recent selling price; how Moody's, S&P, and Fitch rate it; and its coupon rate, price, and current yield (see Chapter 2). You can also find access to TRACE data on the websites of major brokerages.

To get a bird's-eye view of the bond market, go to www.wsj.com/market-data/bonds/benchmarks. The chart there gives you a pretty good idea of what various categories of bonds are paying on any particular day. If you're in the market for a bond, compare the composite yield to the yield you're being offered. If you aren't being offered at least as much as the average yield, ask why. The 52-week range will show you which way bond yields may be moving. But note that yield trends, just like the wins and losses of your favorite sports team, can reverse direction quickly.

Hiring a financial planner

TIP

Lots of people today, including stock and bond brokers, call themselves financial planners. I suggest that if you hire a financial planner, you seriously consider a *fee-only* planner, who takes no commissions and works only for you. To find one in your area, contact the National Association of Personal Financial Advisors (NAPFA) at 847-483-5400, ext. 1, or go online to www.napfa.org.

Some NAPFA-certified financial advisors will work with you on an hourly basis. Others will want to take your assets under management. If you hire a financial planner who takes your assets under management, you typically pay a fee. One percent a year has been pretty standard for many years but that rate may be starting to fall a bit. I think 1 percent is plenty, and only if you're getting help from that planner that extends to insurance, estate planning, and other matters beyond strictly portfolio management.

If you have a sizable bond portfolio, a fee-only financial planner who is trading bonds for you can potentially save you enough money to compensate for the fee. Even though the planner will be dealing with a broker, just as you would, planners with numerous clients can bundle their bond purchases, so the broker often settles for a substantially smaller markup.

Doing It Yourself Online

A growing number of financial supermarkets and specialty bond shops now allow you to trade bonds online, and they advertise that you can do so for a fixed price. In the case of Fidelity, the supermarket with which I'm most familiar, the price is generally $1 per bond.

Whoa, you may say. *That's a great deal!* Well, yes, it is, but you still need to be careful that the price you pay is in line with other recent trades. That's where TRACE data is invaluable.

One way to actually see the cut being taken by others is to buy and sell a few Treasury bonds. The financial supermarkets offer to make this trade at no commission. Yet if you go to place a buy, you'll see one price, and if you go to place a sell, you see a different, slightly lower price. Who's getting this cut? Dealers in far-flung places, buying and selling, selling and buying, shave a little bit off of each trade.

REMEMBER

Regardless of whether you're trading Treasurys, corporate bonds, or muni bonds, you're most likely to get a fair deal online when you're *buying* a bond and dealing in large quantities. You're most likely to get zapped when you're *selling* a bond prior to maturity, especially if you're selling a small number of bonds and if those particular bonds are traded infrequently. In such cases, you may let go of your bonds for one price and, using TRACE, find out that they were sold seconds later for 3 percent (or more) higher than the price you just got. Someone is making quick money in that situation, and it isn't you.

In this section, I explain how online trading generally works.

If you're looking to buy

First, you choose a bond category. Do you want a Treasury bond, an agency bond, a corporate bond, or a municipal bond? (For reminders about each category, see Chapter 3.) What kind of rating are you looking for? What kind of maturity? What kind of yield? (Chapter 2 contains the goods on ratings, maturity, and yield.)

Most online bond shops walk you through this process step-by-step; it isn't that hard. The most difficult piece of the process, and the one I most want to help you with, is making sure that after you know what kind of bond you want, you get the best deal on your purchase.

REMEMBER

Here, plain and simple, is what I mean by getting the best deal for a given type and quality of bond: You want the *highest yield.* The yield reflects whatever concession you're paying the financial supermarket, and it reflects whatever markup you're paying a broker.

Comparing yields, however, can be tricky, especially when looking at callable bonds, because you never know how long you'll have them. Keep in mind that in the past, when interest rates were falling, callable bonds were almost always called because the issuers could issue newer bonds at lower interest rates. In the future, that may not be the case. So, you need to look at two possible scenarios: keeping the bond to maturity or having it called.

As David Lambert, founding partner of Collins Lambert Integrated Wealth Management in Lebanon, New Jersey, suggests, "When considering callable bonds, be sure to examine whether the bonds are selling at a premium or a discount to the call price. If trading at a premium, consider the yield to call first. If trading at a discount, consider the yield to maturity first. (You should see these various yields pop up before you place your online order.) Both of these will give you your most realistic picture of future performance. You can pretty much ignore just about everything else."

What he's saying is that the yield to call on premium bonds and yield to maturity on discount bonds both represent *yield to worst* (or *worst-case basis yield*). That yield is what you're likely going to get, so you may as well factor it into your bond purchase decisions.

If two comparable bonds — comparable in maturity, duration, ratings, callability, and every other way — are offering yields to worst of 4.1 percent and 4.2 percent, unless you have an inside track and, therefore, know more about the issuer than the ratings companies do, go with the 4.2 percent bond. Just make sure you've done your homework so you know that the two bonds are truly comparable.

REMEMBER

To reiterate: The yield reflects the broker's cut. *Focus on the yield* — and especially on the yield to worst — in order to get the best deal. You'll note that the yield shown is based on the current asking price for the bond.

When you go to place your order, you can use either the Limit Yield option or the Limit Price option. You're telling the brokers on the Fidelity network that you'll buy this bond only if it yields, say, 4.2 percent. Or you're telling the brokers that you won't pay a penny more than, say, "102" for a bond. Anything less, and you aren't interested. Putting in a Market order on a bond can get you chewed up, so don't do it. And keep in mind that bond prices are expressed as percentages. "102" means 102 percent of par (the original issuing price of the bond). If you're dealing with $1,000 bonds, then "102" means you're going to pay $1,020 per bond.

Well, that's the price you'll pay more or less. . . . "Accrued interest" often enters into individual bond trades (see the nearby sidebar "All about accrued interest").

ALL ABOUT ACCRUED INTEREST

You place an online order to buy 25 $1,000 bonds inside your brokerage account. The price is marked 102 (which refers to the percent of par), and it includes the broker's markup. Doing the math, which is easy peasy ($1,000 × 102 percent × 25), you figure your account will be debited $25,500. Yet you suddenly see your cash balance fall by $26,000 when you make the trade. Ouch! You feel you've been ripped

(continued)

(continued)

off, so you call the broker, outraged. You yell, you scream, and then you're somewhat embarrassed when the broker explains that the extra $500 was accrued interest.

More often than not, there will be *accrued interest* when you buy a bond. What is that? Most bonds pay interest every six months. If the bond you're buying last paid interest on, say, June 1, and you buy the bond on September 1, then the bond's interest has been accruing for three months without a payment to the former owner of the bond, the one now selling you the bond. You owe that interest to the seller, and the broker will make sure the seller gets it. You then, on December 1, collect six months of interest, and you get to keep all of it, even though you haven't held the bond for that entire time. In other words, you get your $500 back.

Go to sell the bond, and the broker forwards any accrued interest from the bond buyer back to you. It's not unlike buying a house on which the sellers have paid real estate taxes a year in advance. You usually need to front them that money, which you "get back" by not having to pay real estate tax to the city for a year. Similar concept.

If you're looking to sell

Selling bonds online can be trickier business. You have a particular bond you want to dump, and the market may or may not want it.

TIP

The first thing you want to do is check with TRACE to see how much your bond has recently sold for. You can then go onto your brokerage's website and place a Limit Price order to sell. You may get a fair price, or you may not.

Truth be told, you're likely to pay a fairly high markup anywhere if you sell a bond before its maturity. The bottom line for the average investor is to build a bond ladder (see the next section) and hold your bonds until maturity. Don't sell before maturity, and don't try to time rates.

Perfecting the Art of Laddering

Bond laddering is a fancy term for diversifying your bond portfolio by maturity. Buy one bond that matures in two years, another that matures in five, and a third that matures in ten years, and — presto! — you've just constructed a bond ladder.

Why bother? Why not simply buy one big, fat bond that matures in 30 years and kicks out regular, predictable coupon payments between now and then? Well, laddering makes more sense for a few reasons.

Protecting you from interest rate flux

The first rationale behind laddering is to temper interest rate risk. If you buy a 30-year bond right now that pays 4.5 percent, and if interest rates climb over the next year to 6.5 percent and stay there, you're going to be eating stewed crow for 29 more years with your relatively paltry interest payments of 4.5 percent. Obviously, you don't want that. (You could always sell your 30-year bond paying 4.5 percent, but if interest rates pop to 6.5 percent, the price you'd get for your bond isn't going to make you jump for joy.)

Of course, you don't have to buy a 30-year bond right now. You could buy a big, fat two-year bond. The problem with doing that is twofold:

>> You won't get as much interest on the two-year bond as you would on the 30-year bond.

>> You're subjecting yourself to *reinvestment risk*. If interest rates fall over the next two years, you may not be able to reinvest your principal in two years for as much as you're getting today.

REMEMBER

If you ladder your bonds, you shield yourself to a certain degree from interest rates rising and falling. If you're going to invest in individual bonds, laddering is really the only option. Do it!

Tinkering with your time frame

Note that as each bond in your ladder matures, you'd typically replace it with a bond equal to the longest maturity in your portfolio. For example, if you have two-year, five-year, and ten-year bonds, when the two-year bond matures, you'd replace it with a ten-year bond. Why? Because your five-year and ten-year bonds are now two years closer to maturity, so the average weighted maturity of the portfolio would remain the same: 5.6 years.

Of course, over the next two years, your economic circumstances may change, so you may want to tinker with the average weighted maturity. That depends on your need for return and your tolerance for risk.

TIP

A perfectly acceptable (and often preferable) alternative to bond laddering is buying a bond mutual fund or exchange-traded fund (ETF). This option is the heart of Chapter 5. But whether you ladder your bonds or you buy a bond fund, I'd caution you that relying only on fixed income to fund your retirement is probably not the wisest path. You should have a bond ladder or bond funds *and* other investments (stocks, real estate, perhaps commodities).

Chapter **5**

Selecting Bond Funds Wisely

Some bond investors cling to the notion that if you hire a fund manager, you're a wimp. They'd rather get run over trading individual bonds. Doing so is somehow more adult, more intelligent, more sophisticated than buying a bond fund — despite all evidence to the contrary. Yes, even armed with the valuable tips I provide in Chapter 4, a small investor in individual bonds can wind up with tire treads on their back.

I know bonds, and I know dumb. So trust me on this: For the majority of individual investors, funds are the way to go. That was true several years ago, and it's even truer today with the advent of dozens of bond exchange-traded funds (ETFs) that allow the small investor ready access to some darned good and ultra-low-cost (even some *no*-cost) bond portfolios.

There's nothing wimpy about bond funds, and provided you do your homework, they can be as intelligent and sophisticated an investment vehicle as you'll ever find. (Index funds, which include most of the fixed-income ETFs, are seen by some as the wimpiest things under the sky but turn out to be mighty tough themselves.)

In this chapter, I introduce you to the many kinds of bond funds — indexed, active, mutual funds, ETFs, closed-end funds, and unit investment trusts — and reveal that although none is worth dying for, some may well be worth fighting for.

Defining the Basic Kinds of Funds

With hundreds upon hundreds of bond funds to choose from, each representing a different basket of bonds, where do you start? That part is actually easy: You start with the particular class of bonds you want to own. Treasurys? Corporate bonds? Munis? Long-term? Short-term? Investment-grade? High-yield? A blend of all of the above? Chapter 3 helps you answer that question. But knowing what class of bonds you want in the basket isn't enough. You also need to know what kind of *basket* you want.

REMEMBER

Bond baskets (funds) come in five varieties (the first four are covered in the following sections):

>> Open-end mutual funds, typically referred to simply as *mutual funds,* are the most common.

>> ETFs are the newer kids on the block, quickly catching up with mutual funds for good reason.

>> Closed-end mutual funds, usually referred to only as *closed-end funds,* offer comparatively greater return for greater risk.

>> Unit investment trusts (UITs) aren't well known but perhaps are worth knowing.

>> Exchange-traded notes (ETNs) are like bonds within bonds, with bells and whistles and their own unique characteristics.

A multitude of mutual funds

When most investors speak of funds, they're talking about mutual funds. And it's no wonder. According to Morningstar Direct, the total number of distinct mutual funds (ignoring different share classes of certain mutual funds) clocks in at an astounding 7,229 (at the time of writing). Of those 7,229 funds, 1,938 of them — nearly 27 percent — represent baskets of bonds.

Like all funds, a mutual fund represents a collection of securities. You, as the investor, pay the mutual fund company a yearly fee and sometimes a sales charge (called a *load*) to buy the fund. In exchange for your money, the mutual fund company offers you an instant portfolio with professional management.

Most mutual funds are *open-end funds.* This means that the number of shares available isn't limited. Within reason, as many people who want to buy into the fund can do so. As more people buy into the fund, more bonds are purchased. The mutual fund shares then sell at a price that directly reflects the price of all the bonds held by the mutual fund. The interest you receive from the fund is a pro rata portion of the total interest received by all the bonds in the basket, minus whatever management fees are deducted.

You can place mutual fund orders at any time, but they're priced only at the end of the day (4 p.m. on Wall Street), and that's the price you're going to get. If you place an order to buy after 4 p.m., the trade is executed at the next day's closing price.

Most mutual funds are *actively managed,* which means that the managers try to beat the broad bond market by picking certain issues of bonds or by trying to time the markets. Other mutual funds are passively run, or *indexed,* which means they're set up to track standard fixed-income indexes. Index funds tend to cost you a lot less in fees than actively managed funds.

TIP

Regardless of whether you go with active or passive, choose only those bond mutual funds that have solid track records over several years and are reasonably priced. The average yearly operating expense of a bond mutual fund, according to Morningstar, is 0.81 percent. Because total return on bond funds, over time, tends to be less than that of stock funds, the cost ratio is usually a bigger factor. I wouldn't touch anything over 0.5 percent without a compelling reason to do so. You likely don't need to buy more expensive funds; you have many inexpensive alternatives to choose from, and they tend to offer better performance over time.

Exchange-traded funds

ETFs have caught on big in the past decade or so. If you read the latest edition of my book *Exchange-Traded Funds For Dummies* (Wiley), you know that I'm a big fan. ETFs trade on the exchanges like individual stocks. (Yes, even the bond ETFs trade that way.) You usually pay a small brokerage fee if any fee at all (perhaps $5 or so) when you buy and another fee when you sell. But while you own the fund, your yearly fees are very low; they are, in fact, a fraction of what you'd pay for a typical bond mutual fund, closed-end fund, or any other kind of fund.

ETFs usually maintain a price that closely matches the net asset value, or the value of all the securities in the portfolio. But, at least at the present time, the majority of ETFs are index funds, unlike mutual funds. About 18 percent (522) of all 2,836 ETFs available to U.S. investors are bond ETFs (at the time of writing).

There aren't as many fixed-income ETFs as there are bond mutual funds, but I predict that the number will continue to expand. Their popularity is, in part, due to their super-low expense ratio. The average bond ETF charges only 0.3 percent a year in operating expenses, and a good many are less than 0.1 percent. There's one on the market that charges 0.0 percent.

Stock ETFs tend to be much more tax-efficient than stock mutual funds. In the bond arena, the difference isn't as great. ETFs tend to be lower cost, but you may have to deal with small trading commissions (although those commissions have been disappearing). And at times the price of an ETF may appear to rise slightly above, or fall slightly below, the net asset value of its components. This flux shouldn't be a concern to buy-and-hold investors.

Closed-end funds

Most mutual funds are open-end, but some aren't. The closed-end funds are a universe unto themselves. Unlike open-end funds, closed-end funds have a finite number of shares. The price of the fund doesn't directly reflect the value of the securities within it. Nor does the yield directly reflect the yield of the bonds in the basket. In investment-speak, the *net asset value* (NAV) of the fund, or the price of the securities within the fund, may differ significantly from the price of the fund itself.

Supply and demand for a closed-end fund may have more bearing on its price than the actual securities it holds. Closed-end funds tend to have high management fees (almost always more than 1 percent a year), and they tend to be more volatile than open-end funds, in part because they're often leveraged. (Leveraging is part of what adds to the high average cost.) Closed-end funds are traded like stocks (yes, even the bond closed-end funds), and they trade throughout the day. You buy and sell them through any brokerage house — not directly from the mutual fund company, as you can do with most mutual funds.

TIP

All closed-end funds are actively managed. There are 530 closed-end funds at the time of writing, of which 310, or nearly two-thirds, are bond funds. The average yearly fee of these bond funds, per Morningstar, is a relatively chunky 2.03 percent. I suggest very strongly that if you do buy a closed-end fund, you choose one selling at a discount to the NAV, not at a premium. Studies show that discounted closed-end funds tend to see better performance (similar to value stocks outperforming growth stocks, but even more so).

Unit investment trusts

A UIT is a bundle of securities that a manager handpicks. You buy into the UIT as you would an actively managed mutual fund. But unlike the manager of the mutual fund, the UIT manager doesn't actively trade the portfolio. Instead, they buy the bonds (or in some cases, bond funds) — perhaps 10 or 20 of them — and hold them throughout the life of the bonds or for the life of the UIT.

A UIT, which may contain a mix of corporate bonds, Treasurys, and munis, has a maturity date — it could be 1 year, 5 years, or even 30 years down the road. Interest payments (or principal payments, should a bond mature or be called) from a UIT may arrive monthly, quarterly, or semiannually. Management expenses for a UIT range from 0.2 percent to 1 percent, and you pay a commission when you buy them of about 1 percent to 3 percent. (You don't pay anything when you sell them.) Contact any major brokerage house if you're interested.

But *should* you be interested? "A UIT can give you the diversification of a mutual fund, as well as greater transparency by knowing exactly what bonds are in your portfolio," says Chris Genovese, executive vice president of Advisor's Asset Management, a group that provides advice on fixed income to other financial professionals. "They are certainly appropriate for many individual investors, whether in retirement accounts or investment accounts." UITs come and go from the marketplace, explains Genovese. "If you are interested in seeing the currently available selection, talk to your broker. Look at the prospectus. As you would with any other bond investment, weigh the benefits and the risks of the bonds in the portfolio, and determine if it looks like the right mix for you."

Bond ETFs can also give you the diversification and transparency of a UIT, but only a handful of bond ETFs offer target maturity dates, as UITs do.

Knowing What Matters Most in Choosing Any Sort of Bond Fund

For years, alchemists tried to turn common metals into gold. It can't be done. The first rule to follow when choosing a bond fund is to find one appropriate to your particular portfolio needs, which means finding a bond fund made of the right material. After all, bond fund managers can't do all that much more than alchemists.

Selecting your fund based on its components

If you're looking for a bond fund that's going to produce steady returns with little volatility and limited risk to your principal, start with one that's built of low-volatility bonds issued by creditworthy institutions. A perfect example would be a short-term Treasury bond fund. If you're looking for kick-ass returns in a fixed-income fund, you can start looking for funds built of high-yield fixed-income securities, but know that there will be risk involved.

REMEMBER

One of the main characteristics to look for in a bond is its tax status. Most bonds are taxable, but the majority of municipal bonds are federally tax-free. If you want to laugh off taxes, choose a municipal bond fund. But just as with the individual muni bonds themselves, expect lower yield with a muni fund. Also, pick and choose your muni fund based on the level of taxation you're looking to avoid. State-specific municipal bond funds filled with *triple-tax-free bonds* (bonds free from federal, state, and local tax) are triple-tax-free themselves.

Pruning out underperformers

Obviously, you want to look at any prospective bond fund's performance vis-à-vis its peers. If you're examining index funds especially, the driving force behind returns will be the fund's operating expenses. Intermediate-term Treasury bond index fund

X will, all things being equal, do better than intermediate-term Treasury bond index fund Y if less of the profits are eaten up by operating expenses.

Operating expenses are also a driving force with actively managed funds. Year in and year out, the top-performing bond funds are those with the lowest annual fees, and the bottom-feeders of the performance pool are overcharging investors.

TIP

Don't pay more than 0.5 percent per year for any bond fund unless you have a great reason. And don't invest in any actively managed bond fund that hasn't outperformed its peers — and any proper and appropriate benchmarks — for at least several years. (By "proper and appropriate benchmarks," I'm referring to bond indexes that most closely match the composition of the bond fund in question. A high-yield bond fund, given that you can expect more volatility, *should* produce higher yields than, say, a Treasury index. Any comparison of a high-yield fund's return to a Treasury index is practically moot.)

Laying down the law on loads

REMEMBER

An astonishing number of bond funds charge loads. A *load* is nothing more than a sales commission, sometimes paid when buying the fund (called a *front-end load*) and sometimes paid when selling (called a *back-end load* or *deferred load*). My advice? *Never pay a load.* There's absolutely no reason you should ever pay a load of (not unheard of) 5.5 percent to buy a bond fund. The math simply doesn't work in your favor.

If you pay a 5.5 percent load to buy into a fund with $10,000, you lose $550 up front. You start with an investment of only $9,450. Suppose that the fund manager is a veritable wizard and gets a 7 percent return over the next five years, whereas similar bond funds with similar yearly operating expenses are paying only 6 percent. Here's what you'll have in five years with the load fund, even though there's a wizard at the helm: $13,254. Here's what you'd have with the no-load fund, assuming the manager merely shows up for work every morning: $13,382.

REMEMBER

Buying a load bond fund is plain and simple dumb. Unless you get some kind of special deal that allows for the load to be waived, don't buy load funds. Repeat: Don't buy load funds.

Sniffing out false promises

Although morally dubious and in some cases even illegal, some brokerage houses and financial supermarket websites have been known to promote certain bond funds over others not because those funds are any better but because a certain fund company paid to be promoted. (In the industry, this is sometimes known as "buying shelf space.") Buyer beware!

"Investors need to fully understand how their broker is being compensated, and if a firm is promoting certain bonds or bond funds, investors should ask if the firm is being compensated for that promotion," says Gerri Walsh, senior vice president for investor education with the Financial Industry Regulatory Authority (FINRA).

Checking Out My Picks for Some of the Best Bond Funds

In this section, I introduce you to bond funds well worth considering for your portfolio. I lay them out in roughly the same order I introduce you to various kinds of bonds in Chapter 3. I start with short-term, investment-grade bond funds, sometimes referred to as *near cash*. I then proceed to longer-term Treasurys, corporate bonds (investment-grade and junk), agency bonds, municipal bonds, international bonds, and then to some super-diversified bond funds.

TIP

If you have a somewhat modest portfolio (less than $50,000), I wrap up this chapter with some recommendations for good blend funds that allow you instant exposure to a variety of bonds. If you have an even more modest portfolio (less than $20,000), I suggest you consider a fund that allows you instant exposure to a variety of both bonds and stocks, and I name several that fill that bill, too.

Please note that under each section, I list my favorite funds alphabetically. If you were to see a bond fund called Aardvark Bonds (you won't, but humor me) followed by a bond fund called Zygote Fixed Income, don't assume that I like Aardvark any more than I do Zygote.

You'll note that I delineate between actively managed and passively managed (also known as *index* or *indexed*) funds. I prefer index funds because they tend to cost much less and because studies show a strong link between fund performance and costs. I chose any actively run funds in good part for their track records. And because they have positive track records, they're often low cost, too.

Some of the lowest-cost bond funds, such as the first two on the list, may be technically "active," but they charge no more than comparable index funds, and they're often very index-like, with minimal trading, and a lot of hugging the benchmark. In the case of the first entry, the Fidelity Short-Term Treasury Bond Index Fund (FUMBX), for example, the R^2 (R-squared) is 99, meaning that the fund has 99 percent in common with its benchmark. It may as well be an index fund, but the "active" designation gives the manager a bit of leeway, which is fine. The Vanguard Short-Term Investment-Grade Fund (VFSTX) also has an R^2 of 99.

Short-term, high-quality bond funds

These funds will pay slightly higher rates of interest than money-market funds and certificates of deposit (CDs) but less than longer-term bond funds. They carry little risk of default and have minimal volatility. Sometimes referred to as *near-cash*, these bond funds are often the best investments for money that you may need to tap within one to three years.

Fidelity Short-Term Treasury Bond Index Fund (FUMBX)

Type of fund: Actively run (but not very actively run) mutual fund

Types of bonds: Short-term government bonds

Average effective duration: 2.6 years

Expense ratio: 0.03 percent

Russell's review: This is a convenient place to park your short-term money, especially if you're building a portfolio at Fidelity. The low, low expense ratio will barely nick your returns.

For more information: www.fidelity.com

Vanguard Short-Term Bond ETF (BSV)

Type of fund: Index ETF

Types of bonds: About two-thirds short-term government, with some investment-grade corporate

Average effective duration: 2.7 years

Expense ratio: 0.04 percent

Russell's review: You may think that the next fund in this list, this with the words *investment-grade* in the name, would be less risky than this simple fund with its simple name. Actually, it's the other way around. This is the less volatile of the two funds, with more government than corporate bonds. This fund is also available in mutual-fund form under the ticker VBIRX (minimum investment $3,000, with an expense ratio of 0.07 percent).

For more information: https://investor.vanguard.com/corporate-portal

Vanguard Short-Term Investment-Grade (VFSTX)

Type of fund: Actively run mutual fund

Types of bonds: Short-term bonds, mostly high-grade corporate, but with a smattering of government bonds

Average effective duration: 2.7 years

Expense ratio: 0.2 percent

Minimum investment: $3,000

Russell's review: If you have $50,000 to invest in this fund, you're eligible for the Admiral Shares class (ticker VFSUX). You'll be investing in the same fund as VFSTX, but the expense ratio drops to 0.1 percent.

For more information: https://investor.vanguard.com/corporate-portal

iShares ESG Aware 1–5 Year USD Corporate Bond ETF (SUSB)

Type of fund: Index ETF

Types of bonds: U.S. short-term investment-grade corporate bonds, with the aim of investing principally with companies that boast favorable environmental, social, and governance (ESG) ratings

Average effective duration: 2.7 years

Expense ratio: 0.12 percent

Russell's review: I believe that investors can and should invest not only for optimal returns but for a higher purpose. Funds like this one, with reasonable costs and the right components, make ESG investing easy.

For more information: www.ishares.com

Vanguard Short-Term Inflation-Protected Securities ETF (VTIP)

Type of fund: Index ETF

Types of bonds: Short-term Treasury Inflation-Protected Securities (TIPS)

Average effective duration: 2.5 years

Expense ratio: 0.04 percent

Russell's review: Unlike the other funds in this short-term category, this one adjusts for inflation. If inflation rises quicker than expected, you'll score better with this fund than the others in this category. If inflation is suddenly tamed, you stand to earn nothing. In either case, the U.S. government guarantees your principal. You'll find many intermediate-term and long-term TIPS funds, but not many short-term. This one, with its low, low cost, is well worth considering.

For more information: https://investor.vanguard.com/corporate-portal

Intermediate-term Treasury bond funds

You can buy U.S. government bonds on www.treasurydirect.gov without paying a markup. Nonetheless, Treasury bond funds offer instant diversification of maturities at a modest cost. Although conventional Treasury bonds are said to carry little risk of default, they do carry other risks, such as interest-rate risk. And in these days of modest yield, you also run the risk that you may not be able to stay ahead of inflation. (You can find more on Treasury bonds in Chapter 3.)

iShares 7–10 Year Treasury Bond Fund (IEF)

Type of fund: Index ETF

Types of bonds: Intermediate-term Treasurys

Average effective duration: 8.6 years

Expense ratio: 0.15 percent

Russell's review: If intermediate-term Treasurys are what you want, and you want the convenience of storing them in your brokerage with your other investments, then this iShares ETF will do the trick. Note, though, that you can always buy Treasurys directly from Uncle Sam. Just go to www.treasurydirect.gov. You'll have no commission and no management fees whatsoever.

For more information: www.ishares.com

Schwab U.S. TIPS ETF (SCHP)

Type of fund: Index ETF

Types of bonds: U.S. TIPS

Average effective duration: 8 years

Expense ratio: 0.05 percent

Russell's review: If you want inflation protection in a bond fund, this is an excellent choice. Do, however, note the fairly long maturity of the bonds this fund holds; long maturities mean that there will be some volatility. This isn't a fund for money that you may need within the next several months. Note that this fund is similar to the iShares TIPS Bond ETF (TIP), which got to market long before Schwab's and to this day has a much greater amount of money invested. But given the difference in expense ratios — Schwab's 0.05 percent versus TIPS's 0.19 percent — I'd go with Schwab.

For more information: www.schwabassetmanagement.com

Vanguard Intermediate-Term Treasury Fund Investor Class (VFITX)

Type of fund: Actively managed (although with low turnover) mutual fund

Types of bonds: Intermediate Treasurys, mostly, with a sprinkle of agency bonds

Average effective duration: 5.3 years

Expense ratio: 0.2 percent

Russell's review: If you think interest rates are going to continue to rise, and you're fearful of your bond-fund prices dropping, you may prefer this fund, with its shorter duration, to the iShares ETF earlier. If you have $50,000 to invest, go with the Admiral Shares Class (VFIUX). Same bonds, but an expense ratio of only 0.1 percent.

For more information: https://investor.vanguard.com/corporate-portal

(Mostly) high-quality corporate bond funds

Investment-grade corporate bonds have a history of returning about a percentage point higher than Treasurys each year. (For more on corporate bonds, see Chapter 3.)

iShares iBoxx $ Investment Grade Corporate Bond Fund (LQD)

Type of fund: ETF

Types of bonds: Investment-grade and borderline-investment grade (BBB) corporate bonds

Average effective duration: 8.8 years

Expense ratio: 0.14 percent

Russell's review: Not a bad fund at all. But do note the very long duration, which equates to a *lot* of interest-rate sensitivity. I'd recommend that any holder of this fund make doubly sure to also have some short-term bond exposure elsewhere in the portfolio.

For more information: www.ishares.com

Vanguard Intermediate-Term Corporate Bond ETF

Type of fund: Index ETF

Types of bonds: Investment-grade and borderline-investment grade (BBB) corporate bonds

Average effective duration: 6.4 years

Expense ratio: 0.04 percent

Russell's review: Can't beat the low price, can't beat Vanguard's savoir faire where it comes to indexing, and I prefer the duration of 6.4 years to the iShares iBoxx ETF's duration of 8.8 years.

For more information: https://investor.vanguard.com/corporate-portal

Corporate high-yield funds

High-yield bonds can be expected to return more than other bonds over the very long haul, but you can lose your money in times of recession when shakier companies start to default on their loans. (You can find more on junk bonds in Chapter 3.)

iShares Fallen Angels USD Bond ETF (FALN)

Type of fund: Index ETF

Types of bonds: *Fallen angels*, which are high-yield (junk) corporate bonds that were rated investment-grade in recent history prior to being downgraded to junk (hence, "fallen angels"). The majority are currently rated BB.

Average effective duration: 5.6 years

Expense ratio: 0.25 percent

Russell's review: Although this fund hasn't been around nearly as long as iShares HYG and isn't nearly as popular, I prefer it for its lower expense ratio. Plus, some intriguing research indicates that "fallen angels" may, over the long run, offer a slightly higher return per unit of risk than is the case with other junk bonds. At the time of this writing, FALN boasts a five-year return of 5.9 percent versus 3.8 for HYG, despite having a higher duration (greater chance of value tumbling with interest-rate spikes) during a time of rising interest rates.

For more information: www.ishares.com

iShares iBoxx $ High-Yield Corporate Bond Fund (HYG)

Type of fund: Index ETF

Types of bonds: Corporate high yield (also known as junk bonds) with most rated BB, B, or lower

Average effective duration: 3.9 years

Expense ratio: 0.48 percent

Minimum investment: None

Russell's review: This fund opened in April 2007. In its first full year in operation, 2008 (a bad year for corporate high-yield bonds), the fund lost 17.19 percent. The next year, it came back with a return of positive 28.74. This is obviously not your typically sedate bond fund. I include it in this compendium because it's so popular, but the expense ratio makes me wince because it's a bit too high.

Vanguard High-Yield Corporate Fund (VWEXH)

Type of fund: Actively run (but index-like) mutual fund

Types of bonds: Junk bonds, but not enormously junky

Average effective duration: 3.8 years

Expense ratio: 0.23 percent

Minimum investment: $3,000

Russell's review: This is a long-time leader in junk bond investing. Since its inception in late 1978, this fund has returned almost 8 percent, but not without some bumps in the road. In 2008, shareholders lost 21.3 percent. If you have $50,000 to invest in this fund, choose the Admiral Shares version (ticker VWEAX), which carries an expense ratio of only 0.13 percent.

Agency bond funds

As far as default risk, agency bonds are almost as safe as Treasury bonds. However, you get a bit of an extra kick on the coupon payments. These issues lack the liquidity of Treasury funds, which explains much of the premium. They're also mortgage-backed, which means they're subject to greater volatility (due to prepayment risk) but also offer greater diversification from other bonds, such as corporate bonds. (For more on agency bonds, see Chapter 3.)

Vanguard GNMA Fund (VFIIX)

Type of fund: Active index mutual fund

Types of bonds: Intermediate government agency bonds, all mortgage-backed

Average effective duration: 2.6 years

Expense ratio: 0.21 percent

Minimum investment: $3,000

Russell's review: If you happen to have $50,000, invest in the Admiral Shares version of this fund (ticker VFIJX). Your management expenses then drop to a delightful 0.11 percent. This fund is similar to the Vanguard fund that immediately follows. The main difference: This one is actively managed. Plus, this one has a lower duration (less interest rate sensitivity). Is it worth the higher expense ratio? VFIIX's ten-year performance as of the end of April 2022 was 1.18 percent. VFIJX (the Admiral Shares version) was at 1.28 percent. VMBS (the index version) was at 1.14 percent. We're talking pennies here, but this fund is slightly less volatile than the Vanguard ETF that follows, so I'd have to vote the Admiral Share VFIJX as my favorite if we're talking long-term buy-and-hold investments.

For more information: https://investor.vanguard.com

Vanguard Mortgage-Backed Securities ETF (VMBS)

Type of fund: Index ETF

Types of bonds: Intermediate government agency mortgage-backed securities issued by Ginnie Mae, Fannie Mae, and Freddie Mac

Average maturity: 5.9 years

Expense ratio: 0.04 percent

Russell's review: In 2010, Vanguard issued its agency-bond ETF and chose a broad spectrum of bonds using an indexed approach. Among the handful of agency-bond ETFs, this is my favorite. If, for some strange reason, you prefer a mutual fund to an ETF, there's an Admiral Shares version of this fund, VMBSX. It has a $3,000 minimum investment, with an expense ratio of 0.07 percent.

For more information: https://investor.vanguard.com/corporate-portal

Municipal bond funds

These funds don't give you the yield that taxable corporate bond funds do, but you'll be spared, perhaps entirely, from paying federal income tax. (For more on municipal tax-free bonds, see Chapter 3.)

Note that I've included one high-yield muni fund among my choices. *High-yield* doesn't mean quite the same in the world of munis as it does in corporate bonds. Yes, the high-yield funds are more volatile, but municipal bonds rarely go belly-up, and even when they do, you usually get most of your money back. Well, at least that's the way it's been in the past.

Fidelity Tax-Free Bond (FTABX)

Type of fund: Actively run mutual fund, although index-like

Types of bonds: Municipal tax-free, high credit quality (mostly AA to A ratings)

Average effective duration: 6.1 years

Expense ratio: 0.25 percent

Minimum investment: $25,000

Russell's review: This is a well-run bond fund with an impressive long-term track record. Interest is exempt from the alternative minimum tax (AMT), so it's a good deal for people in the northern tax brackets.

For more information: www.fidelity.com

Vanguard High-Yield Tax-Exempt (VWAHX)

Type of fund: Actively run mutual fund

Types of bonds: Municipal tax-free high yield of lower-than-stellar credit quality, but not junk (average credit rating A)

Average effective duration: 5.2 years

Expense ratio: 0.17 percent

Minimum investment: $3,000

Russell's review: If you want high-yield munis in your portfolio, this fund is best in class. Go for it. Most, but not all, of the bonds are free from the AMT. Although the fund does have high-yield bonds, it also has some higher-quality munis. If you have $50,000 to invest, go with the Admiral Shares version of this fund (ticker VWALX), which carries an expense ratio of 0.09 percent. The return since inception of this fund (on November 12, 2001) is 4.3 percent. That's more than a 20-year track record of staying comfortably ahead of inflation. But this fund, given the lower credit quality of some of the bonds, is more volatile than most other muni funds.

For more information: https://investor.vanguard.com/corporate-portal

Vanguard Tax-Exempt Bond Index Fund Admiral Shares

Type of fund: Index ETF

Types of bonds: Municipal tax-free higher-quality bonds (mostly AAA to AA)

Average effective duration: 4.6 years

Expense ratio: 0.05 percent

Russell's review: If you have a minimum of $3,000, you can also go with the Vanguard Admiral Shares version of this fund (VTEAX), which carries an expense ratio of 0.09 percent, but I'd stick with the ETF. Most of the interest is free from the AMT. Your long-term returns on this fund are going to be more modest than the Fidelity fund I list earlier (five-year return is 1.76 percent versus FTABX's 2.18 percent), but the Vanguard fund is exposing you to less default risk and less interest-rate risk.

For more information: https://investor.vanguard.com/corporate-portal

Taxable muni bonds

Taxable munis? Yep. Most municipal bonds are tax-free, so why would you want to invest in the taxable offerings? Because you'll get a higher pretax yield. If you want munis in your bond portfolio for diversification (not a bad idea at all) but you only have room in a tax-advantaged account, such as an individual retirement account (IRA), then taxable munis could make sense.

Invesco Taxable Municipal Bond ETF (BAB)

Type of fund: Index ETF

Types of bonds: Taxable munis of fairly high quality (mostly AA to A)

Average effective duration: 8.7 years

Expense ratio: 0.28 percent

Russell's review: If the only room you have for munis is in a tax-advantaged account, where you aren't going to pay taxes on the interest, then yes, BAB may be a very good option for you. The pretax yield will be more similar to corporate bonds than to tax-free munis.

For more information: www.invesco.com

Global and international bond funds

These funds feature mostly high-quality bonds issued in Japan, Western Europe, and Australia. (For more on international bonds, see Chapter 4.)

Vanguard Total International Bond Index Fund (BNDX)

Type of fund: Index ETF

Types of bonds: Investment-grade bonds from abroad. Top nations are Japan (17 percent), France (12 percent), Germany (11 percent), and Italy (7.5 percent). The average credit quality is AA. The fund is currency hedged.

Average effective duration: 8.2 years

Expense ratio: 0.07 percent

Russell's review: For most investors seeking international diversification, this ETF, with its low cost and excellent diversification, is an excellent choice. Know that the currency hedging makes this fund less volatile than it would be if you were exposed to currency risk. On the other hand, this fund offers limited noncorrelation to U.S. bonds. That's fine. You probably have enough exposure to international currencies on the stock side of your portfolio. (Most international stock funds are currency unhedged.)

For more information: https://investor.vanguard.com/corporate-portal

VanEck Green Bond ETF (GRNB)

Type of fund: Index ETF

Types of bonds: Mostly investment-grade bonds (maybe 14 percent high-yield/junk bonds) issued both in the United States (37 percent) and abroad, all dollar-denominated (no currency risk) and designed "green," in the sense that they're helping to fund environmentally friendly projects. The largest country weightings after the United States are China (12 percent), South Korea (5 percent), and the Netherlands (4.5 percent). The average credit quality is A.

Average effective duration: 5.5 years

Expense ratio: 0.2 percent

Russell's review: If you want a global bond portfolio, this fund isn't a bad choice at all. I'd say that even if it weren't "green." Think of the good you could be doing the world as extra return on your dollar.

For more information: www.vaneck.com

Emerging-market bond funds

If you're willing to deal with the volatility, these bond funds — made up of bonds from South America, Mexico, Central America, the Middle East, and Africa — offer excellent return potential. The bonds are risky, but the risks are somewhat different than the risks you face when you invest in U.S. low-credit-quality bonds. (For more on emerging-market bonds, see Chapter 3.)

Fidelity New Markets Income Fund (FNMIX)

Type of fund: Actively run mutual fund

Types of bonds: Emerging market, mostly government, with some corporate issues; the majority are U.S. dollar–denominated. Average credit quality BBB to BB (moderately junky). Biggest exposure to Mexico (11 percent), Indonesia (5 percent), Qatar (5 percent), and Brazil (4.5 percent).

Average effective duration: 6 years

Expense ratio: 0.8 percent

Russell's review: One of the first emerging-market bond funds. In 1998, the fund lost 22.38 percent, and in 2008, it lost 18.24 percent. Most other years, however, the fund has seen impressive returns. Since its inception, the annualized return has been just a hair shy of 9 percent. Most of the competitors, including a few much lower-cost options, haven't been around for nearly as long. Vanguard's VWOB (see the next listing) has been in existence since 2013. Over the past five years, the Vanguard ETF has returned 0.19 percent; FNMIX, –0.88 percent. Given that bonds have sunk due to rising interest rates and the Vanguard fund has a longer duration (making it more, not less, sensitive to interest-rate flux), you would've expected it to be the other way around, with the Fidelity fund doing better.

For more information: www.fidelity.com

Vanguard Emerging Markets Government Bond ETF (VWOB)

Type of fund: Index ETF

Types of bonds: Emerging-market bonds, with credit ratings all over the map, but at least 45 percent could be deemed junky. Largest country exposure is to Mexico (10 percent), Saudi Arabia (9 percent), Indonesia (7 percent), and Turkey (6 percent).

Average effective duration: 8.2 years

Expense ratio: 0.2 percent

Russell's review: Most emerging-market bond funds cost quite a bit more than this one. If interest rates were higher, that cost difference wouldn't be as important. But with interest rates so low, the other funds are, in essence, running in lead boots. If I had to guess, I'd say that this ETF will outperform most of the competition over the long run.

For more information: https://investor.vanguard.com/corporate-portal

All-in-one bond funds

Instead of picking and choosing, perhaps you'd like to buy up a representative sampling of the total bond market. If that's the case, consider these options.

Dodge & Cox Income (DODIX)

Type of fund: Actively run mutual fund

Types of bonds: With both government and corporate bonds, this fund goes a bit heavier on corporate than the aggregate bond index funds, and it throws in about 11 percent junk bonds.

Average effective duration: 5 years

Expense ratio: 0.42 percent

Minimum investment: $2,500 ($1,000 in an IRA; $1,000 in a custodial account)

Russell's review: This fund costs a lot more than the index varieties, and you're going to be taking more credit risk. But with the lower duration, you're taking less interest-rate risk. As you know, I'm partial to low-cost index funds, which studies show beat the majority of actively managed funds over the long haul. But this veteran among bond funds has had a lot of time to prove itself. Over the past 20 years, it has beaten the index by about half a percentage point a year. Will it do so in the future? I don't know. But if you're going to go with an actively managed, broad-based bond fund, this should be the one.

For more information: www.dodgeandcox.com

Fidelity Sustainability Bond Index Fund (FNDSX)

Type of fund: Index mutual fund

Types of bonds: Seeks to track the Bloomberg Barclays MSCI U.S. Aggregate ESG Choice Bond Index, which includes both government and agency and corporate bonds, handpicked with the aim of supporting more sustainable and eco-friendly concerns.

Average effective duration: 6.4 years

Expense ratio: 0.1 percent

Russell's review: The expense ratio is low, the diversification is excellent, and I'd like this fund even if it weren't an ESG fund. But it is. And that knowledge that you may be doing good for the world is just icing on the cake. There's no reason to think that the ESGness of this fund should change much with regard to performance and volatility. (Some people think that adherence to ESG criteria should raise performance and lower volatility; others argue the opposite. I'm staying neutral. As I said, this is a good fund that should perform well over time. The ESGness is a bonus in terms of sleeping well.)

For more information: www.fidelity.com

Mellon Core Bond ETF (BKAG)

Type of fund: Index ETF

Types of bonds: This fund, born in May 2020, seeks to match the performance of the Bloomberg Barclays U.S. Aggregate Total Return Index. In other words, its composition is similar to the Vanguard fund that follows. It's about two-thirds government, and the rest are investment-grade corporate bonds.

Average effective duration: 6.8 years

Expense ratio: 0.0 percent (Yes, reader, that's correct!)

Russell's review: The main difference between BKAG and Vanguard's BND is the cost. The Vanguard fund costs next to nothing, and the BNY Mellon fund costs zero! Mellon Bank is one of the largest money managers in the world, but it came late to the ETF game. To make inroads, it's offering this one bond fund and one broadly based stock fund for nothing. These are loss leaders, like milk and eggs at the local grocery store. The difference between this fund and Vanguard's — 0.03 percent — will mean that over the long haul, you'd expect this fund to earn you an extra $3 a year for every $10,000 invested.

For more information: https://im.bnymellon.com

Vanguard Total Bond Market ETF (BND)

Type of fund: Index ETF

Types of bonds: Both government (about two-thirds) and corporate bonds make up this broad portfolio of U.S. bonds. The only broad categories of bonds missing are inflation-adjusted bonds and tax-free bonds.

Average duration: 6.7 years

Expense ratio: 0.03 percent

Russell's review: Introduced to the market in April 2007, this fund brings new meaning to low-cost, well-diversified bond investing. This fund would make an excellent core holding to any bond portfolio. If you prefer mutual funds to ETFs, this fund comes in a mutual fund version as well: With $3,000 or more, you can invest in the Vanguard Total Bond Market Index Fund Admiral Shares (VBTLX), which carries an expense ratio of 0.05 percent.

For more information: https://investor.vanguard.com/
corporate-portal

Instant-ladder, defined-maturity bond funds

Two fund providers — iShares and Invesco — offer bond ETFs that hold portfolios of similar bonds with similar maturity dates. In other words, these ETFs mature just like a single bond does. But you're getting diversification and the ability to trade much more easily than you would buying individual bonds. iShares calls its offerings "iBonds" (which is unfortunate, because they're often confused with U.S. Treasury iBonds, a completely different animal); Invesco calls its offerings "Bulletshares."

iShares iBonds

Type of funds: Index ETFs

Types of bonds: Take your pick. There are Treasurys, tax-free munis, investment-grade corporate bonds, and high-yield corporate bonds, and they're all of varying maturities, depending on which ETF you choose.

Maturity: Anywhere from several months away to ten years in the future

Expense ratio: Depends. It's 0.07 percent for the Treasury funds, 0.18 percent for the munis, 0.1 percent for the investment-grade corporate bonds, and 0.35 percent for the high-yield corporate bonds.

Russell's review: I'm lukewarm about Treasury offerings because you can buy Treasurys directly from Uncle Sam and pay nothing. And you really don't need diversification the way you do with other bonds. I'm also lukewarm about the high-yield bonds because the main appeal of these funds is predictability, and high-yield bonds are never predictable. But the munis and the investment-grade corporate bonds can make a lot of sense, especially if you know you're going to need a certain sum of cash by a certain date. These funds are good substitutes for individual bonds.

For more information: www.ishares.com

All-in-one bond and stock funds

For the total bond market *and* the total stock market *and* international stocks all rolled up in one, try this.

Invesco Bulletshares

Type of fund: Index ETFs

Types of bonds: You have a choice: investment-grade corporate bonds, high-yield corporate bonds, tax-free municipal bonds, and emerging-market bonds.

Maturity: From several months to ten years down the road

Expense ratio: Varies. It's 0.1 percent for the corporate bonds, 0.18 percent for the munis, 0.42 percent for the high-yield corporates, and 0.29 percent for the emerging-market bonds.

Russell's review: For the investment-grade corporate bonds and the munis, the Bulletshares are really on par with the iShares iBonds, which is to say, I like them. I don't see much advantage to holding high-yield corporates and the emerging-market bonds in a fund where they all mature around the same time. These aren't good stores of value if you know you'll be needing cash at a certain date. There's too much volatility.

For more information: www.invesco.com

iShares Moderate Allocation ETF (AOM)

Type of fund: ETF that's made up of eight other iShares index funds

Types of bonds: About 40 percent of the portfolio is bonds, and 60 percent is stocks. On both sides of the portfolio, there's a great degree of diversification. On the bond side, you'll be getting U.S. government and corporate bonds, as well as international bonds.

Expense ratio: 0.21 percent

Russell's review: This is the ultimate lazy dude's index portfolio! It's appropriate especially for investing debutants.

For more information: www.ishares.com

Vanguard STAR Fund (VGSTX)

Type of fund: This is a mutual fund constructed of other Vanguard funds. For the most part, it's Vanguard's actively managed funds providing a portfolio of stocks and bonds with an overall moderate risk allocation of 60 percent stocks and 40 percent bonds.

Types of bonds: Across the board

Expense ratio: 0.31 percent

Minimum investment: $1,000

Russell's review: For those with limited funds (less than $10,000), this Vanguard offering allows for an instant and diverse 60/40 (stock/bond) portfolio. Other funds are available that will do the same, but I really like this one and have recommended it to investors with modest-size portfolios. It's been around since early 1985 and returns an average of 9.3 percent a year. Despite the higher expense ratio than AOM (the previous fund), this 60/40 portfolio has returned 8.3 percent over the past ten years versus AOM's 5.6 percent. This is one case where active beats index, at least for the past decade.

For more information: https://investor.vanguard.com/corporate-portal

Target-date funds

Another easy option, best if you have limited funds ($10,000 or less) or a real aversion to dealing with your investments (in which case, granted, you're probably not reading this book), is a target-date fund. Like the Vanguard STAR Fund and the iShares Moderate Allocation ETF, these funds give you the whole ball of wax. Bonds, stocks, and sometimes commodities are all rolled up into one simple fund. Unlike the two funds I just mentioned, which have a static mix of stocks and bonds, target-date funds move you over the years from very aggressive to very conservative, depending on your chosen retirement date.

If you're a typical 30-year-old, or a typical 50-year-old, then a target-date fund may be fine for you. Some of the better ones really aren't bad choices — provided you're typical, with a typical amount of money, a typical projected retirement date, a typical need for return, and a typical stomach for risk. Not everyone is "typical," however, so I can't rave about these funds. They also tend to be a bit more expensive than many other options. Nonetheless, if you think you fill the bill, consider one of the following lineups of funds.

Note that not only are some pricier than others, but one lineup can be considerably more aggressive than another.

Fidelity Freedom Index (2030, 2035, 2040, and so on)

Average expense ratio: 0.08 percent to 0.12 percent

Percent in fixed income for those planning to retire in ten more years: 37 percent

Minimum investment: $1,000

For more information: www.fidelity.com

Vanguard Target Retirement Funds (2030, 2035, 2040, and so on)

Average expense ratio: 0.08 percent

Percent in fixed income for those planning to retire in ten more years: 30 percent

Minimum investment: $1,000

Contact: https://investor.vanguard.com/corporate-portal

Chapter **6**

Fulfilling Your Need for Steady Cash

There's a particular fantasy about money and retirement, and it goes something like this: *You work hard for many years, you give holiday cards to your creep of a boss, you invest in stocks all the while, and the stocks grow. Then, when your portfolio has grown enough, you move your money to safe bonds, you no longer have to give holiday cards to that creep of a boss, you retire, you live off the interest from the bonds, you golf, and you do the early-bird specials.*

In this chapter, I explain why that line of thinking may be as silly as thinking ATMs make money. Maybe even sillier. I explain why a diversified portfolio that includes bonds *and* healthy doses of other investments makes just as much sense to a retiree as it does to working folk. I explain in this chapter and in Chapter 7, how to use your bonds in conjunction with other investments to ride steadily and easily into your financial future long after you've given up your day job.

Reaping the Rewards of Your Investments

At this very moment, as I'm typing this paragraph, I'm feeling rather fortunate. I've had a number of jobs in my life that I didn't particularly enjoy, such as when I was a credit analyst at Maryland National Bank in Baltimore in 1981. But I've also had some jobs that I've enjoyed enormously, such as in 1978, when I was a yoga instructor at Club Med in Al Hoceima, Morocco. Luckily, my current job as a financial planner and author in Philadelphia falls into the latter category.

As much as I enjoy my present work, it comforts me greatly to know that after years of saving and wise investing, whether I get up in the morning to work for pay or sleep in, volunteer my time for a worthy cause, or Zoom with a friend in France, the decision is completely up to me.

In this section, I help you start thinking about what you need to accomplish financially so you, too, can someday choose what each day will bring.

Aiming for freedom

What makes work-for-pay optional (other than being born rich, resorting to crime, or marrying a heart surgeon) is a *freedom portfolio* — a portfolio big enough to produce the income needed to support your lifestyle.

When is a portfolio big enough that employment becomes optional? When it provides enough cash flow to pay both today's and tomorrow's bills. The tough part about retirement planning is that you don't know how many tomorrows you're going to have; estimating bills that are years off is tough; and certain ongoing expenses, such as medical bills, may be well beyond your control. In addition, Congress keeps toying with tax rates and such, so you can't even estimate your future IRS bills.

And on top of all *that,* even though a predictable cash flow for you could be arranged, total predictability, with today's pathetic yields on ultraconservative investments, comes at a heavy price.

Estimating your target portfolio

In Chapter 10, I introduce the *20 times rule:* You figure out how much money you need to live on for a year (being realistic by looking at your bills) and multiply that number by 20. That's the very *minimum* most financial professionals, including me, want you to have in your portfolio before you permanently quit your day job. Anything less, and you can't have reasonable assurance that you aren't going to be living off baked beans and homegrown parsley someday. But this rough rule doesn't factor in the price of beans, the number of beans you can eat, and several other variables over the coming decades.

To do a much better estimation and get a firmer idea of what kind of portfolio you should shoot for, you may want to hire a financial planner with fancy software to create a retirement plan for you. Or you can turn to any number of websites, some of which do a fair to middling job at estimating what size portfolio you'll need. I recommend you use several (just search the web for "retirement calculator"). Just about all brokerage house and financial supermarket websites have calculators. Among my favorites is a website called www.firecalc.com; go to the Start Here box, fill in the three blanks, and then either click Submit for a quick result or go back up to the toolbar and play with the inputs for a more accurate calculation.

Although they're better than any rough rule (even mine), the problem with all retirement plans — yes, even the fancy ones done by professionals — is that they're static. Over the course of your life, things change: interest rates, the inflation rate, your portfolio returns, your spending, your health, and taxes, to name just a few. That said, for the moment, let's accept the 20 times rule, as splintery rough as it is, and move on to the question: Where will your cash actually come from after you're no longer getting a paycheck?

Cash flow, dear reader, is the name of the game. Cash — pure, steady cash — is what you need to quit your paid employment if that's your goal. After all, you may have $7 million in net worth, but if that $7 million is in the form of a framed Picasso or a hilltop house with a big pool in the yard, though you're technically a multimillionaire, you may not have enough in your wallet to buy yourself lunch at Taco Bell.

Lining up your bucks

The gods of retirement offer you a number of options for putting cash in your wallet. If you're one of those lucky Americans who can still bank on a solid fixed pension with health benefits (I'm looking at you, retired senators and executives in the pharmaceutical industry), that's great. Social Security, when you're gray enough, can also provide steady cash, although at the time of this writing, it looks like Social Security may need to start slashing certain benefits within a little more than a decade. Possibly.

Because this is an investment book, I spend the rest of this chapter and Chapter 7 talking about the money you can tap from your savings. Most of us who aren't retired senators will need this money to retire, and it can come from one or all of three sources: interest, dividends, and/or the sale of securities. Your choice among these options or some combination of the three will have a great bearing on how big your portfolio needs to be and how much you can safely withdraw.

REMEMBER

The best option — *always* — is to adopt a cash withdrawal plan from your portfolio that's flexible and potentially allows for all three sources of cash flow to play into your new paycheckless life. One of the biggest and most common investment mistakes that people make is to lock their sights on one form of cash flow (typically, interest income) and ignore the others.

Toward the end of this chapter, I show you how a flexible, sensible, triple-source-of-cash-flow plan works. First, allow me to introduce you to each of the three options I just mentioned and explain why the gods of retirement created them, where to find them, and how to maximize them.

Finding Interesting Sources of Interest

All pigs are mammals, but not all mammals are pigs. All bonds are fixed-income investments, but not all fixed-income investments are bonds. Anything that yields steady, predictable interest can qualify as fixed income. That includes not only bonds but also certificates of deposit (CDs), money-market accounts, and a few other not-as-common investments that I address here. Any and all of these may serve as sources of cash, either to boost a preretirement portfolio or to help mine cash from a postretirement portfolio.

Certificates of deposit

As predictable as the Arizona sunrise, CDs, like zero-coupon bonds, offer your principal back with interest after a specified time frame (usually in increments of three months) for up to five years in the future. Like bank savings accounts, almost all CDs are guaranteed by the Federal Deposit Insurance Corporation (FDIC), a government-sponsored agency, for amounts up to $250,000. Interest rates offered tend to increase with the amount of time you're willing to tie up your money. (If the bank will give you, say, 1.5 percent interest for six months, you can often get 1.75 percent for 12 months.) Take your money out before the maturity of the CD, and you pay a fine, the severity of which depends on the particular issuer.

Because nearly all CDs are federally insured, the security of your principal is on par with Treasury bonds. Interest rates vary and may be higher or lower than you can get on a Treasury bond of the same maturity. (Check www.bankrate.com and your local newspaper for the highest CD rates available.) FDIC-insured internet banking accounts, which tend to pay higher rates of interest than the corner bank, are also often on a par with one-year to two-year CDs.

TIP

Often the three investments — CDs, short-term Treasurys, and internet banking accounts — hug very closely to the same (modest) interest rate. If all three are equal, the CD, a favorite with retirees everywhere, should be your *last* choice. Here are two key reasons:

>> The CD requires you to tie your money up; the FDIC-insured internet bank account doesn't.

>> The CD, as well as the bank account, generates fully taxable income; the Treasury bond or bond fund income is federally taxable but exempt from state tax.

Even though there can be blips in time when CDs are great deals, by and large, CDs are vastly oversold. If you're going to settle for a modest interest rate, you generally don't need your money to be held captive. Lately, some banks have been offering more flexible step-up CDs that allow for interest rates to float upward; these are worth some consideration if the initial rate is competitive.

Most bonds provide higher long-term returns than CDs and tend to be more liquid (meaning you can cash out easier). However, only Treasury bonds carry the same U.S. government guarantee that a CD has.

Mining the many money-market funds

Money-market funds are mutual funds that invest in short-term debt instruments (such as Treasury bills, CDs, and bank notes) and typically offer a modest return. In essence, a money market is a bond turned inside out. It provides a stable price with a floating interest rate, while a bond provides a stable return with a potentially volatile market price if you sell the bond before maturity. Money-market funds aren't guaranteed by the federal government, as are most CDs and bank savings accounts, but they're generally quite safe due to the quality of their investments and the short-term maturities.

In the rare instance that long-term lending pays no more than short-term lending (a *flat yield curve* exists), money-market funds may offer a yield competitive with, or perhaps even exceeding, short-term bond funds. (*Short-term* means that the bonds held by the fund generally mature in one to three years.) But money-market funds typically don't pay as much as bond funds. Some money-market funds, however, may offer yields as high as you can get on any CD.

Money-market funds are often used as the *cash* or *sweep* positions at most brokerage houses. Be aware that when you open an account at a brokerage house, the default, if you fail to specify which sweep account you want, may be a low-yielding money-market fund. And simply for the asking, you may have your money moved to a higher-yielding money-market fund. But you need to ask: "What are my sweep account options?" Some money-market accounts, which hold short-term municipal bonds, offer tax-free interest, but the interest rate is usually less than the taxable money-market accounts and, therefore, usually makes sense only for those in the higher tax brackets.

In 2008, Charles Schwab offered a short-term bond fund to its customers as a sweep option — sort of like a juiced-up money market. As it turned out, Schwab's YieldPlus fund managers were squeezing that extra juice from some risky mortgage bonds, which wound up defaulting during the mortgage crisis. Schwab investors, who thought their money was safe, lost a bundle.

The Securities and Exchange Commission (SEC) brought suit against Schwab, and three years later, investors recouped some, but not all, of their savings. Since then, brokerage houses have been more careful about what funds they present as "stable" reservoirs of cash and what funds they offer as sweep options. However, just in case you come across something that looks like a money-market fund but is offering to pay considerably higher rates than all the others, make sure to read the prospectus carefully.

To date, only two real money-market funds "broke the buck" — returning less principal to shareholders than they invested. In both cases, the principal lost was only about 1 percent (a penny on each dollar invested). And the regulations in place today are a bit tougher than they once were, making such a "break" less likely.

REMEMBER

Expect most bonds and bond funds to provide higher long-term returns than money-market funds. Money-market funds, however, offer greater liquidity and, at least historically, a very high degree of safety.

Banking on online savings accounts

FDIC-insured online banks often offer interest rates on savings accounts comparable to CD rates. Of late, Marcus (www.marcus.com) and Capital One (www.capitalone.com) consistently pay some of the highest rates. You can shop for online rates and local bank rates at www.bankrate.com. Some online banks occasionally offer special enticements, such as a $25 check to anyone opening a new account with at least $250. So, why tie up your money in a CD when you don't have to?

REMEMBER

Expect most bonds to provide higher long-term returns than any savings account. An online savings account, however, may offer fairly handsome rates, with instant liquidity and FDIC insurance.

Considering the predictability of an annuity

A cross between an insurance product and an investment, annuities come in myriad shapes and sizes. The general theme is that you give your money to an institution — usually, an insurance company or a charity — and that institution promises you a certain rate of return, typically for as long as you live. What's the difference between an annuity and a bond? Well, with an annuity, you don't expect to ever see your principal back. In return for giving up your principal, you expect a higher rate of return.

Some annuities, called *variable annuities,* offer rates of return pegged to something like the stock market. Other annuities, called *fixed annuities,* offer a steady rate of return or perhaps a rate of return that adjusts for inflation. Some annuities charge a small fortune in fees. Most annuities ask for surrender charges if you try to change your mind.

WARNING

Be careful out there! Many variable annuities are horrific rip-offs, with all kinds of hidden costs and high surrender charges should you attempt to escape (as many people do when they finally figure out the costs). I'm talking about a very steep penalty here. A typical annuity may charge you, say, 7 percent of the total amount invested if you withdraw your money within a year, 6 percent within two years, and so on, with a gradual tapering off up to seven years.

Most variable annuities are sold with 78-page contracts that no one, not even lawyers, can understand. (I kid you not. I've had lawyer clients who bought these and then later came to me, red-faced, telling me they thought they'd been hoodwinked.)

But some good annuity products do exist. See *Annuities For Dummies,* 2nd Edition, by Kerry Pechter (Wiley) for advice. I have a strong preference for fixed annuities, and I've recommended them for certain clients, although they aren't for everyone. One good place to get an initial quote is www.immediateannuities.com.

An intriguing form of annuity worthy of consideration is the *deferred income annuity* (DIA), often referred to as *longevity insurance.* An increasing number of insurers — including New York Life, Northwestern Mutual, and Symetra Financial — offer these policies. Though they provide a stream of income just as other fixed immediate annuities do, these deferred annuities don't kick in for years to come. If you buy a policy at age 66, you may not see any cash flow for another 20 years, and only if you're still alive.

Because you may not live to see the eventual cash flow — which, thanks to inflation, will be worth a lot less than in today's dollars — and because the insurance company gets to play with your money for 30 years, you don't need to kick in much to potentially get a lot at the back end. For example, I recently asked several insurers for a quote. If I (age 66) cough up $100,000 today, I can buy an immediate annuity that pays me about $6,900 a year for the rest of my life, with payments starting right away. Or, I can buy a deferred income annuity that gives me about $43,500 a year, with payments starting on my 86th birthday — if I'm still around. Of course, even if I'm alive, with future possibilities of raging inflation, $43,500 a year may be just enough income to keep me stocked up in generic dental floss.

Longevity insurance reduces the financial risks associated with living a long life for those who have reason to believe they'll be around a long time. But keep in mind that you have no guarantee of throwing yourself a big birthday party in 20 years, paid for by your deferred income annuity.

TIP

Generally, annuities don't belong in tax-advantaged retirement accounts, such as individual retirement accounts (IRAs). A main advantage to an annuity is the ability to defer taxes. Especially if you're young, putting an annuity into an IRA, which is already tax-advantaged, makes about as much sense as flapping your arms as you board an airplane.

REMEMBER

Payouts on annuities grow larger the longer you hold off on buying one. (Extreme example: Any insurance company would be more than happy, I'd think, to take your money, stick it into an annuity, and pay you 30 percent a year — provided you're 97 years old.) In almost all cases, if you're in your mid-60s or older, you'll get more cash flow than you would by investing in bonds, but you give up your principal, and you may not get more than you would with bonds in the end. (I'm talking here about the *end* end.) The taxing of annuity income can be complicated. Talk to your tax advisor.

Don't confuse the terms *payout* and *return.* An annuity can pay you more than a bond because you are, in effect, getting your own money back. Unless you plan on living to 120, a bond that yields, say, 5 percent will be worth much more than an annuity with a payout of 6 percent because when that bond matures, you (or your estate) get your principal back.

Hocking your home with a reverse mortgage

These babies have been around for a long while but have exploded in popularity the past several years. You own a home? You're 62 or over? You can sell your house back to the bank over time. Each month, you get a check. Each month, you have less equity in your home. Reverse mortgages are complicated. And, like annuities, both good and bad products exist. Do your research. Here are some suggestions:

>> See the booklet "Home Made Money" from AARP (https://assets.aarp.org/www.aarp.org_/articles/revmort/homeMadeMoney.pdf).

>> Talk to a reverse mortgage counselor. AARP has some on board, or try the nonprofit Consumer Credit Counseling Service (https://credit.org/cccs) in your area. Perhaps your best option is to call the U.S. Department of Housing and Urban Development at 800-569-4287 to be referred to a HUD-certified reverse mortgage counselor in your area.

>> Oh, and read *Reverse Mortgages For Dummies,* by Sarah Glendon Lyons and John E. Lucas (Wiley).

REMEMBER

The cash flow you get from a reverse mortgage varies tremendously depending on your age, the equity you have in your home, and the terms of the mortgage agreement. Reverse mortgage income isn't taxable.

Recognizing That Stocks Can Be Cash Cows, Too

Stocks can generate returns in two ways:

>> They can appreciate in value.

>> They can pay dividends.

Historically, dividends have actually accounted for the lion's share of stock returns. Not long ago, however, dividends fell out of favor, reduced to a pittance throughout the '80s and '90s. But in past years, they've come back into vogue. Who can say why? At the time of writing, the dividend yield of an average basket of S&P 500 stocks is now about 1.3 percent, although a fund such as the Vanguard High Dividend Yield ETF is offering a yield of 2.8 percent. In contrast, the yield on a ten-year Treasury bond is now about 3 percent.

Stock dividends, by definition, aren't fixed in stone, as are interest payments on bonds. However, they can, within a diversified portfolio of stocks, deliver a fairly consistent cash flow. And unlike bond interest, which is generally taxed as income, the majority of stock dividends receive special tax treatment. At least under current laws, taxes would rarely be higher than 15 percent.

Not all stocks are equally likely to cough up dividends. If you want, you can add stocks to your portfolio that will do just that (such as with the Vanguard fund cited earlier). You can grab your dividends with either individual stocks or any number of mutual funds or exchange-traded funds (ETFs) that offer high-dividend-paying stocks.

Focusing on stocks with socko dividends

Your yearly dividend yield can produce quite a bit of cash if you choose your stocks selectively or pick up either a high-dividend stock mutual fund or an ETF. Investors who usually jump on board new investing trends have been quick to do just that lately. The reasons? Low yields on bonds and good performance on dividend stocks.

But high-dividend stocks won't see high performance every year or even every decade. High-dividend-paying companies, often categorized as *value companies* (precisely because they pay out higher dividends), tend to invest less in their own growth. Companies that are more miserly with dividends (often called *growth companies*) tend to shovel more into research and development (R&D) and such. Sometimes that "R&D and such" translates into new products, growth, and greater profits that result in gangbuster stock performance. (Think of the entire 1990s; growth stocks were definitely the place to be.)

REMEMBER

There's certainly nothing wrong with dividends per se, but by focusing on them, you may be giving up on absolute return. The best stock portfolios are well diversified: They have both value and growth stocks. I wouldn't want to see you with a stock portfolio of all high-dividend companies, even though the cash flow would be sweet.

Nor would I want to see you with a portfolio too concentrated in a handful of industry sectors. As fate would have it, most high-dividend-paying stocks tend to fall heavily in certain industry sectors, such as utilities, pharmaceuticals, banks, and energy. Gear your portfolio too heavily toward high dividends, and you'll be pretty much locking yourself outside of semiconductors, medical equipment, internet technology, biotechnology, and other sectors that may well turn out to be the superstars of the next decade.

REMEMBER

The cash flow from interest on bonds is more predictable than the cash flow from stock dividends. Although right now dividends on some stocks are offering nearly the same yield as Treasury bonds, that's generally not the case. Over the long haul, however, expect the *total* return on stocks (which includes both dividends and price appreciation) to be higher. Stocks are also much more volatile than bonds. Whereas bond interest is typically issued semiannually and bond funds usually pay interest monthly, stock dividends are more commonly posted quarterly. Note that stock funds may issue dividends quarterly, semiannually, or annually.

Realizing gain with real estate investment trusts

One particular sector of the stock market — real estate investment trusts (REITs) — offers among the highest dividend yields in the land: often double that of the S&P 500. REITs are also slightly different animals from most stocks in that REITs *must,* by law, pay out at least 90 percent of their earnings as dividends. And the dividends that REITs pay generally aren't taxed at 15 percent, as are most other stock dividends, but rather at normal income tax rates.

The real estate sector also shows delightfully limited correlation to the rest of the stock market. So, regardless of whether you want the dividends, it may not be a bad idea to plunk 10 percent or so of the money you've allocated for stocks into REITs — preferably low-cost, indexed REIT mutual funds or ETFs, both U.S. and foreign.

WARNING

REIT distributions aren't only generally taxed as regular income but also may include return of principal, which can make tax reporting tricky. For this reason, your best bet is to house your REIT holdings in a tax-advantaged retirement account.

REITs pay high dividends by stock standards, and when interest rates are as low as they have been lately, the REIT dividends may even exceed the interest from bonds of equal principal value. REITs experience more volatility than bonds, but they also offer significantly greater potential for appreciation.

Taking a middle ground with preferred stock

Often referred to as a sort of hybrid between a stock and a bond, *preferred stock*, issued by companies both public and private, generally offers greater and more secure dividends than common stock. Preferred stock is also safer than common stock in that if a company goes under, the holders of preferred stock must be paid back before the owners of common stock.

Many variations of preferred stock are on the market with varying degrees of payoff and risk. Generally, preferred stock, like most hybrid kinds of investments, wouldn't be my first choice of investment for most people. I'd prefer to see you have a mix of stocks and bonds, which together provide the same benefit as preferred stock but with more diversification power. If the concept of preferred stock floats your boat, however, feel free to discuss it with your broker. There are worse investments.

Preferred stocks' dividends can be just as much as or more than bond interest on a similar amount of money. However, the dividends from the preferred stock may be taxed more gingerly than the interest on bonds. Some preferred stock (convertible preferred) offers an opportunity for substantial capital appreciation. But preferred stock — although safer than common stock — is riskier than most forms of true fixed income.

Seeing a Better Way to Create Cash Flow: Portfolio Rebalancing

I'd like to start this section with two seemingly short and simple questions. Are you ready?

Question #1: You have $100,000 in your portfolio. You withdraw exactly $10,000. How much do you have left?

I know you know the answer.

Question #2: Does it matter whether the money you withdraw — the $10,000 — comes from this past year's interest payments on your bonds or this past year's appreciation in the value of your stock holdings?

Either way, you still have $90,000 left, *right?*

Yes. YES. *YES!*

And yet, despite the simplicity of these two questions, you'd be amazed at how many people get the second question wrong. Then, when I look at them quizzically, they argue with me.

"But . . . but . . . but . . . Russell . . . if I withdraw the money from bonds, because that represents interest, my principal will still be intact. But if I withdraw the money from stocks, I'm tapping my principal, and then I'm eating into a productive asset," they argue.

No. That's wrong. Your portfolio, after withdrawing the $10,000, will be worth $90,000. Period. End of story. Argue all you want, but this is basic math. The resulting balance is the same. It doesn't matter whether the sum withdrawn comes from bond interest, stock dividends, stock appreciation, selling the Picasso from the hallway, renting out the pool, or unicorn droppings. It just doesn't matter.

REMEMBER

I'm not sure where the "Bond interest is okay to withdraw, but stock appreciation isn't okay to withdraw" myth ever started. But for the record, there's no such thing as leaving your bond principal intact. In truth, most of the money that you're ever likely to earn in bonds is simply keeping your principal afloat of inflation. If you withdraw those inflation-neutralizing interest payments from your portfolio, the remainder of your bond holdings won't be "intact" at all. Your bond holdings will slowly but surely lose value due to the steadily rising cost of living, otherwise known as inflation.

Table 6-1 shows what $100 today will be worth in the future, assuming an annual inflation rate of 3 percent, which has been the rate of inflation in the United States over the past several decades. According to these figures, if you have a $100 bond maturing in

20 years and you siphon off all the coupon payments, your "intact" principal will probably be worth only $55 when the bond matures. If you have $100 in stock and you siphon off all the appreciation and dividends (assuming there *is* appreciation and dividends) over the next 20 years, the stock that remains will be worth $55, too.

TABLE 6-1 **The Value of Today's $100 Assuming 3 Percent Inflation**

Years in Future	Value of Today's $100
5	$86
10	$74
15	$64
20	$55
25	$48
30	$41

When you can see that withdrawing $10,000 means withdrawing $10,000 — regardless of the source — and that there's no such thing as leaving your principal "intact," you're ready to create a portfolio that can handle withdrawals objectively.

By "objectively," I'm saying that sometimes it makes sense to take your cash flow from appreciated stock, sometimes from stock dividends, and sometimes from bond interest. As I say at the beginning of this chapter, the best option for withdrawing cash from a portfolio — *always* — is to adopt a cash withdrawal plan that's flexible and potentially allows for all three sources of cash flow.

Buying low and selling high

Here's the best method, far and away, for extracting cash from a portfolio. For illustration purposes, I'm going to use a simple portfolio consisting of a domestic stock fund, a foreign stock fund, a commodity fund, a bond fund, and a short-term cash fund.

Your portfolio allocation today, based on careful analysis of your need for return and your stomach for risk, looks like this:

Investment	Percentage
Domestic stock fund	26%
Foreign stock fund	25%
Commodity fund	5%
Bond fund	38%
Short-term cash fund	6%

You've set up your accounts so that all your interest, dividends, and capital gains are reinvested in (rolled directly into) each security as they accrue.

Six months pass. During that time, you've been pulling regularly from your short-term cash fund, which, at 6 percent of your portfolio, is enough to cover 12 to 18 months' expenses. The world economy is humming, and stocks, especially foreign ones, are sailing. All your allocations have gone awry. Your portfolio now looks like this:

Investment	Percentage
Domestic stock fund	30%
Foreign stock fund	32%
Commodity fund	5%
Bond fund	30%
Short-term cash fund	3%

TIP

What do you do? You *rebalance*. That means you sell off some of your stock fund, and you use the proceeds both to boost your cash position and add to your bond position. Your goal is to bring everything back into alignment so you're once again starting with the same allocation (26 percent domestic stocks, 25 percent foreign stocks, and so on) you had at the beginning of the year. That allocation (your risk/return sweet spot) changes only if your life circumstances change — if, for example, you inherit $1 million from a rich aunt or, conversely, a rich aunt successfully sues you for $1 million.

REMEMBER

Rebalancing not only creates cash flow but puts your portfolio on anabolic steroids. Every six months or so, you're providing yourself with living expenses and keeping your portfolio where it should be in terms of your personal risk/return sweet spot, *and* you're continually selling high and buying low, which is the best formula for long-term investment success.

One more example, yet six months later. During this half-year, the stock market took a nosedive, commodities soared, and bonds did well. Your portfolio at year-end again is out of alignment. It now looks like this:

Investment	Percentage
Domestic stock fund	22%
Foreign stock fund	20%
Commodity fund	9%
Bond fund	46%
Short-term cash fund	3%

At this point, you're going to sell off the bond and commodity portions of your portfolio. And, after you've gotten your cash position back up to where you need it, you may wind up buying more stocks, which are now selling at bargain-basement prices.

Rolling bond interest back in

Earlier in this book, I explain that bonds' main role in your portfolio isn't so much for the income (as nice as income is), but to provide the ballast to keep your portfolio afloat when the waters get choppy. Now you can see why I'm of that opinion.

The coupon payments from your bonds, or the interest payments generated by your bond fund, are to be plowed directly back into the bond side of your portfolio. This practice keeps your bond holdings from getting eaten up by inflation. Historically, stocks have returned much more than bonds. If that holds true in the future (if . . . if . . . if), you'll be skimming much more from the stock side of your portfolio during retirement. If the future turns out to be different from the past, those predictable bond coupons could spare you from destitution, just as they may have spared your grandparents during the Great Depression.

Bless bonds. Bless bond income. I only ask that you don't become a slave to that income.

Dealing with realities

In the real world, rebalancing can sometimes be a bit tricky. If your portfolio is in a taxable account rather than a tax-advantaged retirement account, you may have to contend with tax consequences when you sell any security. You may also have to deal with trading costs, depending on your choice of securities and the brokerage house you use to house your portfolio. Both trading costs and taxes can nibble away at a nest egg. You have to be careful.

Perhaps you feel confident factoring those variables into your rebalancing plan. If not, you should see a financial planner, at least for a single visit, to help you orchestrate and fine-tune your rebalancing strategy.

But before you decide whether to handle it alone, read Chapter 7. In this exciting chapter, I discuss your portfolio allocation during retirement and how to sculpt your portfolio — including putting a good percentage in bonds, of course — to maximize your withdrawal potential without jeopardizing your nest egg.

Chapter **7**

Aiming for Financial Security in Old Age

When it comes to old age, common fears include everything from incontinence and impotence to failing eyesight and loose teeth. But on the financial front, the greatest fear, it goes without saying, is running out of money.

For folks who have money in the first place — enough to build a decent portfolio, enough to confidently give up the day job — two basic things can go wrong. The first is market volatility, in which a growling bear market suddenly turns investment dollars to dimes. The second is unexpectedly high inflation, which results in a slow and steady drain of spending power.

If you fear market volatility most, you may tend to err on the side of what's traditionally seen as investment conservatism. You probably love predictable investments: certificates of deposit (CDs), money markets, savings bonds, annuities, and such. If your big fear is inflation, you likely tend to err on the side of what's traditionally seen as investment aggressiveness. You're going for maximum return with stocks, commodities, real estate investments, and perhaps even high-yield or leveraged bonds.

In this chapter, I present the views of both camps (financial liberals and conservatives), blend them together, and present the view that I believe makes the most sense. Together, you and I figure out the best mix of retirement investments to weather both market volatility *and* inflation.

Grasping the Risk of Being Too Conservative

Most financial pros have moved well beyond the old adage, held dearly for years, that the percent of your portfolio held in bonds should be equal to your age (by age 60, you should be 60 percent in bonds; by age 70, 70 percent; and so on). Some say, as do I, that the formula is as antiquated as the crossbow — and, potentially, just as dangerous. In this section, I introduce you to some newer ways of thinking about how much of a retirement portfolio belongs in bonds.

Considering an aggressive approach

"The real risk to most people's portfolios is, paradoxically, not taking enough market risk with higher-returning but more volatile investments, like stocks," says Steve Cassaday, CFP, chairman and CEO of Cassaday & Company, Inc., an investment management and financial planning firm in McLean, Virginia. "Given what most people have saved by retirement, and the average life span today, a more aggressive portfolio is the only choice if people are going to maintain their lifestyles."

Cassaday has researched the returns of various investments over the past 48 years and opts to put his retired clients in portfolios that are more than 80 percent equities, including U.S. stock, foreign stock, and other traditional diversifiers such as real estate investment trusts (REITs) and commodities. Cassaday's views were published in the *Journal of Financial Planning* and created quite a stir among professional financial types, many of whom are skeptical, at best, of Cassaday's conclusions.

I know you wouldn't expect me, the author of a book on bonds, to agree with Cassaday. However, I've seen his number crunching, and although I don't buy into his strategy completely, I don't think the guy is crazy either. His aggressive portfolios, when back-tested with computers to simulate how they would have done over history, have held up remarkably well through both bull and bear markets. Sure, they dip when the stock market is down, but they come back. Or at least to date they have.

Easing back toward your comfort zone

REMEMBER

The aggressiveness of Cassaday's approach may not be right for all investors. I say that not because I doubt his numbers, but for two other reasons:

>> The future of the stock market may be not quite as rosy as it has been in the past.

>> A portfolio of more than 80 percent equity is subject to huge dips in bad times. People tend to panic and sell their fallen angels just when they should be holding them the most. The stock markets are like giant rubber bands: After the biggest down stretches, you tend to see the strongest snapbacks, and vice versa (although giant rubber bands tend to be more predictable than the stock market).

Keep in mind that a portfolio of 80 percent stocks and 20 percent bonds *will* have short-term setbacks, some of them real gut punches. According to data compiled by Vanguard, such a portfolio has seen negative annual returns in 24 of the past 96 years. But the average annual return has been an impressive 9.6 percent.

"The trade-off for occasional annual returns below the long-term average has historically been long-term returns well above what is possible with a more stable portfolio," says Cassaday. "Our guidance to clients has always been to hold on to the side of the kayak when things get rough. Declines have always become recoveries, and as long as you do not need all of your money in one lump sum and any given point (very few ever do), then it has always paid to wait."

Not every investor can "hold on to the side of the kayak." For those who can't, a somewhat less aggressive portfolio than Cassaday advises will probably work best. (Cassaday himself amends his portfolio for his clients who can't emotionally handle a lot of volatility.)

Another colleague of mine (now retired from financial planning), William P. Bengen, CFP, wrote a book for other financial planners called *Conserving Client Portfolios During Retirement* (FPA Press). His book suggests something of a compromise between Cassaday's portfolio and the traditional age-based portfolio. Most financial planners I know are much more in line with Bengen's thinking than with Cassaday's.

Setting your default at 60/40

Bengen, like Cassaday, crunched the numbers backward and forward. His conclusion: Yes, tweak your portfolio as you approach retirement to include more bonds and less stocks, but don't tweak it too much. "Given that stock returns have historically creamed bond returns, you may need those stock returns if your portfolio is going to last as long as you do," says Bengen.

TIP

For most people, Bengen says, 40 percent nonvolatile, safe investments is probably enough. If you want to get more conservative than that, Bengen suggests that you subtract your age from 120 and allocate that amount to the safe and nonvolatile. For example, at age 60, you might give yourself a 60/40 split (stocks/bonds), and at age 65, you might give yourself a 55/45 split.

"I wouldn't update asset allocation every year — only every fifth year, on a birthday divisible by five," says Bengen. Our 65-year-old might then, at age 70, go for a 50/50 split.

Bengen's formula isn't as far from Cassaday's as it may initially seem. The "stock" part of the equation may include any investment with a potentially high yield but also potential volatility: commodities, investment real estate, junk bonds, and even 30-year Treasurys. The "bond" side of his portfolio would include any kind of limited-volatility investment, including short- and intermediate-term high-quality bonds, CDs, and possibly annuities.

And to some degree, investors should tweak the percentages in accordance with economic conditions. Keep an eye out for extreme changes in market conditions (such as those I discuss next), and tweak as needed. Bengen's advice: "Don't be wooden."

Allowing for adjustments to suit the times

One of the few constants in the world of investing is the tendency for investment returns to revert to their mean. What this means is that if a particular kind of investment (stocks, bonds, what-have-you) typically returns X percent a year, but for the past several years has returned considerably more than X, you have a better than 50/50 chance that the returns are in for a slowdown. If, conversely, the investment has been producing returns in the past several years far less than X, you have a better than 50/50 chance that the returns are about to improve. This rule, appropriately enough, is called *reversion to the mean*.

Stock returns are popularly calculated by what's referred to as the *P/E ratio.* The *P* stands for price, and the *E* stands for earnings. When the average price of all stocks is divided by the average earnings of all companies, you typically, at least in the modern era, come up with a number somewhere around 16. In other words, when corporations historically are making $1 for every share of stock, you can expect the price of a share to be in the ballpark of $16.

REMEMBER

Studies going back decades show that whenever the P/E has risen far north of 16 (as it did in 1999, and again at the beginning of 2022), stock returns usually start to sputter, and they can sputter for a good while. When the P/E drops far below 16, stock returns usually heat up for the following few years. (Think 1980, just prior to the two-decade bull market of the '80s and '90s.)

Not long ago, a Yale economist named Robert J. Shiller adjusted the P/E to reflect not only earnings of the past year (as the P/E typically measures) but earnings over the past ten years, taking inflation into consideration. Testing of the data seems to indicate that the Shiller P/E, or the multiple (which can be found at www.multpl.com), may be a somewhat more accurate predictor of future stock performance than the old-fashioned P/E. This topic is currently an area of hot debate.

TIP

You don't want to go crazy with this stuff, but if both P/E ratios fall well behind historical norms, it may be a good time to beef up on stocks, perhaps adding 5 percent or so to your normal allocation. If the ratios rise well above historical norms, you may want to beef up on bonds, perhaps taking your normal allocation up 5 percent and reducing your stock holdings accordingly.

Choosing my own and your ultimate ratio

Unless my circumstances change, my personal retirement portfolio — which I already have planned, and which I'll be tapping within, oh, four to five years — will be about 60/40: 60 percent stocks and other high-return investments, and 40 percent bonds and other low-return, low-volatility investments. If, at some point, stock prices seem cheap (low P/E ratios), I may move my portfolio toward a more aggressive 65/35 allocation. If the situation is reversed, with seemingly expensive stocks (high P/E ratios), I may move my holdings to a more conservative 55/45. I don't think I'd ever get more conservative than that, even if I live to a very old age, as I hope to.

But I can emotionally stomach more volatility than most people. I know I won't sell if the market takes a flop. If the market sours badly and I need to supplement my portfolio income, I, fortunately, have the kind of career that easily allows me to pick up a few bucks working part-time. Otherwise, I'd aim for a somewhat more conservative retirement position for myself, as I do for some of my clients.

REMEMBER

Bottom (mushy) line: Most people living off their portfolios are advised to have well-diversified ones. A diversified portfolio should contain U.S. stocks, foreign stocks, small-cap and large-cap stocks, and value and growth securities. It's also good advice to include 30 percent to 60 percent fixed income (investment-grade bonds, fixed annuities, and cash). Only a very conservative investor would want 70 percent fixed income. If you go beyond that, your hankering for safety may very well backfire, and your "safe" portfolio could wind up risking your lifestyle as inflation takes its steady toll.

Calculating How Much You Can Safely Tap

Elsewhere in this book, I present the *20 times rule* (a thumbprint that gives you a rough guide of how big a portfolio you need before you retire). In short, figure out how much you need in a year, subtract whatever retirement income you have outside of investment income (such as Social Security), and multiply the remainder by 20. So if you need $50,000 a year and Social Security will provide $20,000, you should build a portfolio of $30,000 × 20 (or $600,000), at the very minimum, before you kiss your office colleagues goodbye forever.

That rough rule, like all rough rules, is the product of a few assumptions. Foremost, it assumes that you have a diversified portfolio returning enough so you can not only keep up with inflation but also withdraw 4 percent to 5 percent a year without depleting your principal before you die.

REMEMBER

That allowable withdrawal amount depends on a whole slew of factors, such as the actual rate of inflation, your tax hit, market conditions, and — a biggie — your life expectancy and current age. (At age 90, it's probably okay to see a slow dwindling in your portfolio size.) A lot of those variables, such as your life span, can be controlled by only a limited extent (eat carrots, walk a lot). What you can control *entirely* — and what will have bearing on how much you can withdraw — is the allocation of your portfolio, especially the ratio of stocks to bonds.

Revisiting risk, return, and realistic expectations

How realistic is a 4 percent to 5 percent withdrawal rate? According to figures from Vanguard, a retirement portfolio with an allocation of 50 percent bonds and 50 percent stocks has about an 85 percent chance of lasting 30 years, provided the initial withdrawal is limited to 4 percent and then adjusted for inflation. The number would be 74 percent over 30 years if using the 5 percent withdrawal rate. I don't know about you, but I find those numbers a bit depressing. It means that you need $800,000, or preferably $1 million, to generate just $40,000 a year, and even then you could still go broke before you die.

According to Steve Cassaday, if you're willing to deal with the volatility that comes with a portfolio of 80 percent equities, you should be able to withdraw up to 7 *percent* a year and be safe for 30 years and beyond. Those numbers are much less depressing: You'd need to generate $40,000 a year, and your portfolio could be considerably less, at about $570,000.

If you go the Cassaday route, know that at times your portfolio will sink, and sink hard, and you'll be wondering whether you're going to run out of money next month. Although I like Cassaday's figure (who wouldn't?), I'm not sure how many people could sit tight and deal with the kind of volatility that would be inevitable with such a market-risk-laden portfolio. Also, if the future is considerably different from the past, things could turn out ugly.

Basing your retirement on clear thinking

Although history rarely repeats, I'm not the first to say that it often echoes. The long-term return on large stocks — at least over the past century or so — has been roughly 10 percent a year. Small stocks (prone to greater price sways) have returned about 12 percent a year. The long-term return on bonds has been about 5 percent. And the inflation rate moving forward, although currently running above the historical norm, will probably stay somewhere close to its decades-long 3 percent. Based on these numbers and your final portfolio allocations, you can best judge whether you can sustain a 3 percent withdrawal, a 7 percent withdrawal, or something in between.

My own 60 percent equity/40 percent bond retirement portfolio, which I don't intend to tap till I'm 70, should safely allow me to withdraw 5 percent for at least 25 years, if I live that long. If the markets don't cooperate, I realize that I may have to tighten my belt. I'm willing to do that. Keep in mind that I plan to have enough from Social Security and a smallish annuity to cover food and shelter. So, worst-case scenario, I figure, I'll be vacationing in New Jersey rather than France.

REMEMBER

But that's my plan. You need to devise your own plan based on your expected longevity, stomach for risk, and the other factors I describe earlier in this chapter. I'd only ask you not to think pie-in-the-sky and, as William Bengen says, "Don't be wooden." Allow yourself some flexibility to adjust your cash flow after you begin to withdraw. No retirement plan should be fixed in stone, or wood.

TIP

Of the many books and articles I've read on retirement planning, one that makes particular sense is *Work Less, Live More*, by Bob Clyatt (Nolo). The author suggests something he calls the "95% Rule." It starts with a retirement plan that incorporates a reasonable rate of withdrawal. Clyatt conservatively advises 4 percent, maybe 4.5 percent, of your initial portfolio ($24,000 to $27,000 a year on a $600,000 portfolio), adjusted each year for inflation. However, if the markets turn sour in any particular year(s), you economize a bit over that time period by withdrawing no more than 95 percent of what you withdrew the previous year. "You'll tighten your belt somewhat, but you won't turn your world upside down," writes Clyatt. (In other words, New Jersey, not France.)

Making the Most of Uncle Sam's Gifts

The Internal Revenue Service (IRS), in cahoots with Congress, gives the U.S. investor two basic kinds of tax-advantaged retirement accounts:

>> Plans that allow for the deferral of income tax until the money is withdrawn — such as individual retirement accounts (IRAs), Simplified Employee Pension (SEP) IRAs, and 401(k) plans

>> Plans that, provided you follow certain rules, allow for tax-free withdrawals after reaching age 59½ — such as Roth IRAs and Roth 401(k) plans

I won't get into the many rules and regulations and the amount you can stash in each kind of account. That information is readily available elsewhere, and it strays a bit from the focus of this book. Instead, I want to discuss in which account you should place your bond allocation and, should you be in the withdrawal phase of your investing career, from which account you should yank your cash.

Minimizing income is the name of the game

Interest payments from bonds or bond funds (other than municipal bonds, covered in Chapter 3) are generally taxable as normal income. In contrast, the money you make off stocks, whether dividends or capital gains, is usually taxed at 15 percent (although this rate is always subject to change). It makes sense, especially if you're in an income tax bracket that's higher than 15 percent, to keep your bonds in a tax-advantaged retirement account where you won't pay any tax on the interest year to year. Even if you're in the 15 percent bracket, this plan still makes sense because bond income, regular and steady, is taxed regardless of whether you withdraw it. Stock appreciation (capital gains) is taxed only when you sell, although stock held in mutual funds may incur capital gains when the fund sells, even if you don't.

REMEMBER

When allocating your portfolio, keep in mind at all times that money in your traditional 401(k) or IRA will eventually be taxed as regular income, and you must, per the IRS, start to withdraw your funds at age 72. Say you decide that you want your retirement portfolio to have a 30 percent allocation to bonds, and all those bonds are in your IRA. If you're within a few years of withdrawing some of that money, you may want to make the allocation of bonds a tad higher, with an emphasis on less-volatile short-term bonds.

TIP

If you have various retirement accounts with more space than you need for just your bond allocation, put the bonds in the tax-deferred accounts and put potentially higher-yielding assets, like stocks, in your tax-free accounts, such as your Roth IRA. That's because the Roth IRA doesn't require you to take required minimum distributions (RMDs) at all, so you may as well fuel up your Roth with assets that can really grow over the years.

Lowering your tax bracket through smart withdrawals

At age 72, you have to start taking something from your 401(k) or your regular or rollover IRA; it's the law. (See the nearby sidebar "Don't miss the required minimum distribution!") But prior to that age, and to a certain degree after that age, it's at your discretion whether your cash comes from your 401(k), IRA, Roth IRA, or taxable account (unless it's an inherited account you received as a beneficiary).

TIP

How to best use that discretion? Balance, Grasshopper, balance. Most likely, you want to pull from your tax-deferred retirement accounts only to the point that doing so doesn't push you into a higher tax bracket. At that point, supplement that cash with money from your Roth account or your taxable brokerage account.

For example, if you're single and withdrawing $45,000 a year from your portfolio, you most likely want to take at least the first $9,950 of that amount from your 401(k) or traditional IRA. You'll be taxed only 10 percent on that money. You may want to consider taking as much as $40,525 from one of these accounts. That amount (according to the 2021 federal tax schedule), and no more, will keep you squarely in the 12 percent tax bracket. Show any more incremental income, and you'll be taxed at 22 percent — a substantial increase. Solution: Withdraw the remaining $4,475 ($45,000 – $40,525) from either your Roth or your taxable brokerage account, and you may keep yourself in the 12 percent bracket. (All of this is subject to any deductions you may have. So the actual numbers may be higher for you if you have, say, substantial medical expenses.)

Having retirement money that's both taxable and tax-free is known in the financial planning world as *tax diversification*. It makes a lot of sense.

Caveat: If you have mucho bucks — more than the federal estate tax exemption (which varies over time) — the rules change. Your heirs will generally fare much better inheriting money outside of your IRA or 401(k) than money within. It may make sense, in your case, to well exceed your RMDs, take the tax hit, but spare your heirs from having to pay a hefty estate tax plus income tax. Talk to an estate planning attorney, tax accountant, or financial planner before setting up your withdrawal strategy. Oh, and Roth money is a great gift for your heirs.

REMEMBER

Do keep in mind that frequent changes in tax laws, as well as your own circumstances, make it a good idea to review your retirement cash-flow plan on a yearly basis.

DON'T MISS THE REQUIRED MINIMUM DISTRIBUTION!

I'm happy to live in a country where people who break the law are given due process and, if found guilty of a crime, they'll neither have their limbs removed nor be stoned to death. Yet we have the RMD on 401(k) plans, as well as regular and rollover IRAs. And woe is you if you miscalculate. No, you won't be stoned, but your finances will certainly be pummeled hard.

Of course, the calculation is easy, says the IRS. You simply take your retirement account's balance as of December 31 the prior year and divide that number by your "life-expectancy factor" (which is found in IRS Publication 590, available at www.irs.gov). Don't get it wrong! The penalty for taking less than your RMD is brutal. If you withdraw less than the required minimum amount, the IRS can nail you for a sum equal to 50 percent of the RMD not taken.

RMDs generally begin at age 72. If you feel uncomfortable doing the calculation yourself, a retirement specialist at the brokerage house where you have your account will help you, or you can ask your tax guru.

There's an entirely different table for RMDs on inherited IRAs. Lots of people mess up there, with potentially expensive consequences.

3

Customizing Your Bond Portfolio

Put together your investment plan by forecasting your future financial needs, knowing your investment style, figuring out how big your nest egg needs to be, and becoming familiar with financial markets.

Develop expectations for risk and return and using bonds to adjust volatility and growth in your portfolio.

Achieve balance in your portfolio by considering many fixed-income and equity investments.

Buy and sell in accordance with a strategy that includes changes in the marketplace, selecting between bonds and bond funds, and factoring in taxes.

» Selecting appropriate investment
vehicles

» Getting a handle on major investment
principles

Chapter **8**

Building Your Portfolio's Foundation

ortfolios, like Cadillacs and minivans, suit certain kinds of personalities. To choose the most appropriate investments — be they bonds, stocks, or pork-belly futures — it helps to know yourself fairly well. I'm not suggesting in a grand, metaphysical, Freudian or Socratic sense, but at least to the point where you — and perhaps your spouse — can formulate some reasonable household financial goals.

Unlike the other chapters in this book, I don't focus squarely on bonds here. First, I help you discover who you are as an investor. (Are you a Warren Buffett or a Nervous Nelly?) After you identify your "inner investor," you'll be more confident in deciding whether a portfolio of primarily bonds may suit you better than, say, dropping your savings into casino stocks, uranium futures, or hush money.

I also discuss some fundamental principles in this chapter, such as reversion to the mean and the cold-clay link between risk and return. These pertain not only to bonds, but to all financial investments. If you're already a seasoned player, these essential market truths could be part of your current game plan. But a quick review certainly couldn't hurt.

Focusing on Your Objectives

Investing in a portfolio of Ginnie Mae bonds is the conservative way to go. (See Chapter 3 for more on Ginnie Maes, Freddie Macs, and various other federal agency bonds.) It's unlikely you'll get rich investing in these — or any bond portfolio. But you won't be waking up at 2 a.m. in a cold-sweat panic, worried about the whereabouts of your money.

Investing your savings in something like the stock of a small technology company can, indeed, make you rich. (Think Microsoft back when a nerdy, young Bill Gates was working out of his garage.) Beware, however: Taking a financial risk on a start-up "Big Idea" with world-changing potential may deprive you of that solid eight hours of sleep your bond-holding buddy is enjoying. Wednesday's investment may be worth a fraction of what you were expecting when you finally crawl out of bed, bleary-eyed, on Thursday morning.

For almost all people, an in-between portfolio — perhaps with Ginnie Mae bonds *and* tech stocks — would make the most sense. Deciding if you want to be smack in the middle of the continuum, or prefer to hang your hat toward the mild side or the wild side, will have a great bearing on just how much you wind up stocking up on bonds or bonding with stocks.

Deciding what you want to be when you grow up

Do you dream of quitting your day job as soon as possible to start a new career writing haiku poetry? Or do you want to pay for your kids' college tuition and expenses and then finish building your retirement portfolio after that point? Do you want to drop out of society after the kids are grown, buy a 52-foot sailboat, and travel the Caribbean from island to island just like in the retirement ads from the brokerage houses? These are the kinds of questions you need to ask yourself in deciding on your optimal portfolio.

REMEMBER

Fortunately, you don't need to be all that specific in your future goals to formulate a fairly good portfolio plan. What you need is a good handle on how much money you'll require to make your dreams a reality and at what age that money will need to be available to you.

Our society has changed a lot in the last generation, and many Boomers now nearing or already having entered traditional retirement age aren't looking for anything even closely resembling a traditional retirement. As for me, I love most of the work I do and hope to continue doing it for as long as I'm capable. However, I wouldn't mind clocking fewer hours at my desk and spending more time traveling and taking courses. My future lifestyle comes with a certain price tag, and I have a fairly good idea what that will be.

Picturing your future nest egg

In Chapter 10, I provide you with the tools to help you fine-tune your retirement goals and figure out what lump sum you'll likely need — given the kind of lifestyle you envision — to replace your weekly paycheck. (This is otherwise known as *financial independence*.) But for now, I'm just going to share some loose guidelines.

TIP

It doesn't much matter whether you're like me and you intend to keep working past traditional retirement age or whether you want a more old-fashioned retirement (complete with checkered pants, green golf shirts, blue hair, and mah-jongg games). Most financial planners suggest that your ultimate savings goal be something on the order of 20 times — or even better, 25 times — your annual anticipated expenses, minus any income from Social Security, pension, or part-time employment.

In other words, if you think you'll need $60,000 a year to live comfortably at age 65 or so, and you anticipate yearly income of $30,000 from a combination of Social Security payments and, say, hobby income, your goal should be to grow a nest egg worth at the very least $600,000. Simple arithmetic: $60,000 (your desired yearly income) minus the $30,000 you're anticipating from other sources equals $30,000. That's what you'll need from your portfolio. Multiply that number by 20, and you'll need to have, at a minimum, a nest egg of $600,000 — or, even better, multiply that $30,000 by 25, and you'll need a nest egg of $750,000.

Understanding the Rule of 20 (preferably 25)

Before I explain the (rough — very rough) Rule of 20, let me first say that I know that the number 20 may scare the heck out of you if you haven't put away much so far, but try to remember that compound interest is a powerful force.

If you're still the young age of 30, investing wisely in a diversified portfolio, you'd likely have to put aside only about $300 a month to have a darned good chance of building a $600,000 nest egg by age 65. If you have a job where the employer matches your 401(k) contributions by kicking in 50 percent on top of whatever you put in, $200 a month would likely do the trick. Many readers of this book will be well over 30, but, still, you get the idea: Start saving today, and you can likely make great headway.

Okay, so where does the multiplier of 20 come from? It simply gives an approximation of how much you should have by age 65 to cover your yearly expenses, based on the average life expectancy for someone your age (that is, roughly 20 years). With 20 times your annual withdrawal needs, the chances are good that you won't run out of money before you make your final exit. Obviously, if you can save more, so much the better. After all, you may live longer than the average life expectancy. And the markets may perform very poorly. Baked into these safe-withdrawal rate assumptions is the assumption that the markets will perform more or less as they have in the past.

TIP

If you think that you're likely to live an exceptionally long life, or if you're planning to quit work before age 65, you should plan to save more than 20 times your annual living expenses. The longer you plan to live a life of ease, the more money you'll need to tap.

TIP

Here's another very rough rule: If you plan to live in retirement for 30 years, have 30 times your annual anticipated portfolio withdrawals; 40 years, 40 times; and so on.

For those of us who would like to keep working as long as we can, there's still nothing whatsoever wrong with financial independence, so I would advocate the same goal: Try to amass at least 20 times what you might need to pull from your portfolio to live for a year. (Don't forget to factor in that you'll be getting Social Security.) Again, I'm talking rough estimates here, and I can't emphasize that enough. I believe it's important, though, to illustrate how the nest egg goals you establish now have everything to do with how heavily you invest in bonds.

Choosing your investment style

Okay, what does the Rule of 20 have to do with your choice of investments and the wisdom of holding bonds? Simple: The further away you are from achieving that financial goal, the higher the rate of savings you need or the higher the rate of return you require from your portfolio — or both.

TIP

In Chapter 10, I try to answer the very difficult question, "What percent of your portfolio should be in bonds?" For now, I simply want to point out that people who need a higher rate of return generally don't want too bond-laden a portfolio. A heavy position in bonds is more appropriate for investors who don't need a lot of growth but, rather, can sit back and enjoy the steady, slow growth their portfolio will offer.

Say, for example, you're 55 or 60 years old and, thanks to your good savings habits, you're now on the cusp of having your "20x" portfolio. If much of that portfolio is now in stocks or stock mutual funds, it may be time for you to start shifting a good chunk of your portfolio into bonds. Why take much risk with things like stocks or commodities if you don't need to?

WARNING

You should know, however, that simple portfolio-construction formulas (that typically use age as a main determinant) often don't work. These are some very rough rules just to get you thinking about investment allocation. As I explain in Chapter 10, a 55- or 60-year-old investor who may be considering adding more bonds to their portfolio may do better by shifting back to stocks 20 years later — if the portfolio is worth millions. (Yes, it would be great to find yourself in a position where this is an option.)

Making Your Savings and Investment Selections

True, you can shove your money under the mattress, but with inflation running about 3 percent a year at the time of writing, $1,000 in today's dollars will have only about $940 in purchasing power two years from now and $860 in purchasing power five years from now. Economists call that loss in purchasing power *inflation risk*, and it is, indeed, a real risk. Moral of the story: Don't keep money under the mattress. You have to do *something* with it.

In my mind, *savings* refers to money socked away that has at very best a chance of keeping even with inflation. *Investments* refers to money socked away that's projected to grow at least at the rate of inflation (over the long haul) and likely greater than the rate of inflation.

REMEMBER

The whole point of investing is to earn a *real return*, which is to say the rate of return after inflation. If your nominal return is 8 percent but inflation is 5 percent, your real return is approximately 3 percent. Getting a nominal return of 2 percent when there's no inflation is much better than getting a 15 percent return when the inflation rate is 20 percent.

Different types of bonds can fall into either category: savings or investments. Some bonds — like U.S. savings bonds — generally keep about even with inflation (although they haven't quite done that in the past few years). Other bonds, such as high-yield corporate bonds, will usually keep you ahead of the game if you hold them for a long while.

TIP

In general, money that may be needed in the upcoming months, or even a few years down the pike, should be kept in safe savings; you can't risk a loss of principal. (Yes, loss of principal is possible with most bonds, especially long-term bonds. You discover why in Chapter 2.) Money that you most likely won't need for many years to come should be invested for growth; even if there's a loss of principal, you will likely earn that back, and then some, before you require withdrawals.

Following are some of the most popular options for saving and investing, which I briefly compare and contrast with bond investing.

Saving your money in safety

With the following savings options, the principal is guaranteed (or close to guaranteed), but the rate of return may not keep you even with inflation:

>> **Your local savings bank:** There's something to be said for keeping at least a small balance at the neighborhood bank. I do. Need a loan someday? It may be easier if you're a regular customer. Local businesses are also more likely to accept a check drawn on a local bank. (Well, just in case you still write checks, that is. I've mostly been using Venmo and PayPal lately.) Then there's the "bank experience," which may be

especially important if you're a parent. When my two children were younger, each had a savings account at the corner bank, and they loved going there for the plate of free cookies.

At all savings banks in the United States, deposits are insured up to $250,000 by the Federal Deposit Insurance Corporation (FDIC). Even if the bank goes under, you're covered (up to that $250,000 limit). The interest rates paid by local banks tend to be modest — especially in the low-interest-rate environment of recent years — more modest than those paid by most bonds.

TIP

>> **Certificates of deposit (CDs):** The longer you're willing to commit your money to the bank, the higher the interest rate. Generally a 6-month CD may pay an interest point greater than a regular savings account; a 12-month CD may pay a bit more; and an 18-month CD, even a wee bit more than that. If you have one to several thousand dollars sitting around, perhaps you might put one-third into each. That way, you're not tying up all your money for the entire time, and if interest rates go higher in six months, you'll be free to take part of your money and upgrade to a higher-yielding CD.

Shop for the best rates at www.bankrate.com or www. moneyrates.com. Especially if you're dealing with a local bank, ask to talk to the manager and see if you can negotiate something higher than the advertised rate. CD rates are usually comparable to short-term bonds but are not on par with longer-term bonds.

TIP

>> **Internet banking:** Consider opening an account with a web-based, FDIC-insured savings bank, such as Marcus (www.marcus.com) or Bread Savings (https://savings. breadfinancial.com). The rates on savings accounts are often comparable to one-year CDs, and you don't need to tie up your money at all.

>> **Money-market mutual funds:** Money-market mutual funds aren't insured by the FDIC, so they may not be as safe as bank accounts or U.S. savings bonds. It depends on the particular fund. Some are invested in Treasurys, and they would be as safe as an FDIC guarantee. Most money-market funds, however, are invested more in corporations and such, and they aren't quite as safe, although the risk of default is very small. Both kinds of money-market funds tend to offer

returns similar to what you get in bank accounts but not as much as a bond portfolio. If you hold one of these funds outside of your retirement account, you may want to choose a tax-free money-market fund, especially if you're in a higher tax bracket.

Note that with money-market funds, your principal is quite secure, but the interest rate is not; it can, and often does, vary from day to day. That's just the opposite of a bond, by the way: With a bond, your interest rate is fixed, but the value of your principal can vary day to day. (I explain this in Chapter 2.)

>> **Short-term, high-quality bonds:** Short-term bond mutual funds and exchange-traded funds (ETFs), both taxable and tax-free, government and corporate, are similar to money-market funds and often pay slightly higher earnings, but they also subject you to modest volatility. Read all about them, and how to choose the best one for your portfolio, in Chapters 5 and 10.

HOME SWEET HOME

Yes, of course, home equity represents a form of savings. It's also your most *illiquid* savings. (*Liquidity* refers to the ease with which you can cash out on an investment, if you need to.) You need a place to live, and you always will. So, for your home to ever do you much good as a store of value, you'll need to downsize. At that point, you can sell the more expensive home, pick up a cheaper abode (or rent one), and pocket the difference.

Home values in the United States rose steadily for many years — until 2006–2007, when prices dropped in many areas of the country by 50 percent or more. Since then, and especially in the past couple of years, housing prices have risen sharply. But the lesson of 2006–2007 should stand.

You never want all your net worth tied up in any one asset, particularly the asset you call home. Even if housing prices remain stable or trend upward, it isn't like you can carve off a piece of your living room if you ever need a dose of cash.

Investing your money with an eye toward growth

By sinking your savings into investments such as the ones I list here, your payoff can be handsome. But remember, of course, you can also lose money.

TIP

>> **Stocks:** Whereas bonds represent a loan you're making to a company or government, stocks represent partial ownership in a company. Over the long run, few investments pay off as well as stocks, which have an 80-year track record of returning nearly 10 percent a year (before inflation) — about twice the return of bonds.

The problem with stocks is that they can be extremely volatile, perhaps going up 20 percent or 30 percent one year and tumbling 37 percent the next. (Remember 2008?) You can somewhat reduce that volatility by holding a variety of different kinds of stocks, most easily done with stock mutual funds or ETFs (which, like mutual funds, represent baskets of securities but, unlike mutual funds, trade like stocks). You can also temper the volatility of a stock portfolio by blending into that portfolio certain other kinds of investments — such as bonds — that tend to hold their own or may even head north when stocks head south.

>> **Gold and other commodities:** In the past, commodities — gold, silver, oil, wheat, coffee — have been difficult to invest in and extremely volatile. The volatility remains. However, investing in commodities has recently become easy. A bevy of ETFs introduced in the past several years allow you to plunk your money into just about any commodity imaginable.

Like bonds, certain commodities may hold their own, or even go up, when stocks go down. Commodities tend to increase value over time because the world is becoming an awfully crowded place, with more and more people consuming limited resources. But in the short run, commodity prices are subject to the whims of weather, politics, and investor enthusiasm.

>> **Investment real estate:** Whether you invest in apartments to rent, shopping centers, or office space, there's money to

be made in investment real estate. (Like commodities, real estate is a limited resource.) However, tending to real estate, as any landlord knows, can be a lot of work. And some tenants tend to be real pains in the butt — calling you at midnight to fix a leaky faucet.

TIP

Real estate investment trusts (REITs) operate much like stocks and let you enjoy the fruits of others' labors, profiting merely by depositing your money. (No leaky faucets!) Of course, as with stocks, there's risk involved — more so than there is with most bond offerings. REITs, like stocks, are generally best purchased in the form of a mutual fund or ETF. Brokerages, the likes of a Fidelity or a Schwab, can offer you dozens of REIT funds. (See Chapter 6 for more info.)

>> **Entrepreneurial ventures:** Open a restaurant, a dry-cleaning shop, a dance studio, a gas station. Several million Americans have the bulk of their savings invested in small businesses. You're in control that way, and there's a chance that your small business could go big. Running a business does require tons of work, and there's always a risk that profits won't materialize. When small business owners come into my office, I certainly try not to discourage them from growing their businesses, but I also advise funneling some money toward other investments, such as bonds and stocks. Yes, diversification is good for the entrepreneur, as well as the employee.

Understanding Five Major Investment Principles

When I first became a serious student of investments, I was amazed at how much hard academic research existed. Most of it contradicts anything and everything you've ever been told about investments by the magazines and books that shout, "Get Rich Now!" or "Five Hot Stocks for the New Year!" If you know nothing else about investing, know the following five eternal, essential investment truths — all real-world tested — and you'll be way, way ahead of the game.

Risk and return are two sides of the same coin

REMEMBER

If you see an investment that has gained 50 percent in the past year, sure, consider taking a position. But know this: Any investment that goes up 50 percent in a year can just as easily go down 50 percent in a year. That's the nature of the investment world.

Risk and return go together like fire and oxygen. Short-term, high-quality bonds bring modest returns but bear little risk. Long-term, low-quality bonds bring more handsome returns but bear considerable risk. Lower-quality bonds *must* offer greater potential for return, or no one but maybe a few loonies would invest in them. Higher-quality bonds *must* offer lower rates of return, or so many investors would flock to them that the price would be bid up (which would effectively lower the rate of return).

Financial markets are largely efficient

If someone says to you that a particular investment is "guaranteed" to return 15 percent a year with no risk, take that with a big, big, big grain of salt. Financial markets tend to be *efficient*, which means that thousands upon thousands of buyers, sellers, fund managers, and market analysts are constantly out there looking for the best deals. If a truly safe investment were to offer a guaranteed return of 15 percent, so many people would make offers to buy that investment that the price would surely be bid up — making the return drop.

To clarify, markets can be terribly inefficient (sometimes downright mad!) in the short run where emotion and hype can take the price of stocks and commodities (and to a lesser degree bonds) all over the map, but after time, things tend toward the more rational.

The efficiency of the markets is why even so few professional investors can beat the indexes. In numerous studies — each supporting the findings of the others — actively managed mutual funds (funds whose managers try to pick stocks or bonds that will outperform all others) rarely manage to beat the indexes. Over the course of a decade or more, the number is infinitesimally small, and even those chosen few fail to beat the indexes by very much.

In Chapter 5, I tell you where to find the best bond *index funds* — funds that try to capture the returns of the entire market rather than attempting, usually in vain, to beat the market.

Diversification is about the only free lunch you'll ever get

REMEMBER

So, if you can't pick certain securities that will outperform, how can you become a better investor than the next person? It's not that hard, really. Keep your costs low. Keep your taxes minimal. Don't trade often. Most important, diversify your portfolio across several *asset classes* — various kinds of investments, such as bonds, stocks, and real estate — so that all the components can contribute to your returns. Because the components move up and down at different times, the volatility of your entire portfolio is kept to a minimum.

The essence of *modern portfolio theory* (MPT) is this: You can add a highly volatile (high risk, high return) investment to a portfolio, and — if that investment tends to zig while other investments in your portfolio zag — you may actually lower the volatility (and risk) of the entire portfolio. So, who says there's no such thing as a free lunch?

Reversion to the mean — it means something

Most things in this world — from batting averages to inches of rainfall to investment returns — tend, over time, to revert back to their historical averages. This phenomenon is called *reversion to the mean* (or sometimes *regression to the mean*).

Suppose, for example, that a certain kind of investment (say, intermediate-term Ginnie Mae bonds) showed extraordinary returns for the past two to three years (perhaps 18 percent a year). That kind of return on a bond would be rare, but it does happen (I explain how in Chapter 2). We know from the past several decades that intermediate-term, high-quality bonds such as Ginnie Maes typically return about one-third as much. Would you be well advised to assume that Ginnie Mae bonds will continue to earn 18 percent for the next two years?

In fact, most investors assume just that. They look at recent returns of a certain asset class and assume that those recent returns will continue. In other words, most fresh investment money pours into "hot" investment sectors. And this often spells tragedy for those who don't understand the concept of reversion to the mean. In reality, hot sectors sooner or later turn cold — and, in general, you should avoid them.

In fact, if anything, you might expect an asset class that overperforms for several years to underperform in the upcoming years. Why? Because all investments (like batting averages and inches of rainfall) tend to return to their historical average return.

To look at it another way, investments tend to move in and out of favor in cycles. It's hard, if not impossible, to imagine that any one investment that has historically yielded modest returns would suddenly, for any extended period of time, become a major moneymaker.

Investment costs matter — a lot!

Oh, sure, 1 percent doesn't sound like a prodigious sum, but the difference between investing in a bond mutual fund that charges 1.25 percent annually in management fees and one that charges 0.25 percent is enormous. And given the low interest being paid on bonds today, the difference in dollars is enormous. Over the course of the next ten years, assuming the bonds yield 3 percent, compounded annually, a $50,000 investment in the more expensive fund would leave you, after paying the fund company, with about $59,500. That same investment in the less expensive fund would leave you with about $65,600 — a difference of $6,100.

Of course, fund companies that charge more tend to have a lot of money to spend on advertising, and they do a great job conning the public into thinking that their funds are somehow worth the extra money. That's rarely true. In mutual bond-fund advertising, mediocre funds are often dolled up to look much better than they are. And by the way, if you're thinking about investing in individual bonds, your profits are going to similarly be eaten away by the bond broker's cut. That's unavoidable, but you need to know what that cut is and how much will be eaten away. Some bond brokers are amazingly deft at hiding this from you.

Studies galore show that the investors who keep their costs to a minimum do best. That's especially true with bonds, where the returns tend to be more modest than with stocks even in normal times. Whether you're buying bond funds or purchasing individual bonds, transaction costs and operating expenses need to be minimized. That's largely what Chapters 4, 5, and 11 of this book are all about.

Chapter 9

Considering Return, Risk, and Realism

N
o trade-off between risk and return? A thousand years from now — nay, ten times ten thousand years from now — there will *still* be a trade-off between risk and return. This chapter explains why that's so, why understanding that trade-off is integral to building a successful portfolio, and why trying to do so without bonds is as silly as, well, questioning the existence of Santa Claus.

Searching for the Elusive Free Lunch

A trade-off between risk and return exists for roughly the same reason that a shiny new Lexus costs more than a 2013 Honda Civic. If both vehicles cost the same, everyone except maybe Ralph Nader would buy a new Lexus. Similarly, if you thought you could earn as much investing in Federal Deposit Insurance Corporation (FDIC)–insured certificates of deposit (CDs) as you could investing in shiny tech stocks, backed only by the capriciousness of the market, would you invest in tech stocks? No, I don't think so.

A risk-free investment that paid high returns would be the equivalent of a free lunch. Sorry, but free lunches are very hard to find. No stable investment should be expected to pay a high rate of return. No luxury car should be expected to sell for the same amount as an old jalopy. The capitalist market, as Adam Smith once said and even Ralph Nader can't deny, has an invisible hand.

Making a killing in CDs . . . yeah, right

What I'm saying, and what Professor Smith was saying (sort of), is that risky investments — or at least investments perceived as risky — tend to return more than less risky investments for the same reason that old jalopies sell for less than new luxury cars: At least over the long run, they must.

Look, if you could invest in the stock market, commodities, real estate, or money-market funds and CDs, all returns being equal, you'd invest in money-market funds and CDs, right? Everyone would invest in money-market funds and CDs. There'd be no market for more volatile investments. Similarly, if luxury cars and old jalopies were available at the same price, there'd be no market for old jalopies.

Only because of differing rewards (higher return potential or greater price bargain) is there a market for both. Honk, honk. Ka-ching, ka-ching.

Defining risk and return

REMEMBER

In just a moment, I talk about the particular risk and return characteristics of bonds. But first, I want to make clear what risk and return really are. (No, it isn't obvious to everyone.)

>> **Risk is the potential of losing money.** Although you can lose or gain money a lot more easily in certain investments than others, all investments carry some risk — including the safest of bonds, and even including cash. When most people think of risk, they think of wild market swings such as those that often occur in the market for, say, cocoa bean futures. They think of how much money they could potentially lose in a week, a month, or a year. But you can lose money in an investment in other ways, which I address in the next section.

>> **Return is the potential of making money.** Most of the money made in bonds is made in the form of interest

payments. Sometimes, bonds also appreciate (or, alas, depreciate) in value. Overall, the return potential of bonds is modest compared to certain other investments, like an investment in the S&P 500 or a dry-cleaning franchise in a local strip mall. As I make clear, I hope, throughout this book, the benefit of bonds is more to temper risk and provide steady, predictable income than to capture huge gains.

Appreciating Bonds' Risk Characteristics

The majority of bond offerings are rather staid investments. You give your money to a government or corporation. You receive a steady flow of income, usually twice a year, for a certain number of years. Then, typically after a few years, you get your original money back. Sometimes you pay taxes. A broker usually takes a cut. Beginning and end of story.

The reason for bonds' staid status is not only that they provide steady and predictable streams of income, but also that, as a bondholder, you have first dibs on the issuer's money. A corporation is legally bound to pay you your interest before it doles out any dividends to people who own company stock. If a company starts to go through hard times, any proceeds from the business or (in the case of an actual bankruptcy) from the sale of assets go to you before they go to shareholders.

However, bonds offer no ironclad guarantees. First dibs on the money aside, bonds are not FDIC-insured savings accounts. They're not without some risk. For that matter, even an FDIC-insured savings account — even stuffing your money under the proverbial mattress — also carries some risk.

Following are seven risks inherent in bond investing. As a potential bondholder, you need to know each of them.

REMEMBER

As you read the following sections, please don't think that I'm trying to convince you not to buy bonds. Despite all the risks I mention, bonds still belong in your portfolio. And in the meantime, check out Figure 9-1. To the left, see where bonds tend to fit into the investment risk spectrum as compared to other kinds of investments. To the middle and the right, see where different kinds of bonds rank in order of relative risk.

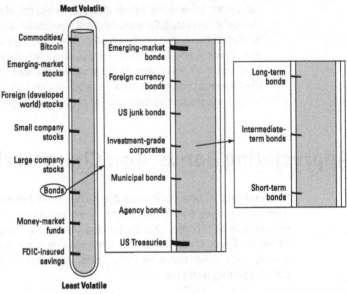

© John Wiley & Sons, Inc.

FIGURE 9-1: Where bond risk falls in the spectrum of investments.

I'm talking here about risk as in volatility. Short-term Treasurys aren't very volatile in that the prices remain stable. But they *are* subject to inflation risk. Over the long run, a portfolio of short-term Treasurys (like money-market funds or an FDIC-insured savings account) won't keep up with inflation and will lose money in real-dollar terms.

Okay, on to the risks.

Interest rate risk

Interest rates go up, and interest rates go down. And whenever they do, bond prices move, almost in sync, in the opposite direction. Why? If you're holding a bond that pays 4 percent, and interest rates move up so that most new bonds are paying 6 percent, your old bond becomes about as desirable to hold as a bedbug-infested mattress. Any rational buyer of bonds would, all things being equal, choose a new bond paying 6 percent rather than your relic, still paying only 4 percent. If you try to sell the bond, unless you can find a real sucker, the price you're likely to get will be deeply discounted.

I recall a cartoon I saw once in a financial journal that had Batman throwing a punch at the Joker. *BAM!* Across Batman's chest was written *interest rates*, and across the Joker's chest was written *bond prices*. How perfect an analogy.

The longer off the maturity of the bond, the louder the *BAM!* — in other words, the more its price will drop with rising interest rates. Thus, long-term bonds tend to be the most volatile of all bonds. Think it through: If you have a bond paying 4 percent that matures in a year, and the prevailing interest rate moves up to 6 percent, you're looking at relatively inferior coupon payments for the next 12 months. If you're holding a 4 percent bond that matures in ten years, you're looking at potentially ten years of inferior coupon payments.

No one wants to buy a bond offering ten years of inferior coupon payments unless they can get that bond for a steal.

WARNING

That's why if you try to sell a bond after a period of rising interest rates, you take a loss. If you hold the bond to maturity, you can avoid that loss, but you pay an opportunity cost because your money is tied up earning less than the prevailing rate of interest. Either way, you stand to lose.

Of course, interest rate risk has its flip side: If interest rates fall, your existing bonds, paying the older, higher interest rates, suddenly start looking awfully good to potential buyers. There are no longer bedbugs in the mattress. If you decide to sell, you'll get a handsome price. (I discuss the formulation of bond prices in Chapter 2.)

This flip side to interest rate risk is precisely what has caused the most peculiar situation in the past 40 years, where the longest-term government bonds have actually done as well as the S&P 500 in total returns. The yield on these babies has dipped and dipped and dipped, from over 14 percent in the early 1980s to about 2 percent today. Hence, those old bonds turned to gold. Will this happen again in the next 40 years? Not unless long-term Treasurys in the year 2062 are being issued with a −12 percent interest rate. Of course, that isn't going to happen. More likely, interest rates are going to climb back to historical norms.

You can probably figure out now why I'm putting interest rate risk first on this list. Interest rate risk has perhaps never been greater than it is today. You would be foolish to put your money into 30-year Treasurys and assume that you're going to get 10 percent a year annual return, as some very lucky investors have done over the last 40 years. Chances are, well, anything can happen over 40 years, but keep your expectations modest, please.

Inflation risk

WARNING

If you're holding a bond that's paying 4 percent, and the inflation rate is 4 percent, you aren't making anything. You're treading water. And that's only if your interest is coming to you tax-free. If your bond is paying 4 percent and inflation moves up to 5 percent, you're losing money. Inflation risk is perhaps the most insidious kind of bond risk because you can't really see it. The coupon payments are coming in. Your principal is seemingly intact. And yet, when all is said and done, it really *isn't* intact. You're slowly bleeding purchasing power.

Although inflation rarely hits you as fast and hard as rapidly rising interest rates, it's the fixed-income investor's greatest enemy over the long run. Interest rates, after all, go up and down, up and down. But inflation moves in only one direction. (Well, we could have *deflation*, where prices fall, but that hasn't happened since the Great Depression except for a month or two here and there. I don't believe deflation is likely to happen again anytime soon.) Inflation takes its toll slowly and steadily, and many bondholders don't even realize that they're losing ground.

Some bonds — Treasury Inflation-Protected Securities (TIPS) — are shielded, at least theoretically, from the risk of inflation. (It's complicated; see Chapter 3.) Most bonds (and bondholders), however, suffer when inflation surges.

Reinvestment risk

When you invest $1,000 in, say, a 20-year bond paying 6 percent, you may be counting on your money compounding every year. If that's the case — if your money does compound, and you reinvest all your interest payments at 6 percent — after 20 years, you'll have $3,262.

But suppose you invest $1,000 in a 20-year bond paying 6 percent and, after four years, the bond is *called.* The bond issuer unceremoniously returns your principal, and you no longer hold the bond. Interest rates have dropped in the past four years, and now the best you can do is to buy another bond that pays 4 percent. Let's suppose you do just that, and you hold the new bond for the remainder of the 20 years. Instead of $3,262, you're left with $2,387 — about 27 percent less money.

The risk I describe here is called *reinvestment risk*, and it's a very real risk of bond investing, especially when you buy callable or shorter-term individual bonds. Of course, you can buy non-callable bonds and earn less interest, or you can buy longer-term bonds and risk that interest rates will rise. Trade-offs, baby, trade-offs. It's what investing is all about.

Note that one way of dealing with reinvestment risk is to treat periods of declining interest rates as only temporary investment setbacks. What goes down usually goes back up.

Default risk

Default risk is what most people think of when they imagine investment risk. Many bond investors focus on default risk — sometimes, too much. In fact, most bond investors worry so much about default risk that it often blinds them to the more common and more insidious risks of bond investing, such as those I mention in the previous sections.

What's default risk? Simple: The issuer of your bond starts to go under; limited or no money is left to pay creditors; and not only do your interest payments stop coming in the mail every six months, but you start to wonder if you'll ever get your principal back. If the issuer actually declares bankruptcy, your mailbox, instead of offering you interest payments, will be flooded with letters from lawyers explaining in explicit Latin that you're a sucker and a fool.

With Treasurys and agency bonds, a default has never happened. Rarely do municipal bonds or investment-grade corporate bonds default. Default risk is mostly an issue when you invest in high-yield (junk) corporate bonds. When the economy is humming along, defaults are rare. When the economy slides and even companies that make hotcakes can't sell their wares, default rates jump. That's an especially nasty time to be losing money on your bonds because chances are good that your other investments are doing poorly also.

TIP

Certain foreign bonds, especially emerging-market bonds, carry default risk as well. But emerging-market bonds — bonds issued mostly by the governments of poor countries — unlike U.S. junk corporate bonds, have limited correlation to the U.S. stock market. For that reason, although emerging-market bonds may have somewhat higher volatility than U.S. junk bonds, I might recommend them first for a portfolio (see Chapter 3).

Downgrade risk

Even if a bond doesn't go into default, rumors of a potential default can send a bond's price into a spiral. When a major rating agency, such as Moody's, S&P Global Ratings, or Fitch Ratings, changes the rating on a bond (moving it from, say, investment grade to below investment grade), fewer investors want that bond. This situation is the equivalent of *Consumer Reports* magazine pointing out that a particular brand of toaster oven is prone to explode. Not good.

Bonds that are downgraded may be downgraded a notch, or two notches, or three. The price of the bond drops accordingly. Typically, a downgrade from investment grade to junk results in a rather large price drop because many institutions aren't allowed to own anything below investment grade. The market, therefore, deflates faster than a speared blowfish, and the beating to bondholders can be brutal.

On occasion, downgraded bonds — even those downgraded to junk, which are sometimes referred to as *fallen angels* — are upgraded again. In the rare case that happens, prices zoom right back up again. Holding tight, therefore, sometimes makes good sense.

But trust me when I tell you that bond ratings and bond prices don't always march in sync. Consider, for example, that when U.S. Treasurys were downgraded by S&P in 2011 from an AAA to an AA rating, the bonds didn't drop in price but actually rose, and rose nicely. Why? In large part, it was because of the credit crisis in Europe and the realization of Japan's rising debt. In other words, although the United States appeared to be a slightly riskier place to invest vis-à-vis other nations, it actually started to look safer.

Tax risk

When comparing taxable bonds to other investments, such as stocks, some investors forget to factor in the potentially high cost of taxation. Except for municipal bonds and bonds kept in tax-advantaged accounts, such as an individual retirement account (IRA), the interest payments on bonds are generally taxable at your income-tax rate, which for most people is in the 25 percent to 28 percent range but could be as high as 35 percent — and, depending on the whims of Congress, may rise higher.

In contrast, stocks may pay dividends, most of which, thanks to favorable tax treatment enacted into law just a few years back, are generally taxable at 15 percent to 20 percent. If the price of the stock appreciates, that appreciation isn't taxable at all unless the stock is actually sold, at which point, it's usually taxed at 15 percent to 20 percent. So, would you rather have a stock that returns 5 percent a year or a bond that returns 5 percent a year? From strictly a tax vantage point, bonds lose. Paying even 25 percent tax represents a 67 percent bigger tax bite than paying 15 percent. (Of course, getting back to the whims of Congress, these special rates are also subject to change.)

WARNING

Tax risk on bonds is most pronounced during times of high interest rates and high inflation. If, for example, the inflation rate is 3 percent, and your bonds are paying 3 percent, you're just about breaking even on your investment. You have to pay taxes on the 3 percent interest, so you actually fall a bit behind. But suppose that the inflation rate were 9 percent and your bonds were paying 9 percent. You have to pay three times as much tax as if your interest rate were 3 percent — and possibly even more than three times the tax, if your interest payments bump you into a higher tax bracket — which means you fall even further behind.

I don't believe that inflation and interest rates will go to 9 percent. But if they do, holders of *conventional* (non-inflation-adjusted) bonds may not be happy campers, especially after April 15 rolls around.

Fear-of-missing-out (FOMO) risk

Despite all the other risks I mention, bonds, when chosen wisely and well diversified, usually make good, safe investments. But the return on bonds generally isn't going to be anything to write home about. From a strictly financial point of view, that may not be so bad. Some people who live within their means and already have good nest eggs don't need — and really shouldn't take — much risk with their investments. But if you're not taking that risk and your neighbors are, and the markets are good, and the economy is humming, your neighbors you're concerned about keeping up with may be making much more on their investments than you are. Ouch.

Studies show that *relative wealth* (making more than your neighbors) is more important to many people than *absolute wealth* (how much you actually have in the bank). Can you handle dinner with your neighbors and friends when, between bites, they boast about their major gains in the markets?

Reckoning on the Return You'll Most Likely See

If all bonds were the same, this would be a very short book. Bonds differ greatly when it comes to risk, expected return, taxability, sensitivity to various economic conditions, and other factors. Up until now, this chapter has focused more on risk than on expected return. I now discuss expected returns.

I can hear you say with confidence, "But a bond yielding 5 percent can be expected to return 5 percent over the life of the bond, and a bond yielding 6 percent can be expected to yield 6 percent. How hard can this be?" Keep on reading, Grasshopper.

Calculating fixed-income returns: Easier said than done

So, you invest in a $1,000 bond that yields 6 percent and matures in 20 years. What do you do with the $30 coupon payments that you receive every six months? Do you reinvest them or spend them on Chinese dinners? Do you keep the bond for the entire 20 years or cash it out beforehand? (If the bond is callable, of course, you may have no choice but to take back your principal before maturity.) And if you do cash out before maturity, what kind of price will you be able to get for the bond?

And what about the *real* (after-inflation) rate of return — the return that really matters? If inflation runs at 2 percent, your real return will be a lot greater than if inflation runs at 8 percent. But how can future inflation be predicted?

And what if you invest in a bond fund? Just because the fund yielded, say, 5 percent annually over the past seven years, does that mean it will yield that much moving forward?

And (sorry, just a couple more questions here — I'm almost done) what about *after-tax* real return — the return after both inflation *and* taxes? Ultimately, that's the return that matters the most of all. That's the return that moves you ahead financially or sets you back. Do you know what your tax bracket will be in ten years? Do you know what *anyone's* tax bracket will be in ten years?

These are just some of the questions that make bond investing — or any kind of investing — so much fun. I now pull out my crystal ball.

Looking back at history: An imperfect but useful guide

Not to tickle a dead horse or anything, but I said something earlier about the markets pretty much compensating long-term investors for the risks they take. And so it stands to reason that if we know what kind of returns a certain kind of bond has seen in the past, oh, 30 years, that information may give us a pretty good indication of the kind of returns that kind of bond is likely to provide in the next 30 or so years — at least relative to other bonds. Granted, history is only a guide. (Repeat: *History is only a guide.*) But aside from tea leaves and tarot cards, history is one of the only guides we have.

As it happens, we have pretty good data about bond returns over the past 94 years, largely thanks to Ibbotson Associates, a Morningstar company. Here are the figures for the average annual *nominal* (before inflation) return of three categories of bonds since 1926:

>> **One-month Treasury bills:** 3.3 percent

>> **Long-term government bonds:** 5.6 percent

>> **Long-term corporate bonds:** 6.2 percent

And here are those same figures translated into *real* (after inflation) returns for the same time period:

>> **One-month Treasury bills:** 0.4 percent

>> **Long-term government bonds:** 2.7 percent

>> **Long-term corporate bonds:** 3.3 percent

Um, I suppose as the author of this book, I'm not supposed to point this out, but quite honestly, the numbers aren't too awe-inspiring, are they? Keep in mind that these figures don't even factor in taxes, and you're taxed on the nominal (preinflation) returns of your bonds, not the real (postinflation) rate of return.

Investing in bonds despite their lackluster returns

So, what would you have earned, after taxes, investing in long-term government bonds over the past nine decades or so? Well, compared to stocks, which have returned about 10 percent a year before inflation and 7 percent after inflation, you would've earned squat. With corporate bonds, you would've earned slightly more than squat. And with short-term government bonds, you would've earned less than squat.

Keep in mind that all squat figures are rough approximations. If you force me to get technical, the long-term return on all bonds, judging by the past nine decades, is about half that of all stocks. The real return on bonds (after inflation but before taxes) is about one-third that of stocks. For the average taxpayer, the after-tax, long-term return on bonds is very roughly one-quarter that of stocks. (I *told* you this wasn't a book on getting rich quick!)

REMEMBER

So, why even bother investing in bonds? There are several *very* good reasons:

>> Even squat adds up when compounded year after year. Start with $10,000. Give yourself a mere 2 percent annual return, and — voilà! — within a century, you'll have $72,450. Granted, you're not going to live another century unless you're from extremely good stock and you're reading this in diapers, but you get the point, right?

>> In the last 90-plus years, stocks clearly clobbered bonds, but the next 90-plus years could be entirely different. Data from the 1800s show that the returns of stocks and bonds weren't all that different way back when.

>> Investment-quality bonds have practically no correlation to stocks, so they provide excellent balance to a portfolio. If you want to make sure that you're holding investments that don't all crash at once, stocks and bonds are a sweet mix to have.

>> At certain times when stocks have tanked, bonds (especially long-term Treasury and high-quality corporate bonds) have rallied, providing comfort to investors when comfort was most needed. Remember 2008.

>> Unlike just about any other kind of investment, bonds provide steady income for people who need it.

>> Bonds' limited volatility, as compared to many other investments, makes them good bets for people who can't afford to take much short-term risk.

>> Even though bonds have earned squat compared to stocks, they're virtual money machines compared to keeping your money in a savings account or money-market fund. Savings accounts and money-market funds are generally not going to pay you enough to even keep up with inflation. These days, they don't even come close.

>> Because you're going to take my advice on regularly rebalancing your portfolio (see Chapter 10), the "drag" of bonds on total portfolio performance will likely be much less than you think.

YIKES! BONDS THAT "PAY" NEGATIVE INTEREST RATES

You think interest rates are low here? Consider how investors in Germany and Japan must feel. In those countries, and several others in Europe, interest rates on government bonds have teetered around zero, and several times in the past few years they've actually dipped *below* zero. That's right. It could one day happen here as well. You buy a government bond for, say, $1,000, and the government agrees to

(continued)

(continued)

pay you back $992 in ten years. Who would purchase such a bond?! Well, if you have no choice but to either lose a few dollars in bonds or keep your money under the mattress, you might choose the former, for the sake of safety and convenience.

But safety and convenience are only worth so much, which is why, although we've seen interest rates turn slightly negative in certain countries, we've never seen the interest rate dip all that far below zero. . ... Never less than –1 percent. If any government tried to sell a $1,000 bond with an interest rate of, say, –2 percent, people would choose to keep their money under the mattress (or in a safe-deposit box). Or, they would pay for their currency to be converted to another currency so that they could invest in bonds elsewhere in the world where interest rates were paying more, like the United States, where, for a short time in March 2020, ten-year Treasurys were yielding an all-time low of 0.318 percent. That's awfully pathetic, but better than Germany's government bonds in 2020, which reached an all-time low yield of –0.84 percent.

Finding Your Risk-Return Sweet Spot

Portfolio A is as jumpy as a springer spaniel puppy but offers high return potential. Portfolio B is as sedate as a three-toed sloth (it hangs in trees) and offers modest return potential. Portfolio C is halfway between the two. Without knowing anything else about these three hypothetical portfolios, I'd say that Portfolio A is made up mostly of stocks, Portfolio B is constructed mostly of bonds, and Portfolio C is a more even mixture of both.

How you split your portfolio between fixed income (bonds, cash, CDs) and equity (stocks, investment real estate, commodities) will usually affect your risk-return profile more than any other decision. For that reason, I have an entire chapter (Chapter 10) designed to help you make that one crucial decision. Do you want a 70/25/5 (stocks/bonds/cash) portfolio? A 50/45/5 portfolio? A 30/55/15 portfolio? Silly formulas abound. I want you to get it right, which you will.

But certainly, the *kind* of equity (large-company stocks, small-company stocks, foreign stocks, dry-cleaning franchise) and the *kind* of fixed income (Treasurys, corporate bonds, junk bonds, munis) you choose for your portfolio play very much into your risk-return profile as well. In Chapter 10, I ask you to tell me something about yourself so I can help you decide what kinds of bonds are best for you. For now, I want you to start thinking about your risk-return "sweet spot."

REMEMBER

Your age, your income, your wealth, your expenses, your retirement plans, your estimated Social Security, and your health all come into play when deciding where your risk-return sweet spot should fall. As far as choosing your bonds, the less-volatile bonds (short term, high quality) naturally edge your portfolio toward safety but more modest returns. The higher-volatility bonds (long term, high yield) move your portfolio toward greater risk but potentially higher return.

Chapter **10**

Slicing the Pie: Determining How Much Should Be in Bonds

As a teenager, my family had a little boat. It was 15 feet from bow to stern, yellow with two white vinyl bucket seats up front and a small bench in the back. We kept it behind our home on Long Island, tied to a floating dock in an inlet that led to the Atlantic Ocean. It was propelled (if you can even use that word) by a 25-horsepower engine. The boat, when it had the currents running against it, moved at a snail's pace. When three passengers were in the boat, it was lucky to move at all.

My father bought that boat from an elderly gentleman who used it for lake fishing. Dad wanted a boat with little horsepower because he figured the severely limited speed might keep his son safe. Dad's motivation was good, but his reasoning wasn't. A boat that size with a 25-horsepower engine may be perfect for lake fishing, but out in the ocean it was something of a floating death trap, prey to strong currents and the wakes of behemoth yachts.

After such a wake blew me into the side of a concrete bridge and cracked the hull, I was finally able to convince my father to up the horsepower a bit — for safety's sake, of course. I wasn't exactly going *vroom-vroom* with our new 35-horsepower engine, but I no longer had to listen to "Slooow down, Russell!" from my boating schoolmates. And that felt awfully good.

Funny how some things never change. Many years later, I would become an investment advisor. And my dad, by then retired from years as a New York City attorney, was living along with my mom off a portfolio of mostly bonds and certificates of deposit (CDs). It took some doing, but I was finally able to convince them to "up the horsepower" of the portfolio by adding some stocks. Like many retirees I've worked with, especially those who lived through the Great Depression, my parents had the notion that bonds and other slow and steady fixed-income investments, such as bank CDs, meant safety.

REMEMBER

True, a bond portfolio, unlike a stock portfolio, tends to move at a steady pace. But as with an underpowered boat in a large ocean, lack of horsepower can be as dangerous as too much horsepower. Bond portfolios lack volatility, but they're easy prey to the currents of the economy and the tides of inflation. The truly safest portfolios, as we've seen in both the Great Depression and the high inflation of the 1970s and 1980s, have both the horsepower of stocks *and* the stability of bonds.

Ah, but how much horsepower and how much stability? How do you find that perfect blend? Well, that depends on whether, investment-wise, you're an elderly lake angler, a youngster with a hankering for speed, a retired attorney with a spouse, or a yachtsman leaving a big wake. In this chapter, I ask you some questions about your life and, by examining your answers, help you determine the proper allocation of bonds for your portfolio. In other words, I help you find just the right *vroom-vroom/slooow-down* ratio.

Seeing Why the Bond Percentage Question Isn't as Simple as Pie

A 28-year-old with $2,800 in savings shouldn't invest money the same way as a 56-year-old with $620,000 in savings. A 67-year-old with a $500,000 nest egg and no pension should invest differently than a 67-year-old with the same nest egg but a generous pension. A gazillionaire with a spouse and kids and a desire to leave half a gigillion to charity may invest differently than a gazillionaire whose greatest interest is throwing big parties in Morocco in drag with dozens of camels. These are only some of the factors ignored by simplistic formulas. They *won't* be ignored in this chapter.

Minimizing volatility

If I may briefly recap what I say about bond returns in Chapter 9, the long-term return on all bonds, judging by the past 80-plus years, is about *half* that of all stocks. The real return on bonds (after inflation but before taxes) is about a *third* that of stocks. For the average taxpayer, the after-tax, long-term return on bonds is roughly a *quarter* that of stocks. So, what percent of your portfolio do you want in bonds? If an easy formula existed, it would be this:

> Ideal percent of your portfolio in bonds = The necessary amount and no more (or less, for that matter)

TIP

The *no more* part, in my book (hey! — this *is* my book!), is the easier part of the formula. The answer is *75 percent*. No kidding. Except perhaps in very rare circumstances, no one needs or wants a portfolio that's more than 75 percent bonds. Why? Because stocks and bonds together provide diversification. With all bonds and no stocks, you lack diversification. Diversification smooths out a portfolio's returns.

REMEMBER

Believe it or not, even though stocks are much more volatile than bonds, a modest percent of stocks added to a portfolio of mostly bonds can actually help lower the volatility of the portfolio. Including less than that (or more than 80 percent bonds) can actually raise volatility and lower the odds of favorable returns both over the short run and over the long run. So, why would anyone ever want to go there? Unless you have good reason to expect an economic apocalypse anytime soon (you don't), it doesn't make a whole lot of sense to invest only in bonds.

Maximizing return

The highest returning portfolios over the past few decades — over any few decades, for that matter — are made up predominantly of stocks. But those are also the portfolios that go up and down in value like popcorn kernels on a fire. So, the question "How much do you need in bonds?" is largely a question of how much volatility you can or should tolerate.

How much volatility you can or should stomach, in turn, is largely a factor of time frame: Are you investing for tomorrow? Next year? A decade from now? Five decades from now? If you run an endowment fund, or if you happen to be immortal, your time frame may be infinite. Most of us human-being types will want to tap into our treasured nest egg at some point. But when?

Bonds' long-term gains pale compared to stocks, but when things get rough, bonds don't take it on the chin the way stocks do.

Peering into the Future

You may be saving and investing to buy a new home, to put your kids through college, or to leave a legacy for your children and grandchildren. For most people, however, a primary goal of investing (as well it should be) is to achieve economic independence: the ability to work or not work, to write the Great (or not-so-great) American Novel, to do whatever you want to without worrying about money. In this section, I help you start thinking about how to achieve your investment goal, whatever it may be.

In Chapters 6 and 7, I discuss in some depth how big a nest egg you'll likely need for economic independence and how much you'll be able to withdraw from your portfolio, should you stop working, without running out of money. I'll save the nitty-gritty for those chapters. For now, the pertinent question is this: Just how far along are you toward achieving your nest-egg goal?

Estimating how much you'll need

TIP

For reasons I divulge in Chapters 6 and 7, think of how much you'll need to withdraw from your nest egg each year when you stop getting a paycheck. Don't forget that you'll likely be getting Social Security and perhaps you'll have other income. Whatever that number that you'll need to withdraw may be ($30,000? $40,000?), multiply it by 20. That's the amount, at a minimum, I'd like to see you have in your total portfolio when you retire. (I'd prefer 25 times, however.) Now multiply that same original-year withdrawal figure ($30,000? $40,000?) by 10. That's the amount, at a minimum, that I'd like to see you have in fixed-income investments, including bonds, when you retire.

I'm assuming here a fairly typical retirement age, meaning somewhere in your mid-60s. If you want to retire at 30, you'll likely need considerably more than 20 times your annual expenses (or else very wealthy and generous parents).

Assessing your time frame

REMEMBER

Okay, got those two numbers: one for your total portfolio, and the other for the bond side of your portfolio at retirement? Good. Now how far off are you, in terms of both years and dollars, from giving up your paycheck and drawing on savings?

>> **If you're far away from your goals, you need lots of growth.** If you currently have, say, half of what you'll need in your portfolio to call yourself economically independent, and you're years from retirement, that likely means loading up (to a point) on stocks if you want to achieve your goal. *Vroom vroom.*

>> If you're closer to your goals, you may have more to lose than to gain, and stability becomes just as important as growth. That means leaning toward bonds and other fixed-income investments. *Slooow down.*

If you're far beyond your goals (you already have, say, 30 or 40 times what you'll need to live on for a year), an altogether different set of criteria may take precedence.

Factoring in some good rules

TIP

No simple formulas exist that determine the optimal allocation of bonds in a portfolio. That being said, there are some pretty good rules to follow. Here, I provide you with a few, and then I ask you to join me for a few case studies to help clarify:

» **You should keep three to six months of living expenses in cash (such as money-market funds or online savings bank accounts like** www.ally.com **or** www.emigrantdirect.com**) or near-cash.** If you expect any major expenses in the next year or two, keep money for those in near-cash as well. When I say *near-cash,* I'm talking about CDs or very short-term bonds or bond funds, such as those I introduce in Chapter 5.

» **The rest of your money can be invested in longer-term investments, such as intermediate-term or long-term bonds, or equities, such as stocks, real estate, or commodities.**

» **A portfolio of more than 80 percent bonds rarely, if ever, makes sense; on the other hand, most people benefit with some healthy allocation to bonds.** The majority of people fall somewhere in the range of 70/30 (70 percent equities/ 30 percent fixed income) to 30/70 (30 percent equities/ 70 percent fixed income). Use 60/40 (equities/fixed income) as your default if you're under 50 years of age. If you're over 50, use 50/50 as your default. Tweak from there depending on how much growth you need and how much stability you require.

» **Stocks, a favorite form of equity for most investors, can be very volatile over the short term and intermediate term, but historically that risk of loss has diminished over longer holding periods.** Over the course of 10 to 15 years, you're virtually assured that the performance of your stock portfolio will beat the performance of your bond-and-cash portfolio — at least if history is our guide. (It shouldn't be our only guide. History sometimes does funny things.) Most of the money you won't need for 10 to 15 years or beyond could be — but may not need to be — in stocks, not bonds.

» **Because history does funny things, you don't want to put all your long-term money in stocks, even if history says you should.** Even very long-term money — at the very least, 20 percent of it — should be kept in something safer than stocks.

Recognizing yourself in a few case studies

Different strokes for different folks. The following vignettes are all based on real, live clients who have asked me to massage their portfolios. All names and most identifying information have been changed to protect the identities of these good people. Perhaps you'll see some similarities between their situations and yours.

Jean and Raymond, 61 and 63, financially quite comfortable

Jean and Raymond have raised three children; the third is just finishing up college. Jean and Raymond are both public school teachers, and both will retire (he in two years; she in four) with healthy traditional pensions. Together, those pensions, combined with Social Security, should cover Jean and Raymond's living expenses for the rest of their lives. The couple will also likely bring in supplemental income from private tutoring. Jean's mother is 90. When her mom passes away, Jean, an only child, expects to receive an inheritance of at least $1.5 million. Her mom's money is invested almost entirely in bonds. So, what should Jean and Raymond do with the $710,000 they've socked away in their combined 403(b) retirement plans?

Jean and Raymond are in the catbird seat. Even if they were to invest the entire $710,000 nest egg in stocks, and even if we were to see the worst stock market crash in history, Jean and Raymond would likely still be okay. The couple certainly doesn't need to take the risk of putting their money in stocks because they don't need to see their portfolio grow to accomplish their financial goals. But given their pensions, is investing in stocks really that risky? No. If Jean and Raymond want to leave a large legacy (to their children, their grandchildren, or charity), a predominantly stock-based portfolio may be the way to go. Because equities tend to be so much more lucrative than fixed income in the long run, a greater percentage in equities would likely generate more wealth for the future generations.

Ignoring for the moment a slew of possibly complicating factors from the simple scenario here, I would feel comfortable suggesting an aggressive portfolio: perhaps two-thirds in equity (stocks and such) and one-third in fixed income (bonds and such). This breakdown isn't what most people think of as appropriate for an "aging" couple, but to me, it makes a whole lot of sense, provided Jean and Raymond are fully on board and promise me that they won't cash out of stocks (as many investors do) the first time the market takes a dip.

Kay, 59, hoping only for a simple retirement

Kay, divorced twice, earns a modest salary as a medical technician. She scored fairly well in her last divorce. (Hubby was a condescending jerk, but a well-paid condescending jerk.) Thanks to a generous initial cash settlement, as well as having made a good profit on the sale of her last home, Kay has a portfolio of $875,000. Kay doesn't hate her work, but she isn't crazy about it either; she would much rather spend her days caring for stray animals. After careful analysis, she figures that she can live without the paycheck quite comfortably if she's allowed to pull $45,000 a year from savings. Her children are grown and self-sufficient.

REMEMBER

I use Kay to illustrate why simple formulas (such as your age = your proper bond allocation) don't work. Kay is roughly the same age as Jean in the previous example. And Kay, like Jean, is financially comfortable. But it would be a great mistake for Kay to take the same risks with her money. Unlike Jean, Kay doesn't have a spouse. Unlike Jean, Kay doesn't have a pension. Unlike Jean, Kay isn't expecting a big inheritance. Unlike Jean and Raymond, Kay can't afford to lose any significant portion of her nest egg. She's dependent on that nest egg to stay economically afloat.

At her current level of savings and with a fairly modest rate of growth in her portfolio, Kay should be able to retire comfortably within four to five years. In Kay's case, she has more to lose than to gain by taking any great risk in the markets. On the other hand, if things work out as she plans, Kay may be spending 30 or more years in retirement. So, an all fixed-income portfolio, which could get gobbled up by inflation, won't work. In Kay's case, I'd likely recommend a portfolio, somewhat depending on Kay's tolerance for risk, of 50 percent to 55 percent stocks and 45 percent to 50 percent bonds.

Juan, 29, just getting started

Three years out of business school with an MBA, Juan, single and happy in his big-city condo, is earning an impressive and growing salary. But because he's been busy paying off loans, he has just started to build his savings. Juan's 401(k) has a current balance of $3,700.

Juan — yet another example of why simple formulas don't work — should probably tailor his portfolio to look something like Jean and Raymond's, despite the obvious differences in age and wealth. Juan is still many years off from retirement and doesn't see any major expenses on the horizon. Juan's budding 401(k) is meant to sit and grow for a very long time — at least three decades. History tells us that a portfolio made up of mostly stocks will likely provide superior growth. Of course, history is history, and we don't know what the future will bring. So, I'd still allocate 20 percent to 25 percent bonds to Juan's portfolio, with the rest going to stocks.

Before moving any money into stocks or bonds, however, I'd want Juan to set aside three to six months' worth of living expenses in an emergency cash fund, outside of his 401(k), just in case he loses his job, has serious health issues, or becomes subject to some other unforeseen crisis.

Miriam, 53, plugging away

Never married, with no children, Miriam wants to retire from her job as a freelance computer consultant while still young enough to fulfill her dreams of world travel. Her investments of $75,000 are growing at a good clip, because she is currently socking away a full 20 percent of her after-tax earnings — about $20,000 a year. But she knows that she has a long way to go.

Miriam is right: She does have a long way to go. To fulfill her dreams of world travel, Miriam needs considerably more than a nest egg of $75,000. In this case, the bond allocation question is a tough one. Miriam needs substantial growth, but she isn't in a position to risk what she has either. Cases like Miriam's require delicate balance. I'd likely opt for a starting portfolio of mostly stocks and about 25 percent to 30 percent bonds, but as Miriam gets closer to her financial goal in the coming years, I'd urge her to up that percentage of bonds and take a more defensive, conservative position.

DO YOU HAVE A "BOND" CAREER OR A "STOCK" CAREER?

Part of your entire net worth, most likely the largest part, is your own human capital — in other words, your present and future earnings. Some people have argued that you must factor in this human capital when fashioning your optimal investment portfolio. If, for example, you're firmly entrenched in a staid and steady career in a staid and steady industry (you're an actuary for a life insurance company, an X-ray technician at the local hospital, or a bill collector for the utility company), the human potential part of your portfolio may be seen as more bond-like than stock-like. If, however, you're in a potentially very lucrative but unpredictable career in an unpredictable industry (you're a high-ticket and high-tech commissioned salesperson, a Hollywood producer, or a fashion model with string-bean legs), the human potential part of your portfolio may be seen as more stock-like.

To achieve the best diversification, individuals with bond-like careers should tilt their investments more toward stocks, while those with stock-like careers should tilt their portfolios the other way, with more bonds. Of course, the kind of personality that would choose a staid and steady career could also be the kind of personality to choose a staid and steady investment portfolio. In other words, in fashioning your optimal investment portfolio, it may serve you well to fight your gut instinct to go in one direction or the other.

Noticing the Many Shades of Gray in Your Portfolio

REMEMBER

Although the world of investments offers countless opportunities — and dangers — all investments qualify as one of these two types:

>> **Equity:** Something you own (such as stocks, real estate, or gold)

>> **Fixed income:** Money you've lent in return for interest (such as bonds, CDs, or money-market funds), or possibly money you've given up in return for steady payments (annuities)

For the sake of simplicity, my portfolio discussion thus far has dealt largely with stocks and bonds, ignoring the many shades of gray that define both of these large umbrella terms. I've also ignored other forms of fixed income, such as annuities, and other forms of equity, such as real estate and commodities. It's time now to stop ignoring and start addressing.

Bonds of many flavors

If the point of investing in bonds is to smooth out the returns of a portfolio that also includes stocks (Yes! That *is* the point!), it makes sense to have bonds that tend to zig when stocks zag. By and large, you're looking at Treasurys, including Treasury Inflation-Protected Securities (TIPS), corporate investment-grade bonds, or agency bonds. If you're in the higher tax brackets and you have limited space in your retirement accounts, you may consider municipal bonds. If you have a very large bond port-folio, you may consider a smattering of international bonds. (See Chapter 3 for an introduction to all these types of bonds.)

WARNING

High-yield bonds may also play a role in your portfolio, along with other forms of more exotic bonds, but they need to be added with some finesse. As alluring as high-yield bonds can be (especially at a time when quality bonds are yielding so little), they don't offer the same diversifying power as quality bonds do. When stocks sink, high-yield bonds tend to sink as well, for the same reason: Companies are closing doors. Don't be a yield-chaser. Higher-returning bonds always carry more risk.

Whatever your choice in bonds, it's best to seek some diversification: different issuers, different maturities. I make specific recommendations for diversifying the bond side of your portfolio later in this chapter, again in Chapter 4 where I dis-cuss individual bonds (diversification mandatory!), and yet again in Chapter 5 where I talk about bond funds. You can probably tell that I'm something of a stickler when it comes to diversification.

Stocks of all sizes and sorts

This is a book about bonds, so I won't dwell on what you should do with the stock side of your portfolio. In this chapter on portfo-lio building, however, it seems fair to devote at least a few para-graphs to the subject. So, here goes!

Because stocks can be so volatile, you must diversify. The best way to diversify is with a portfolio of mostly, if not all low-cost, no-load mutual funds (index funds are often best) or exchange-traded funds (almost all of which are index funds).

REMEMBER

Just as stocks and bonds tend to correlate poorly, different kinds of stocks and different kinds of bonds have limited correlation. That's especially true on the stock side of the portfolio. Smart investors make sure to have domestic and foreign stocks, stocks in large companies and small companies, and growth and value stocks. (*Growth stocks* are stocks in fast-moving companies in fast-moving industries, such as technology. *Value stocks* are stocks in companies that have less growth potential; you may be able to get these stocks on the cheap, at times making them better investments than growth stocks.)

TIP

Just as you get more bang for your buck but also more bounce with stocks versus bonds, you also get more potential return and additional risk with small-company stocks versus large-company stocks. Although international stocks aren't any more volatile than U.S. stocks per se, differences in exchange rates can make them much more volatile to U.S. investors. The greater your tolerance for risk, the more small-company stocks and the more international stocks you may want to incorporate.

After your portfolio grows and you have all the broad asset classes covered, you may consider branching out into narrower (but not too narrow) kinds of investments. Possibilities include certain industry sectors, especially those that tend to have limited correlation to the market at large, such as real estate, timber, and energy. Beyond that, you may consider holdings in commodities, such as precious metals. And beyond that, perhaps think about certain high-yield bonds that offer the potential for stock-like growth.

TIP

For more tips on investing in stocks, *don't* go to your local pub or to various and sundry get-rich-quick websites. Instead, see *Stock Investing For Dummies,* by Paul Mladjenovic; *Mutual Funds For Dummies,* by Eric Tyson; or my own entertaining and highly educational *Exchange-Traded Funds For Dummies* (all published by Wiley). Sure, there are many other good books out there (and lots of bad ones, too), but the *For Dummies* series is a darned good place to start.

Other fixed income: Annuities

For some people, sticking an annuity on the fixed-income side of the portfolio makes sense. When you purchase an annuity, you typically surrender your principal to the annuity issuer. You then receive cash at regular intervals at a rate of return that's (sort of) considerably higher than you receive by buying a Treasury or municipal bond. (I say "sort of" because part of the "return" is actually your own money being given back to you. Yeah, it's complicated.)

REMEMBER

Let me be clear: I'm not talking about *variable annuities,* most of which are pretty terrible investment products sold by people who make outrageous commissions and conveniently forget to mention that most of the money you'll be seeing is your own money being returned to you. Instead, I'm talking about *fixed annuities.* The difference? With a variable annuity, you receive payments that are largely based on the performance of some piece of the market, such as the S&P 500 or another stock index. A fixed annuity gives you a certain fixed amount of income (which may be inflation-adjusted) at fixed intervals. Your payments aren't contingent on the performance of the markets or anything else. And the interest earned may be tax-deferred.

With either kind of annuity, the rate of return usually is largely determined by your age. The fewer years the annuity provider thinks it'll be sending you checks, the more generous it'll be with payments.

At the time I'm writing this, a 65-year-old man with $100,000 could get about 5.5 percent on an immediate fixed annuity for the rest of his life. Treasurys are currently paying 2 percent. But keep this in mind: If the investor dies tomorrow after taking out an annuity today, his estate loses $100,000. He could get an annuity with a death benefit (so his spouse or kids would continue to get payments if he dies), but that lowers the rate of return.

TIP

The best candidates for annuities are generally healthy people with good genes in their 60s and 70s who don't mind dying broke and don't care about leaving behind any chunk of money. And you must remember that an annuity is only as good as the company issuing it. Don't even consider buying an annuity from anything less than a huge and stable issuer. (However, each state has a guaranty association that provides annuity protection plans up to a certain sum; go to www.immediateannuities.com/state-guaranty-associations to check the limits in your state.) I'd generally recommend inflation-adjusted annuities for anyone under 70; otherwise, you risk seeing inflation swallow up your income to the point that your monthly checks will seem like pin money.

Shop around. ImmediateAnnuities.com isn't a bad place to start. You're looking for an annuity issued by a highly rated company, offering the highest payout. But be sure this is something you really want. Typically, if you sign up for an annuity and then change your mind and want your principal back, you're penalized to the tune of 7 percent if you try to withdraw your money within a year, 6 percent if you try to withdraw within two years, and so on.

TIP

For more on annuities, check out the latest edition of *Annuities For Dummies* (Wiley), written by a friend of mine, Kerry Pechter.

Other equity: Commodities and real estate

Equity is investment-speak for "something you own." It doesn't have to be a share in a company. You can own real estate, silver, gold, or corn futures. Real estate, if it refers to your own home, generally shouldn't be considered part of your nest egg simply because you'll always need a place to live. Selling your home and downsizing or moving to an apartment may someday add to the size of your nest egg, and you always have the option of a reverse mortgage (although it's expensive), but you shouldn't count on your home as your main retirement fund.

Investment real estate can, indeed, be profitable, but only if you know what you're doing and you're willing to clock some serious hours landlording. It helps to know something about plumbing. And have the patience to deal with some not-so-ideal tenants. And my own personal nightmare a number of years ago involving a property in Maryland tells me that no one should *ever* be a long-distance landlord. If you want to learn about buying houses for a profit, check out the latest edition of *Real Estate Investing For Dummies* by Eric Tyson and Robert S. Griswold (Wiley).

TIP

Commodity investing was once a sticky business, with high fees and complicated strategies. Lately, with the advent of exchange-traded funds (ETFs) and exchange-traded notes that allow you to buy into commodities without a lot of mess, commodity investing has become much like investing in stocks or bonds. Commodities have limited correlation to both stocks and bonds, and I recommend a modest position in commodities for many people's portfolios.

Making Sure That Your Portfolio Remains in Balance

Say you've decided that you want a portfolio of 60 percent equities and 40 percent fixed income (commonly expressed as a *60/40 portfolio*). You have $100,000, so you aim to construct a portfolio that's $60,000 in stocks and $40,000 in bonds. Over the ensuing months, the stock market takes off. At the end of a great year, you count your blessings and realize that you now have not $60,000, but $75,000 in stocks. Your bonds, however, have hardly budged. Let's say you have $41,000 in bonds. Your entire portfolio is now worth $116,000 ($75,000 + $41,000). But you no longer have a 60/40 portfolio. Now you have a 65/35 portfolio. Funny how that happens.

What to do? It's time to rebalance.

Rebalancing means getting your investment house back in order. Unless your life circumstances have changed, you probably still want a 60/40 portfolio. That means that your new $116,000 portfolio should be $69,600 in stocks ($116,000 × 60 percent), and $46,400 in bonds ($116,000 × 40 percent). To get to that point, you're going to have to sell $5,400 in stocks ($75,000 – $69,600) and buy $5,400 in bonds ($46,400 – $41,000).

It won't be easy. You've seen your stocks go up while your bonds have languished. But rebalancing is the smart thing to do. I explain why in the following sections.

Tweaking your holdings to temper risk

The primary reason to rebalance is to keep you from losing your shirt. If your personal situation a year ago warranted a 60/40 portfolio, then a 65/35 split is going to be more volatile than the portfolio you want. If you continue to leave the portfolio untouched and stocks continue to fly, you'll eventually wind up with a 70/30 portfolio, and then a 75/25 portfolio. And what happens if the stock market reverses at that point, moving as quickly backward as it was moving forward a year or two before? You'll see a much larger loss than you ever bargained for.

Wouldn't you rather lock in some of your profits and start afresh with the proper portfolio mix?

Savoring the rebalancing bonus

Rebalancing also helps you realize larger returns over time. Think about it: Most investors buy high, choosing whatever asset class is hot, and sell low, getting rid of whatever asset class is lagging. The financial press is continually pushing us to do this; "10 HOT FUNDS FOR THE NEW YEAR!" inevitably focuses on ten funds that have risen to new heights in the past months, largely because of the kind of asset class in which they invest (U.S. stocks, foreign stocks, long-term bonds, or whatever).

Studies show that, as a result of continually buying high and selling low, the average investor barely keeps up with inflation. It's sad. But you, by rebalancing regularly, are destined to wind up ahead. Instead of buying high and selling low, you'll continually be selling high and buying low. In the preceding example, you were selling off your recently risen stocks, for example, and buying more of your lagging bonds.

Over the long run, not only will rebalancing temper your risk, but your long-term returns, if we're simply talking about rebalancing stocks and bonds, will tend to be about ½ percent higher. Need proof?

Consider the ten-year average annual return of the Vanguard Total Stock and the Vanguard Total Bond Index funds. At the time of writing, they clock in at 14.28 percent average annual return for the stock fund and 2.19 percent for the bond fund. Adding the two together, giving the stocks a 60 percent weighting and the bonds a 40 percent weighting, you would expect the average annual ten-year return of the two to be 9.44 percent. But when you look at the Vanguard Balanced Index Fund, which combines the total stock market with the total bond market and continually rebalances, the average annual return for the same period isn't 9.44 percent — it's 9.53 percent, despite an expense ratio slightly higher than either the stock or the bond index fund.

If you invest in multiple asset classes (including commodities, foreign and domestic stock, and so on), regular rebalancing may add a full percentage point or more each year to your long-term returns.

Scheduling your portfolio rebalance

With the miracle of modern technology, Excel spreadsheets and whatnot, rebalancing can be easy — too easy! Rebalancing your portfolio every week, or even every month, is most likely going to be counterproductive. You may get hit with transaction costs, as well as potential capital gains taxes, with every sale you make. But another important (and often overlooked) factor is the *momentum* of markets: When an asset class shoots up, all those yokels who like buying something that's up will often, by the very fact that they're buying, force the price a bit higher.

The question of how often to rebalance has been studied to death, and those studies show that someone who rebalances as often as they brush their teeth tends to lose out to momentum — in addition to paying more in transaction costs and taxes.

TIP

So, what's the perfect time to rebalance? Well, there is no perfect time. It depends on the volatility of the markets, the correlation of the securities in your portfolio, the cost of your personal transactions, and your tax status. In general, however, rebalancing should be done once every year or two. If you're retired and pulling cash from your portfolio, you may want to rebalance twice a year to make sure your cash reserve doesn't dip too low. But do be careful whenever selling securities to watch your trading costs and monitor your potential tax hit.

REMEMBER

The division between stocks and bonds, be it 70/30 or 50/50 or 30/70, is often the most important risk-and-return determiner in your portfolio. Even if you allow everything else to get out of balance, keep your balance of stocks and bonds on an even keel.

If you really hate the idea of rebalancing yourself, you may need to hire a professional money manager, or buy an all-in-one, stock-and-bond fund that will rebalance automatically (see Chapter 5 for some options). There are also robo-advisors available that will not only rebalance but make investment suggestions as well. I've seen both good and bad investment suggestions spit out from robo-advisors, and I just don't think, as a broad category, that they're quite ready for prime time.

Whichever way you chose to maintain balance, do it. Such balance, grasshopper, will keep you afloat and spare you from getting slammed into financial bridges or swamped by the wake of inflation.

Sizing Up Your Need for Fixed-Income Diversification

As you know, some stocks can double or triple in price overnight, while others can shrink into oblivion in the time it takes to say, "CEO arrested for fraud." Unless you're investing in individual high-yield bonds (not a good idea), your risk of default — and the risk of your investment shrinking to oblivion — is minimal. But diversifying your bonds is still a good idea.

REMEMBER

Although you can reduce your risk of default to near zero simply by buying Treasury and U.S. agency bonds, you still incur other risks by having too concentrated a bond portfolio.

Diversifying by maturity

Regardless of whether you invest in Treasurys, corporate bonds, or munis, you always risk swings in general interest rates (which can depress bond prices) and *reinvestment risk* (the fact that interest or principal invested in a bond may not be able to be reinvested in such a way that it can earn the same rate of return as before).

You can greatly improve both risks with the fine art of *laddering* (staggering your individual bond purchases to include bonds of differing maturities). I discuss laddering in Chapter 4. You can also lessen risks by investing in (the right) bond funds, discussed in Chapter 5.

Diversifying by type of issuer

In addition to diversifying by maturity, you also want to divide up your bonds so they represent different kinds of bond categories, such as government and corporate. This is true with both individual bonds and bond funds. Different kinds of bonds do better in certain years than others. Holding various types of bonds helps to smooth out your total bond portfolio returns.

Let's take two years — 2008 and 2009 — as examples. Why those two years? I'm using 2008 because it was the last time we've seen a really bad recession and bear market in stocks. I'm picking 2009 because, well, it was very different from 2008.

The year 2008 was an extraordinarily bad year for the economy, and stock markets worldwide plummeted. Investor confidence fell hard. As is always the case in hard economic times, money rushed to safety — primarily U.S. Treasurys. At the same time, inflation came to a standstill. Interest rates also fell, as the Fed attempted to pump-prime the flagging economy. All of this meant good times for owners of conventional Treasurys and U.S. agency bonds, whereas other bondholders didn't fare quite as well. That year, from January to December, we saw the following returns:

>> **Long-term conventional government bonds**: +25.8 percent

>> **Investment-grade corporate bonds:** +8.8 percent

>> **TIPS:** –2.4 percent

>> **Municipal bonds:** –2.7 percent

Now let's jump to 2009. Investor confidence was back, the stock market shot up, the yearning for safe harbor was gone, and inflation was back in vogue. Many investors kissed their Treasurys goodbye and moved back into stocks and higher-risk, higher-returning bonds. Munis and corporates fared better that year than Treasurys, although TIPS (a variety of Treasury) evidenced excellent returns:

>> **Municipal bonds:** +12.47 percent

>> **TIPS:** +11.4 percent

>> **Investment-grade corporate bonds:** +3 percent

>> **Long-term conventional government bonds:** –14.9 percent

REMEMBER

Generally, muni bonds and investment-grade corporate bonds do better than government bonds when the economy is strong. When the economy is in trouble and people flock to safety, government bonds — especially conventional longer-term Treasurys — tend to do better. If you think you can tell the future, buy all of one kind of bond or the other. If you aren't clairvoyant (hint: you're not), it makes the most sense to divide your holdings.

Diversifying by risk-and-return potential

The returns on high-quality corporate bonds, Treasurys, and munis (after their tax-free nature is accounted for) generally differ by only a few percentage points in any given year. (The years 2008 and 2009 both saw unusually high spreads.) But some other kinds of bonds, such as high-yield corporates, convertible bonds, and international bonds, can vary much, much more.

In general, because the potential return on stocks is so much higher than just about any kind of bond, I favor stomaching volatility on the stock side of the portfolio. For some people, however, more exotic, "cocoa-bean" type bonds make sense. High-yield bonds, for example, act like a hybrid between stocks and bonds. They often produce high returns (higher than other bonds, lower than stocks) when the economy is growing quickly, and they tend to dive (more than other bonds, less than stocks) when the economy falters. Because of this hybrid nature, they make particular sense for relatively conservative investors who need the high yield but can't take quite as much risk as stocks involve.

TIP

Emerging-market bonds (issued by the governments of less-developed countries) also can produce very high yields, but they're highly volatile. Unlike U.S. high-yield bonds, they tend to have limited correlation to the U.S. stock market. For this reason, I often include a small percentage of emerging-market bonds in many people's portfolios.

Diversifying away managerial risk

Where I discuss bond funds in Chapter 5, I suggest that you put most of your bond money into *index funds* (funds run by managers who work on the cheap and don't attempt to do anything fancy). But occasionally, taking a bet on a talented manager may not be such a terrible thing to do. And regardless of what I say, you may turn up your nose at index funds anyway. You may attempt to beat the market by choosing bond funds run by managers who try to score big by rapidly buying and selling, going out on margin, and doing all sorts of other wild and crazy things.

Whenever you go with an actively managed fund (as opposed to a passively managed fund, otherwise known as an *index fund*), you hope that the manager will do something smart to beat the market. But you risk that the manager will do something dumb. Or perhaps your manager will get hit by a train, and the incompetent junior partner will wind up managing your fund. That's called *managerial risk.*

Managerial risk is real, and it should always be diversified away. If you have a sizable bond portfolio and are depending on that portfolio to pay the bills someday, you shouldn't trust any one manager with that much responsibility. Recall the numbers from the earlier section "Diversifying by type of issuer," which reflect the differences among returns of different kinds of bonds in a couple of sample years? That's *nothing* compared to the differences you find between well-managed and poorly managed active bond funds.

At one point in recent history, the following occurred:

>> The ten-year cumulative return on the well-run Loomis Sayles Bond Fund was **169.08 percent** (meaning $10,000 invested ten years prior would have been worth $26,908).

>> The ten-year cumulative return on the not-so-well-run (and now defunct) Oppenheimer Champion Income Fund, Class C, was **-58.46 percent** (meaning $10,000 invested ten years prior would have been worth $4,154).

If you're going to take a shot at beating the market by giving your bond money to managers who tinker and toy, do it in moderation.

Weighing Diversification versus Complication

Most individual bonds sell for $1,000. But buying individual bonds (not Treasurys, but most other bonds) means paying a broker, and that can be expensive. You can't very well build a diversified bond portfolio — different maturities, different issuers — out of individual bonds unless you have quite a few grand sitting around.

Diversifying with funds is much easier, and that's a big reason I usually recommend them. But which funds? We get into specifics in Chapter 3, but for now, here are some overarching thoughts.

Keeping it simple (for people with less than $2,000)

TIP

Best solution: Consider a *balanced fund*, a one-stop-shopping fund that allows you to invest in stocks and bonds in one fell swoop. Some balanced funds are static; they allocate, say, 60 percent of your money to stocks and 40 percent to bonds, and that's how it will always be. Others are dynamic; these are often called *life-cycle funds.* A life-cycle fund, a favorite of company 401(k) plans, shifts your money, usually from the stock side to the bond side, along what is called a *glide path,* to become more conservative as your retirement date nears. (See my recommendations for several all-in-one funds in Chapter 5.)

Moving beyond the basic (for people with $2,000 to $4,000)

TIP

In the ballpark of $2,000 to $4,000, you may be looking to invest a grand or two in stocks and perhaps another thousand in bonds. Your best bet for building a diversified portfolio would be a handful of low-cost, no-load mutual funds or ETFs. Perhaps you want one total-market bond fund, one total U.S. stock fund, and one diversified foreign stock fund. (See Chapter 5 for my recommendations for total-market bond funds.)

Branching out (with $4,000 or more)

TIP

When you pass $4,000 or so, you can begin to entertain a more finely segmented portfolio of either mutual funds or ETFs. But you'll probably want more than $4,000 dedicated to the bond side of your portfolio alone before you sell your total-market bond fund and start diversifying into the various sectors of the bond market.

WARNING

I wouldn't suggest dabbling in individual bonds unless you have a bond portfolio of $500,000 or so. Otherwise, the trading costs will eat you alive. The exception would be Treasury bonds because you can buy them at www.treasurydirect.gov without a markup. Even some large brokerage houses allow you to buy Treasurys without a markup.

Finding the Perfect Bond Portfolio Fit

Earlier in this chapter, I introduce four portfolios, belonging to Jean and Raymond, Kay, Juan, and Miriam. There, I suggest what percentage of their portfolios should be in bonds. I revisit our friends here to suggest what specific kinds of bonds they might consider.

Case studies in bond ownership

You'll notice that just as there are no hard-and-fast rules for the percentage of a portfolio that should be in bonds, there are no absolutes when it comes to what kind of bonds are optimal for any given investor.

Jean and Raymond, 61 and 63, financially fit as a fiddle

These folks have a solid portfolio of nearly three-quarters of a million dollars, and a fat inheritance is likely coming. They're both working in secure jobs, and when they retire, their pensions and Social Security should cover all their basic bills. With their children and grandchildren in mind and having little to risk with volatility in the markets, Jean and Raymond have decided to invest about two-thirds of their savings (all in their retirement accounts) in equities — mostly stocks, with some commodities. They've chosen to invest the other third (about $235,000) in fixed income.

What to do with the fixed income? Financially fit as they seem, Jean and Raymond still could use an emergency kitty. Because both are older than 59½ and they're allowed to pull from their retirement accounts without penalty, I'd suggest three months' living expenses ($15,000) be kept in cash or in a short-term bond fund, of the kind I suggest in Chapter 5.

That leaves them with $220,000. Chances are, this money won't be touched for quite some time — perhaps not until after Jean and Raymond have passed to that great teachers' lounge in the sky and their children and grandchildren have inherited their estate. That being the case, it warrants investing in higher-yielding bonds. Just in case the economy takes a real fall and the lion's share of the estate goes with it, these bonds should be strong enough to stand tall.

Tax-free munis make no sense in this case because Jean and Raymond have room in their retirement accounts, and tax-free munis, which pay lower rates of interest than bonds of comparable quality and maturity, *never* make sense in a tax-advantaged retirement account.

I'd suggest they put about 30 percent of the remaining pot (approximately $66,000) into intermediate-term conventional Treasurys, either in a bond fund or in individual bonds. They should put another 30 percent into a fund of investment-grade corporate bonds. Corporate bonds over time tend to return higher interest than government bonds but may not do quite as well if the economy hits the skids. They should allocate another 30 percent of their bonds to TIPS, again either in a TIPS fund (see my recommendation in Chapter 5) or in individual TIPS purchased free of markup on the Treasury's own website.

Then Jean and Raymond might devote 10 percent of their bond allocation to a foreign bond fund. These funds have their pros and cons (see Chapter 3). Whether Jean and Raymond should go with a foreign bond fund depends on how much exposure they have to foreign currencies on the equity side of their portfolio. I present some good international bond funds in Chapter 5.

See Figure 10-1 for a chart that reflects my recommendations to Jean and Raymond.

Kay, 59, approaching retirement

Kay, the divorced medical technician, is currently on her own. She needs a larger emergency fund than Jean and Raymond do. Having no pension, she'll be reliant on her portfolio when she retires, and she can't take quite as much risk as Jean and Raymond can. (Simple formulas that say you need to take less risk as you get older simply aren't very helpful much of the time.) Kay's healthy portfolio of $875,000 is divided 50/50 between equities and fixed income. That equates to $437,500 in fixed income.

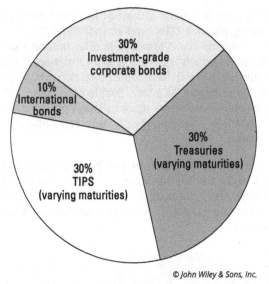

FIGURE 10-1: My recommended bond allocation for Jean and Raymond.

Where to put it?

Kay needs a somewhat larger cash cushion for emergencies than Jean and Raymond do. She is, after all, on her own, although her adult children could help her in a real emergency. I'd allot four to five months of her fixed income to either a money-market fund or a short-term bond fund. That would still leave $418,000 or so to invest in higher-yielding instruments.

Kay doesn't care about leaving an inheritance. Her kids are grown and doing well. She also has good genes, eats oatmeal and grapefruit for breakfast, and expects to live a long life. In four or five years, when Kay plans to retire, she may be a good candidate for an inflation-adjusted fixed annuity that would guarantee her an income stream for the rest of her life.

I'd set up a bond portfolio for her with the intention of moving some part of it to an annuity when Kay is in her mid- to late 60s (provided interest rates at that time are favorable). Kay needs a bond portfolio that will be there for her in four or five years, providing income and, more important, the cash she'll need to live on in retirement should the other 50 percent of her portfolio — the stocks — take a dive. With $418,000 to invest in bonds, almost twice what our teacher couple has to invest, I'd suggest a somewhat more diversified bond allocation.

Kay may start by taking a third of her bond money ($139,000) and buying either a TIPS fund or individual TIPS through www.treasurydirect.gov. These bonds offer modest rates of return but adjust the principal twice a year for inflation. If inflation goes on a rampage, Kay will have some protection on the fixed-income side of her portfolio. As a rule, people with higher allocations to fixed-income should have more inflation protection on that side of the portfolio, because they'll have less inflation protection from stocks.

With the other two-thirds of her bond portfolio ($279,000 or so), I'd suggest equal allocations to intermediate-term conventional Treasurys, intermediate-term investment-grade corporate bonds, and international, developed-market bonds, as shown in Figure 10-2.

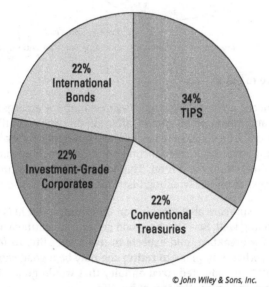

© John Wiley & Sons, Inc.

FIGURE 10-2: My recommended bond allocation for Kay.

Juan, 29, building up his savings

Juan's 401(k) has a current balance of just $3,700, but he's making a good salary. I'd first encourage Juan to save up enough so he can set aside three to six months' living expenses in an emergency cash fund.

Given that Juan won't be touching his 401(k) money until he's at least 59½, when he's able to make withdrawals without penalty, he's decided to allocate only 20 percent of his retirement fund to bonds, which is just about right. The purpose of those bonds is to somewhat smooth out his account's returns, provide the opportunity to rebalance, and be there just in case there's an economic apocalypse. Juan, of course, is prisoner to his 401(k) investment options, whatever they may be.

If his employer's plan is like most, he may have the option of one mixed-maturity Treasury fund and one mixed-maturity corporate-bond fund. Because we're talking about only 20 percent of his portfolio, whichever way he goes shouldn't make a huge difference over the next few years. I'd suggest going half and half (see Figure 10-3).

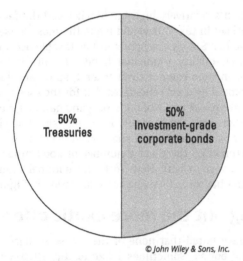

© John Wiley & Sons, Inc.

FIGURE 10-3: My recommended bond allocation for Juan.

If Juan leaves his job, he may be able to transfer his 401(k) to his new place of employment, or he may be able to roll it into an individual retirement account (IRA). I'd usually advise the latter because IRAs typically offer better investment choices at lower costs. At that point, if Juan opens an IRA, and if the balance grows beyond several thousand dollars, I'd encourage greater diversification of his bonds.

Miriam, 53, behind on her goals

With $75,000 in savings and the good majority in stocks, Miriam's 25 percent in bonds ($18,750) must serve two purposes:

>> Provide ballast to smooth out the year-to-year return of her investments.

>> Help provide cash flow when (within a decade, we hope) Miriam is able to retire and fulfill her dreams of world travel.

Miriam is currently making serious bucks in her job as a freelance computer consultant — about $160,000 a year. But she lives in New York City, paying high city and state taxes. She rents rather than owns her home, so she gets no mortgage deduction. Most of her $75,000 in savings sits in a taxable brokerage account.

Given Miriam's relatively high tax bracket and the fact that she pays a boatload in taxes, it would make the most sense for Miriam to have her $18,750 of bonds in her taxable account socked away in high-quality municipal bonds. Locally issued munis would offer income exempt from federal, state, and local taxes, and these would be good candidates. But for the sake of diversification, I'd like to see a mix of both local and national muni bonds. With less than $20,000 to invest in munis, she'd be chewed up and spit out by the markups if she started dabbling in individual issues. Fortunately, there are a number of good funds in which she might invest in both New York and national munis. I give examples in Chapter 5. (See Miriam's allocation in Figure 10-4.)

Seeking out the more exotic offerings

TIP

You may have noted that none of these case scenarios calls for more exotic bonds. Sometimes I like exotic. High-yield bonds from abroad, for example, have handsome historical returns and, unlike U.S. high-yield bonds, tend to rise and fall *somewhat* independently of the U.S. stock market. That's especially true of so-called *emerging-market bonds* (bonds from less economically advantaged countries). Because of their extreme volatility, however, I recommend putting emerging-market bonds, in modest allocations, on the equity side of the portfolio. (See further discussion of emerging-market bonds in Chapter 3.)

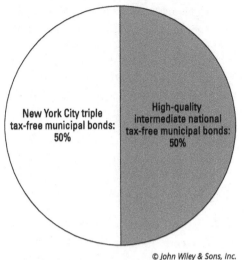

© John Wiley & Sons, Inc.

FIGURE 10-4: My recommended bond allocation for Miriam.

Earlier in this chapter, I discuss rebalancing. After you set up a properly allocated portfolio, it's crucial to go in once a year or so to make sure that if you allocated, say, 60 percent to equities and 40 percent to fixed income, those allocations haven't gone too far astray. At the same time, you want to check every year or so that your bond allocations — your division between Treasurys, corporates, munis, and other kinds of bonds — are where you want them to be.

Perhaps you can rebalance your portfolio every spring, just about the same time you spread your mulch. I don't know if Mike-with-the-truck does that, but that's what I do.

Chapter **11**
Figuring Out Your Bond Buys

A short number of years ago, if you wanted to invest in bonds, you had a bitter choice. You could walk into the office of your local bond broker and face fierce markups on individual bonds, or you could sail into the sea of funds and deal with hostile management fees and loads. Whichever option you chose, bond investing was often a perilous journey.

Today's bond market has become a friendlier place. Let me introduce you.

Discovering the Brave New World of Bonds

Regardless of which way you decide to invest your money — bond funds or individual bonds — the going is easier today than it was just several years ago. And over time, it's likely to get easier still. And when interest rates climb back to historical norms, bond investing will also prove to be more lucrative.

Finding fabulously frugal funds

Expensive bond funds still exist. There are still plenty of them that charge 1 percent or more in annual fees. The overall average bond-fund fee at the time of writing, per Morningstar Direct, is 0.77 percent. Imagine. At today's modest interest rates, most high-quality bonds are yielding 2.5 percent to maybe 3.5 percent. That's a *nominal* — before inflation — 2.5 percent to 3.5 percent a year. After inflation, you're looking at a total *real* return of about, well, you *may* beat inflation, but it won't be by much. After taxes, you're looking at less than that. And you're going to fork over more than ¾ percent to a fund manager? Lots of people do, but they haven't read this book yet.

Keep in mind that paying such fees, once a hard thing to avoid, is now strictly optional. Yes, the times they are a changin'. In 1998, 36 bond funds had expense ratios below 0.5 percent. As I write these words, that number is in the thousands. In the past few years, we've seen a virtual revolution in the world of investment funds. Many of the bond funds I now recommend have annual fees of 0.1 percent or less, and some charge *nothing!* A decade or so ago, that was unheard of.

TIP

The lowering of fees is due largely to the introduction of exchange-traded funds (ETFs). If you want to know more about ETFs, well, I wrote an entire book about them titled *Exchange-Traded Funds For Dummies* (Wiley). ETFs are wonderful investment vehicles in their own right because they're both inexpensive and tax-efficient. They've also given some serious competition to mutual funds, resulting in a lowering of fees across the board.

A lineup of ETFs from Vanguard, State Street SPDRs, BlackRock's iShares, Schwab, and a host of others allows anyone with minimal money to invest in numerous bond index funds — Treasury or corporate, short-term or long-term, taxable or tax-free — for annual fees of a mere 0 percent to 0.1 percent. A number of bond index mutual funds from Vanguard and Fidelity, the two largest U.S. financial supermarkets, are charging annual fees in the same ballpark.

Dealing in individual bonds without forking over a fortune

The transaction costs on individual bonds, which have traditionally been way higher than stock transaction costs, have also been dropping faster than hail.

One 2004 study from the Securities and Exchange Commission (SEC) found that the average cost of a $5,000 corporate bond trade back then was $84, or 1.68 percent — equivalent to several months' interest. Smaller trades (less than $5,000) tended to whack investors with much higher costs.

Trade costs of municipal bonds (a favorite flavor of bond among individuals in high tax brackets), according to the same study, averaged 2.23 percent — equivalent perhaps to a full year's return after inflation — for trades of $25,000 or less. For trades from $25,000 to $100,000, the average price spread was 1.12 percent.

Since 2004, the cost of bond trading has dropped considerably and continues to do so. Although I haven't seen any recent comprehensive studies, my guess (and the guess of a few industry insiders I speak to regularly) is that savvy bond investors can now buy typical corporate or municipal bonds with half to a third of the trading costs they would have incurred in 2004. But, of course, interest rates are awfully low today. So, paying even a markup of half a percent could represent several months of interest.

TIP

Bond sales, as opposed to buys, can still be a tougher and more expensive game. That's one reason I generally recommend buying single bonds only if you plan to hold them until maturity or until they're called. (I discuss individual bond trading in Chapter 4.)

The changing environment, which has actually thrown many bond brokers out of business, is due in part to the advent of internet trading but more so to something called the *Trade Reporting and Compliance Engine* (TRACE), a government- and securities industry–imposed national database that allows bond traders — both professional and amateur — to see what other bond traders are up to. Brokers can no longer charge whatever markup they want.

Deciding Whether to Go with Bond Funds or Individual Bonds

Before I get into the nitty-gritty of buying and selling bonds, you need to decide between individual bonds and bond funds. Thanks to the many recent changes in the bond markets that I discuss in the previous sections, either choice can be a good one. My own bias, built on years of experience, is that most investors are better off, most of the time, with bond funds.

Calculating the advantages of bond funds

Bond funds are best for more investors for a number of reasons, but far and away the largest reason is the diversification they allow.

Diversifying away certain risks

The obvious appeal of going with a bond fund over individual bonds is the same as the appeal of going with stock funds over individual stocks: You get instant diversification. If you build an entire portfolio of McDummy Corporation bonds (or stocks), and the McDummy Corporation springs a serious leak, you could take a serious hit on the McChin. With bond funds, you don't need to worry so much about the crash of a particular company.

Just as important, bond funds allow you to diversify not only by issuer but by credit quality (you can have AAA-rated bonds and B-rated bonds — see Chapter 3) and by maturity. Some bond funds allow you to diversify even more broadly by including completely different *kinds* of bonds, such as Treasurys, agencies, and corporates, both U.S. and international.

WARNING

How much money should you be able to invest before you forget about bond funds and build a truly diversified bond portfolio out of individual bonds? I ran this question by several financial-planning colleagues, and although the answers were all over the map, few gave a number of less than $500,000.

Making investing a lot easier

Sure, you can own a boatload of individual bonds and *ladder* them (which means to use a diversification technique I discuss in

Chapter 4), but owning one or a handful of bond mutual funds or ETFs is often a lot simpler. Also, given that $500,000 to put into bonds is an amount well beyond what most investors have, bond funds are really the key to a low-cost, diversified fixed-income portfolio.

WARNING

Individual bonds are also more work than bond funds. A lot more work. There's the buying and selling part, which requires expertise, research, and some cunning. But the work doesn't end there. There's also the matter of reinvesting. A bond-fund portfolio can be put more or less on autopilot. There's no such thing with individual bonds.

When you own an individual bond, the interest payments generally come to you twice a year. If you aren't going to spend that money, you'll need to reinvest it, lest it sit in cash earning diddly-squat. In other words, a portfolio of individual bonds takes ongoing care and maintenance, sort of like an old car that needs to go to the shop every few months.

Having choices: Index funds and actively managed funds

If you want to capture the gains of the entire bond market, bond index funds allow you to do that. If you want to bet (yes, it's always something of a bet) that you can do better than the bond market at large, you can hire an active manager who tries to eke out extra returns for you by looking for special deals in the bond market.

REMEMBER

I lean strongly toward index investing (for both stocks and bonds) because beating the market is hard to do. Study after study shows that index investors, in both equities and fixed income, wind up doing better than the majority of investors. That's largely because index funds tend to be the least expensive funds. Index fund managers take less for themselves, and they incur far fewer trading costs.

Still, if you put the time and effort into finding the right active bond manager, and you pay that manager a modest fee, you may wind up ahead of the indexes. Just know the odds are against it. According to S&P's midyear 2021 SPIVA Scorecard, 90 percent of investment-grade intermediate bond funds have underperformed their benchmarks over the past five years. So have 85.6 percent of all high-yield bond funds, 91.2 percent of all muni funds, and 68.4 percent of all government intermediate funds.

If you want to try to beat the market using individual bonds, you may be able to find a really good bond broker who knows the markets inside and out and charges you only a reasonable markup for each trade or a reasonable flat fee for services. Finding such a broker, however, is a lot more difficult than researching bond-fund managers. And most such talented brokers aren't going to work with you if you have chump change to invest.

Keeping your costs to a minimum

For the savvy investor, the cost of trading individual bonds is cheaper than ever. But so, too, is the cost of investing in bond funds. You can buy Treasury bonds online (www.treasurydirect. gov) with no fee or markup. Any other kind of bond, however, costs you something to trade. Given the volume that bond fund managers trade, they can trade cheaper than you can.

"Institutional buyers can buy and sell bonds and get much better prices than the retail investor," says Helen Modly, CFP, executive vice president of Focus Wealth Management in Middleburg, Virginia. "Because of that, bond funds, especially bond index exchange-traded funds (ETFs), make a lot of sense."

If you pay a fund manager a pittance per year (such as the 0.035 percent that the Vanguard Total Bond Market ETF manager receives), Modly says (and I agree) you're nearly always going to get off cheaper with the fund than with building your own bond ladder.

REMEMBER

Note that popular wisdom has it that individual bond investing is cheaper than investing in bond funds. Don't buy it. Except perhaps for Treasury bonds and maybe new issues on agency bonds or municipals, the small investor dealing in individual bonds is unlikely to wind up ahead.

REMEMBER

I should add that many buyers of individual bonds easily get lazy about reinvesting and wind up incurring one frequently forgotten cost: the cost of having idle cash. If you collect your semiannual coupon payments and don't spend them, they may sit around in a low-interest money-market account. Many of the clients I've seen show me their existing "bond" portfolios, and I immediately notice wads and wads of cash sitting around earning next to nothing. That doesn't happen with bond funds, where the monthly interest can easily be set up to roll right back into the fund, immediately, earning money without pause.

Debunking myths about individual bonds

Please don't get me wrong. I'm not saying that bond funds are manna from heaven. There are good bond funds and bad. I'm also not saying that individual bonds are bad investments. Sometimes, for some investors, individual bonds can be a wise choice. But do know the pros and cons, and don't fall prey to a number of popular myths.

Dispelling the cost myth

People who defend the trading of individual bonds often say that bond funds are more expensive than investing in individual bonds. Although this statement is often untrue, the expenses associated with bond funds have traditionally been more *visible* than those associated with trading individual bonds.

REMEMBER

Overall, funds tend to be less expensive unless the individual bonds are bought for very large amounts and held till maturity (provided maturity is at least several years away).

Dispelling the predictability myth

Another misconception is that individual bonds are much more predictable than bond funds. After all, you get a steady stream of income, and you know that you're getting your principal back on such-and-such a date. Technically, these things are true. But they're more complicated than they seem.

Say you had all your money in one big, fat bond worth $100,000 with a coupon rate of 5 percent, maturing in 20 years. You'd know that you'd get a check for $2,500 every six months and that, in 20 years, provided the company or municipality issuing the bond is still around, you'd get a final check for $102,500 (your final interest payment, plus your principal returned).

But that's not how things work in the real world. In the real world, investors in individual bonds typically have bonds of varying maturities. As one bond matures, a younger bond takes its place. Except by rare coincidence, the new bond won't have the same maturity period or the same coupon rate. So, the argument that the returns on a portfolio of individual bonds are as predictable as the sunrise is weak.

In addition, consider the effects of inflation. Yes, $100,000 invested in individual bonds today will be returned to you in 10, 20, or however many years, depending on the maturity of the bonds. But what will that money be *worth* in 10 or 20 years? You simply don't know. Because of inflation, it could be worth quite a bit less than the value of $100,000 today. I'm not arguing that inflation wallops the return on individual bonds any more than it wallops the return on bond funds; I'm only arguing that the effect of inflation renders final bond returns kind of mushy, whether we're talking individual bonds or bond funds.

REMEMBER

To look at it another way, individual bond ladders (see Chapter 4) fluctuate — in both interest payments and principal value — just as bond funds do. So, you won't convince me that individual bonds (except perhaps for short-term bonds that aren't as vulnerable to inflation or interest rate fluctuations) are much better than bond funds for reasons of either price or consistency.

Dispelling the interest rate risk avoidance myth

In Chapter 9, I discuss interest rate risk. *Interest rate risk* — the risk that general interest rates may go up, making the value of your existing bonds (paying what are now no longer competitive rates) go down — can really put a damper on the life of a bond investor. That's especially true when interest rates are so low that they can really only move in one direction: up.

Sometimes when people get scared, they get stupid. And stupid is, I'm afraid, the word that comes to mind when I hear the argument — and I've heard it a *lot* lately, even from people who should know better — that buying individual bonds is a way of avoiding interest rate risk.

Here's how the argument goes: Buy an individual bond, hold it until maturity, and you'll be immune from interest rate risk. Let those bond fund buyers suffer from depressed prices. You'll get your principal back, in full, in 20 (or whatever) years. So, the interest rate can go up and down, down and up, and it won't affect you at all!

Um, yeah. Although this argument is technically true, it is, like the predictability argument, more complex than it first seems. Sure, go ahead and buy a bond for $1,000 that pays 3 percent for

20 years. Then let's say that next year, interest rates on similar bonds pop to 6 percent. You, gosh darn it, are going to hold that bond for another 19 years. You aren't going to sell and take a loss like all those nincompoops who bought into bond funds last year, *are you?*

Well, that's your option. But know the cost: For the next 19 years, all things being equal, you'll collect 3 percent on your initial investment. Everyone else, perhaps even those bond fund holders, will be collecting 6 percent a year. Sure, you'll get your $1,000 back eventually. But you're taking a loss in the form of locking in your principal at the lower interest rate. And that loss could be a significant one.

Dispelling the tax myth

This one isn't so much a myth. The reality is that bond mutual funds can incur capital gains tax where individual bonds — until perhaps you sell them — do not. When fund managers sell individual bonds for more than they paid for them, the funds make capital gains that are passed onto the shareholders (if there are no offsetting capital losses). With individual bonds, you often don't incur a capital gains tax unless you yourself sell the bond for a profit — or you buy a bond at a discount to par and you hold it to maturity.

TIP

But although capital gains on stock funds can be very large, capital gains on bond funds generally aren't. Most bonds simply don't appreciate in price the way stocks can. Also, if you're concerned with capital gains on your bond funds, you can always put them into a tax-advantaged retirement account, and your capital gains tax problems disappear. Or, instead of investing in an actively managed bond mutual fund, you can choose a bond index mutual fund or ETF that rarely sees much in the way of capital gains taxes because less trading is involved. Both index investing and putting your bond funds in retirement accounts are strategies that I recommend. I discuss tax-advantaged retirement accounts more in just a few pages. You can find more on ETFs and indexed mutual funds in Chapter 5.

Embracing the precision of single bonds

Neither price nor consistency makes individual bonds much better than bond funds. What *can* sometimes make individual bonds a better option is control. If you absolutely need a certain amount of income, or if you need the return of principal sometime in the next several years, individual bonds can make sense. For example:

- ›› If you're buying a house, and you know that you're going to need $40,000 in cash in 365 days, buying one-year Treasury bills may be a good option for your money.

- ›› If your kid is heading off to college in two years, and you know you'll need $20,000 a year for four years, Treasury bills and bonds may be the ticket.

- ›› If you're comfortably retired and your living expenses are covered by your pension and Social Security, but you need to pay out $500 twice a year for property taxes, it may be wise to put away enough in individual bonds to cover that fixed expense, at least for several years down the road. (Beyond several years, you can't be certain what your property taxes will be.)

- ›› If you're pulling in a sizable paycheck, you find yourself in the upper tax brackets, you live in a high-tax city and state, and your reading of Chapter 3 tells you that investing in triple-tax-free munis makes the most sense, then a ladder of triple-tax-free munis may be your best portfolio tool. (*Triple-tax-free* means free from federal, state, and local taxes.)

- ›› If you're getting seriously on in years, your life expectancy isn't that great, and you suspect that your heirs will inherit your bond portfolio in the next several years, you may want to consider a bevy of individual corporate bonds with death puts (see Chapter 3).

REMEMBER

Individual bonds allow for a precise tailoring of a fixed-income portfolio, with certain potential estate benefits. Quite simply, most people don't need that kind of precision or insurance. That's why the advantages of funds usually outweigh the advantages of single bonds.

Spotting other scenarios when individual bonds may make sense

There may be a few instances where precision in payment isn't your main motivation to buy an individual bond rather than tap into a bond fund. If any of the following scenarios apply to you, individual issues may make sense:

>> **You meet a bond broker extraordinaire.** If you find a bond broker who's so talented in the ways of bond trading that they can do for you what a bond fund manager can do, only better, then I say go for it. Such bond brokers are very rare birds, but maybe after reading Chapter 4, you'll have the prowess to spot one.

>> **You plan to become a bond expert.** If you yourself intend to make such an intense study of bonds that you can serve as your own expert, researching individual bond issues and issuers to the point that you feel you have an edge on the market, then individual bonds are for you. My guess is that because you're reading the words on this page, you, Luke, have a *lot* of studying to do before you become a true fixed-income Jedi warrior.

>> **You have an inside edge.** If you have inside information that allows you to know that a particular bond is worth more than the market thinks it's worth, you may take advantage of it by investing in that bond. Of course, true inside information, such as the information available to directors of a company, is illegal to take advantage of — in stock trading or bond trading. And false insider information — the kind of information available *free* all over the internet — is worth every penny you pay for it!

>> **You plan to spend a lot of time and energy on your portfolio.** You can use certain strategies to juice your returns with individual bonds that you can't use with funds (although a good fund manager may very well follow these strategies). One strategy, called *rolling down the yield curve,* entails holding long-term bonds paying higher interest until they become intermediate- or short-term bonds and then selling them and replacing them with other higher-yielding long-term bonds until they become intermediate- or short-term bonds. Such a strategy takes time, energy, a good head for finance, and strong trading skills.

INTRODUCING FUNDS THAT ACT LIKE INDIVIDUAL BONDS

Any edge that individual bonds may have had over bond funds as far as predictability in getting your money back is quickly losing ground to a new breed of bond fund. For investors who want the diversification of a fund but the knowledge that their principal is coming back to them at a certain date, a lineup of ETFs from iShares and another from Invesco may offer the perfect blend.

Although introduced not all that long ago, the Invesco BulletShares ETFs, such as the Invesco BulletShares 2028 Corporate Bond ETF (BSCS), gives you instant exposure to a bevy of bonds that mature at about the same time. The expense ratio is 0.1 percent, which is quite reasonable. And the predictability of payout is similar to that of a single bond. You can buy BulletShares ETFs that mature in 2028, or sooner, or later. You can also buy high-yield bonds, muni bonds, or emerging-market bonds in ETF form. What happens when all these bonds in a BulletShares ETF mature? The ETF itself "matures," and you wake up one morning to see cash, rather than the ETF, sitting in your brokerage account.

Similarly, iShares has a lineup of defined maturity bond funds called the iBonds series, such as the iShares iBonds December 2030 Term Treasury ETF. The expense ratio is 0.07 percent at the time of writing. All the Treasury bonds in the ETF mature at the end of 2030. iBonds, like BulletShares, come in many varieties. They have different maturity dates and different bonds — Treasurys, corporates, high-yield, munis, and even a few very targeted funds, such as one that invests in corporate bonds ex-financials — that all mature around the same time.

These funds — both iShares's and Invesco's — offer the precision of an individual bond with the diversity of a fund. They're a near-perfect hybrid. I like them, and I use them in my portfolios, where appropriate — most notably when the client needs a certain amount of money on a certain date.

Wondering When It's Time to Buy Bonds

After suggesting a bond portfolio — or any other kind of portfolio — to a new client, I often hear, "But is *now* a good time to invest?"

The answer is *yes*. And most of the people in the investment world would say the same. "An investor that warranted a portfolio with 50 percent bonds ten years ago, still, all things being equal, would warrant a portfolio today with 50 percent bonds," says Matthew Gelfand, PhD, CFA, CFP, executive director of Tricolor Capital Advisors, based in Chevy Chase, Maryland.

Predicting the future of interest rates . . . yeah, right

With stocks, the big concern people have is usually that the market is about to tumble. With bonds, the big concern — especially these days — is that interest rates are going to rise, and any bonds purchased today will wither in value as a result.

But interest rates are almost as unpredictable as the stock market. Yes, the government has more control over interest rates than it does the stock market, but it doesn't have complete control, and the actions it decides to take or not take aren't for you to know.

The "financial experts" on TV are forever predicting which way interest rates are going to move. They seem to be right about half the time. Maybe less. Flipping a coin would serve you just as well as listening to these clowns.

Furthermore, I'd argue that even if you *could* predict interest rates (which you can't), and even if you *did* know that they were going to rise (which you don't), now *still* is a good time to buy bonds.

I'm assuming, of course, that you've done the proper analysis (see Chapter 10), you've decided that more bonds belong in your portfolio, and you have cash in hand. What do you do with it? You have three savings/investing options, really:

>> Keep it in cash.

>> Invest it in equities.

>> Invest it in fixed income.

If you invest in equities (stocks, real estate, commodities), you mess with your overall portfolio structure, making it perhaps too risky. If you keep cash (a savings or money-market account), you earn enough interest to *maybe* keep up with inflation — but after taxes, probably not. In either scenario, you lose.

Now, suppose you choose to go ahead and buy the bonds, and interest rates, as you feared, do rise. That isn't necessarily a bad thing. Yes, your bonds or bond funds — especially those with long maturities — will take a hit. The value of the bonds or the price of the bond-fund shares will sink. In the long run, though, you shouldn't suffer, and you may even benefit from higher interest rates.

After all, every six months with individual bonds, and every month with most bond funds, you get interest payments, and those interest payments may be reinvested. The higher the interest rate climbs, the more money you can make off those reinvestments. Waiting for interest rates to fall — which they may or may not do — just doesn't make sense.

I'll concede that when interest rates are very low, as they are at the time of writing, it makes sense to lean your bond portfolio more toward the short-intermediate side than the long-term side. Yes, you'll get a lesser yield, but you'll take a softer punch when interest rates do rise.

Paying too much attention to the yield curve

Another difficult decision for bond investors putting in fresh money occurs when we see a flat or inverted yield curve, which is rare. The *yield curve* refers to the difference between interest rates on long-term versus short-term bonds. Normally, long-term bonds pay higher rates of interest. If the yield curve is *inverted*, it means the long-term bonds are paying lower rates of interest than shorter-term bonds. That situation doesn't happen often, but it happens. The reasons for the yield curve are many and complex, and they include inflation expectations, feelings about the economy, and foreign demand for U.S. debt.

Whatever the reasons for an inverted yield curve, it hardly makes sense to tie up your money in a long-term bond when a shorter-term bond is paying just as much interest or possibly a slight bit more. Or does it?

Some financial planners would disagree with me on this one, but I'm not averse to investing in longer-term bonds even when the yield curve is slightly inverted. Keep in mind that a large reason you're investing in bonds is to have a cushion if your other investments (such as stocks) take a nosedive. When stocks plunge, money tends to flow — quickly — into investment-grade bonds, especially Treasurys. Initially, the "rush to safety" creates the most demand for short-term bonds, and their prices tend to rise.

Over time, however, a plunge in the stock market often results in the Fed lowering interest rates (in an attempt to kick-start the economy), which lifts bond prices — especially the price of longer maturity bonds. In other words, longer-term Treasurys are your best hedge against a stock market crash. If that hedge is paying no more interest, it may still be worth having it, rather than shorter-term bonds, in your portfolio.

Consider another reason for investing in longer-term bonds, even if they aren't paying what short-term bonds are. What if interest rates drop, regardless of what's going on in the stock market? Sometimes interest rates fall even when the stock market is soaring. If that's the case, once again, you may wish that you were holding long-term bonds, says Chris Genovese, executive vice president of Advisor's Asset Management, a group that offers advice on fixed income to other financial professionals. "If interest rates are falling when your short-term bonds mature, you may be forced to reinvest at a lower rate," he says. "In the context of an entire bond portfolio, having both short-term and long-term bonds, regardless of the yield curve, may be advisable."

The recent yield curve hasn't been inverted, but it has been rather flat. As of mid-2022, longer-term Treasurys are paying pretty darned close to what short-term Treasurys are paying. In both cases, we're seeing crew-cut rates: 2.5 percent for two-year Treasurys, and 2.6 percent for ten-year Treasurys.

TIP

By the time you're reading this chapter, however, who knows? (By the way, if you want to get a quick look at current yield curves, here's the place to do it: www.bloomberg.com/markets/rates-bonds.)

Adhering — or not — to dollar-cost averaging

Instead of throwing all your money into a bond portfolio right away, some people say it makes more sense to buy in slowly over a long period of time. As the argument goes, you spread out your risk that way, buying when the market is high *and* when the market is low. And if you invest equal amounts of money each time, you tend to buy more product (bonds or fund shares) when the market is low, potentially adding to your bottom line. This approach to investing is called *dollar-cost averaging*.

REMEMBER

Dollar-cost averaging makes some sense if you're taking freshly earned money and investing it. If you have an existing pool of cash, however, it simply doesn't. The cash you leave behind will be earning too little for the whole scheme to make sense.

If you have a chunk of money waiting to be invested, and you have an investment plan in place, go for it. Buy those bonds you were planning to buy. There's no reason to wait for just the right moment or to buy in dribs and drabs. (I feel a little differently about stocks, but stocks, by and large, are way more volatile than bonds.)

Choosing Retirement Accounts for Your Bonds

Yesteryear, when corporations and municipalities were still offering *bearer bonds* (bonds that came with a certificate and were registered nowhere, with no one), you didn't have to concern yourself with keeping them in any particular account. You could keep your bearer bonds in your safe, your glove compartment, or your underwear drawer. Today, it's a different matter.

Chances are, you have both a taxable account where you can store your investments and a tax-advantaged account, such as an individual retirement account (IRA), a Roth IRA, a 401(k), or a 529 college savings plan. Think of these as "containers" of sorts, which you fill up with your various investments. In which container do you keep your bonds?

Positioning your investments for minimal taxation

REMEMBER

Say you're in the 28 percent federal tax bracket. You'll pay 28 percent tax (plus state income tax) on any bond interest dividends paid from any bonds held in a taxable account — except for tax-free municipal bonds. Plain and simple, tax-advantaged accounts exist to allow you to escape — or at least postpone — paying income tax on your investment gains. It generally makes the most sense to keep your taxable income-generating investments, such as taxable bonds, in your retirement accounts.

TIP

Here are some other things to keep in mind:

>> Treasury bonds are free from state tax. Therefore, if you have room in your retirement accounts for only one kind of bond, it makes the most sense for it to be corporate bonds.

>> Foreign bonds often require the paying of foreign tax, which usually is reimbursed to you by Uncle Sam, but only if those bonds are kept in a taxable account.

>> Tax-free municipal bonds always belong in your taxable accounts.

Figure 11-1 illustrates where you want to keep your bond holdings.

Keep in retirement account	Keep in either	Keep in taxable account
Corporate bonds	Treasuries	Foreign bonds	Tax-free munis

© John Wiley & Sons, Inc.

FIGURE 11-1: Where your bonds belong.

Factoring in early-withdrawal penalties and such

REMEMBER

Keep in mind that any money withdrawn from an IRA, 401(k), or simplified employee pension (SEP) IRA prior to age 59½, except under certain special circumstances, is subject to a 10 percent penalty. (Income tax must be paid regardless of when you withdraw.) So, you shouldn't put any bonds you're planning to cash out prior to that age into your retirement account.

On the flip side, at age 72, you must start taking minimum required distributions from most retirement accounts. That fact should be figured into your allocation decisions as well. If your required minimum distributions (RMDs) — the amount the IRS requires you to pull from your account each year after age 72 — are substantial, it can mess with your balance of investments.

As I discuss more in Chapter 7, Roth IRAs are different animals. You pay no tax when you withdraw, and you're not required to withdraw at any particular age. The money grows and grows, tax-free, potentially forever.

The Part of Tens

Recognize the ten most common misconceptions about bonds.

Avoid ten mistakes that bond investors often make.

Chapter **12**

Ten Common Misconceptions about Bonds

A bond selling for 100 and paying 5 percent looks like the clearest, most easy-to-understand investment possible. Yet it is, in reality, a much more complex organism. Read through these ten common bond misconceptions, and you'll no doubt see what I'm talking about.

A Bond "Selling for 100" Costs $100

Welcome to the first complexity in bonds: jargon! When a bond broker says that a bond is "selling for 100," it means that the bond is selling not for $100, but (typically) for $1,000. If that same bond were "selling for 95," it would be on the market for $950. If it were "selling for 105," you could buy it for $1,050.

Ready for more jargon? The *par value* or *face value* of a $1,000 bond is $1,000. But the *market value* depends on whether it's selling for 95, 100, 105, or whatever. In addition, that $1,000 face bond may be said to "pay 5 percent," but that doesn't mean you'll get 5 percent on your money. It means you'll get 5 percent on the par value — that is, 5 percent on $1,000, or $50 a year, which may mean a yield of greater or less than 5 percent to you. If you paid 105 for the bond (that's called a *premium*), you'll actually be making less than 5 percent on your money. If you paid 95 for the bond (that's called a *discount*), you'll be making more than 5 percent on your money.

Confused? Turn to Chapter 2.

Buying a Bond at a Discount Is Better Than Paying a Premium

REMEMBER

Discounted bonds sell at a discount for a reason; premium bonds sell at a premium for a reason. Here's the most common reason: Those premium bonds typically have higher coupon rates than prevailing coupon rates. Discount bonds, in contrast, typically have lower coupon rates than prevailing coupon rates. Both in theory and in practice, two bonds with similar credit ratings and similar maturities, all other things being equal, will have similar yields to maturity (the yield that really matters) whether sold at a premium or a discount.

Here's an example: Bond A, issued in 2012, has a coupon rate of 6 percent. Bond B, issued in 2022, has a coupon rate of 4 percent. Everything else about the bonds is the same — same issuer, same maturity date (let's say 2042), same callability. Currently, similar bonds are paying 5 percent. You'd fully expect Bond A to sell at a premium and Bond B to sell at a discount. But in both cases you'd expect their yields to maturity to be roughly 5 percent.

A Bond Paying X% Today Will Pocket You X% Over the Life of the Bond

A bond paying a coupon rate of 5 percent may (if the bond is purchased at a discount) be yielding something higher, like, say, 6 percent. But every six months, as you collect that 6 percent on your money, you'll either spend it or reinvest it. If you reinvest it at an even higher rate of interest (suppose interest rates are going up) — say, 8 percent — then your *total return* on your money, over time, will be higher than both the coupon rate of 5 percent and the current yield of 6 percent. When you're done holding the bond, the price you get for it will also be factored into your total return. That amount, if you hold the bond to maturity, will be the bond's par value. But if you sell the bond before its maturity, you'll get the bond's market value (minus the broker's cut) at the time, which could be higher or lower than the par value.

REMEMBER

In sum, the total return on the money you invest in bonds is often unknowable. Bonds aren't at all as predictable as they seem at first glance — or even second glance!

Rising Interest Rates Are Good (or Bad) for Bondholders

In general, rising interest rates are good for *future* bondholders (who will see higher coupon payments); for those who *presently* own bonds, rising interest rates may not be so good because rising interest rates push bond prices down. (Who wants to buy your bond paying 5 percent when other bonds are suddenly paying 6 percent?)

On the other hand, rising interest rates allow present bondholders to reinvest their money (the coupon payments that arrive twice a year) for a higher return.

REMEMBER

In the end, however, what matters most for bondholders both present and future is the *real* rate of return. The real rate of return is the nominal rate of interest minus the rate of inflation, minus your tax hit. You'd rather get 6 percent on a bond when inflation is running at 2 percent than 10 percent on a bond when inflation is running at 8 percent, especially after taxes, which tax the nominal rate and ignore inflation.

What I'm saying is that there are certainly good times and not-so-good times to be a bondholder, but whether interest rates are falling or rising is only part of the larger picture, and sometimes not even the most important part.

Certain Bonds, Such as Treasurys, Are Completely Safe

Our national government has been spending money like a drunken sailor on payday. But the U.S. government can also print money and raise taxes, so there isn't much chance of Uncle Sam going bankrupt and Treasurys becoming worthless. I can safely say that Treasurys have only a negligible risk of default. That's not to say, however, that Treasurys are completely safe. They're still subject to the other risks that bonds face, such as inflation risk and interest-rate risk.

There's also the risk that some future bevy of government leaders may find the government so much in debt, and the thought of raising taxes or risking inflation so intolerable, that they decide to skip a monthly payment or to pay 90 cents on the dollar to bondholders. Other governments have done this.

Although the United States doesn't seem likely to follow that lead, read Chapter 9 before plunking your entire savings into Treasury bonds.

Bonds Are a Retiree's Best Friend

If you rely on an all-fixed-income portfolio to replace your paycheck, you'd better have an awfully big portfolio, or you'll risk running out of funds. Bonds, unfortunately, have a long-term track record of outpacing inflation by only a modest margin. If you plan on a long retirement, that bit of extra gravy may not be enough to get you through the rest of your life without resorting to an awfully tight budget. The retiree's best friend is a *diversified* portfolio that has stocks (for growth potential), bonds (for stability), and cash (for liquidity), with maybe some real estate and commodities mixed in.

For more information on shaping your post-paycheck portfolio for maximum longevity, see Chapters 6 and 7.

Individual Bonds Are Usually a Better Deal than Bond Funds

Some of the newer exchange-traded funds (ETFs) offer an instant diversified bond portfolio with a total expense ratio of peanuts — or even less than peanuts. These ETFs are excellent ways to invest in bonds. Many other bond funds offer professional management with reasonable expenses and impressive long-term performance records.

Buying individual bonds may be the better route for some investors, but the decision is rarely a slam dunk, especially for those investors with bond portfolios of, say, $400,000 or less. Less than that, and it may be hard to diversify a portfolio of individual bonds. Plus, the markups you pay on your modest buys and sells may be significantly more than you'd pay for a bond fund — especially if you wind up not keeping the bond till maturity. Despite popular myth, individual bonds don't offer up all that much more predictability than do bond funds. More, yes. Much more, no.

Chapter 11 provides greater insight into the question of individual bonds versus bond funds.

Municipal Bonds Are Free from Taxation

Most income from municipal bonds is free from federal income tax. But the income from many municipal bonds is taxed at the local and state level, especially if you buy bonds that were issued outside of your own backyard. If you see a capital gain on the sale of a muni or muni fund, that gain is taxed the same way any other capital gain would be. And some municipal-bond income is subject to the alternative minimum tax (AMT), designed so that those who make six figures and more can't deduct their way out of paying taxes.

Do municipal bonds make sense for you? The tax question is the primary one. Unfortunately, it isn't as straightforward as it looks.

TIP

Don't invest in "tax-free" munis, which generally pay lower rates of interest than do taxable bonds, without having the entire picture. Crunch the numbers. Talk to your tax guru. Always diversify. And read Chapter 3.

A Discount Broker Sells Bonds Cheaper

Often, a discount broker has the best deals on bonds, but sometimes not. That's especially true for new offers on municipal bonds and corporate bonds when a full-service broker may actually be packaging the bond for the public. It always, *always* pays to shop around. And by all means, when buying a corporate bond or an agency or municipal bond, use TRACE so that you know how much the bonds have been trading for. (Read all about TRACE in Chapter 4.)

TIP

When buying Treasurys, don't go to just any broker; either find a broker who charges zero commission, or shop direct on www. treasurydirect.gov.

The Big Risk in Bonds Is the Risk of the Issuer Defaulting

Even in the world of corporate junk bonds, where the risk of default is as real as dirt, I'm still not sure if actual default qualifies as the biggest risk that bondholders take. Maybe sometimes. But investors, in general, focus too much on default risk. A bond can also lose plenty of market value if the issuing company is simply downgraded by one of the major credit rating agencies. Most commonly, however, a bond's principal crashes if interest rates soar. No matter how creditworthy the issuer, a swift rise in interest rates will cause your bond's value, or your bond fund's value, to dip. That's not so much an issue if you hold an individual bond till maturity, but you may be less than thrilled to be holding a bond that's paying 5 percent when all other bonds are paying 8 percent.

Another large risk with bonds, especially if your entire portfolio is made up mostly of bonds, is that the much lower returns can leave you behind. There have been plenty of years in which bond interest, especially after you deduct trading costs and taxes, simply hasn't kept up with inflation.

Chapter **13**

Ten Mistakes That Bond Investors Should Avoid

nvesting in bonds is easy, but investing *well* in bonds is hard. The hard part, in good measure, is that some hungry brokers out there are more than willing to share in your profits. In addition, bonds, by their very nature, can be more complicated than they appear. It's easy to get bamboozled, easy to make dumb mistakes. But if you watch out carefully for the following ten do's and don'ts, you'll be far ahead of the game.

Allowing the Broker to Churn You

Bond brokers generally make their money when you buy and sell bonds. They rarely make anything while the bonds are simply sitting in your account, collecting interest. Largely for that reason, your broker may find several reasons to call you with special deals. Perhaps it will be to tell you that the bond issue you bought last year is — oops! — no longer worth holding.

In truth, a bond you bought last year is almost always still worth holding. The major rating agencies downgraded the company? You probably already lost whatever money you're likely to lose; selling the bond now will result in your locking in that loss. Why not hold the bond till maturity if that was your original plan? Interest rates have risen or fallen? Yeah, so? Don't they always? Bond B has a more favorable tax status than Bond A? Well, why weren't you told that when you bought Bond A?

REMEMBER

I won't say that you'll *never* encounter a good reason to swap one bond for another. But you're almost always going to be better off as a buy-and-hold-till-maturity investor than you are riding the bond merry-go-round. If your broker calls with reasons to buy or sell, ask lots of questions, and make sure you get clear answers as to why it's to *your* benefit, not theirs, to start trading.

Not Taking Advantage of TRACE

Buying and selling bonds is more transparent than ever before. That means lots of information is available if you know where to look. Until just a few years ago, bond brokers could charge you any kind of markup they wanted to, and you'd have no idea what that markup was. Now, with a system called the Trade Reporting and Compliance Engine (TRACE), you can go online and, often within moments, find out how much your broker paid for the bonds you're now being offered. If you don't have luck doing that, you can find out how much similar bonds are selling for. Conversely, if your broker sells some bonds for you, you can find out how much they were sold for. You have a right to know.

At the same time you're checking TRACE to see what the broker is looking to score, you can compare the yield on a prospective bond purchase with the yields of comparable bonds. In fact, the better yield on comparable bonds often results from a lesser markup by the broker. The two are closely intertwined.

See Chapter 4 for complete instructions on checking a bond's price history and the yield on comparable bonds.

Choosing a Bond Fund Based on Short-Term Performance

A bond fund's performance figures, especially going back for any period of less than, say, three years, can often look impressive, but they may not mean squat. In most cases, a fund's performance, especially over such a short time period, has more to do with the kind of bond fund it is than with any managerial prowess. If, for example, high-yield bonds have had a great year, most high-yield bond funds — even the lousy ones — will see impressive performance. If foreign bonds have had a great year, foreign-bond funds will rally as a group. If interest rates have recently taken a nosedive, *all* bond funds will likely look good.

REMEMBER

What matters most isn't raw performance but performance in relation to other similar funds and performance over the long haul — five or six years and beyond. Turn to Chapter 5 for more tips on choosing the best bond fund(s) for your portfolio.

Not Looking Closely Enough at a Bond Fund's Expenses

Bonds historically haven't returned enough to warrant very high management expense ratios on bond funds. But that certainly hasn't stopped some bond fund managers from slapping on high fees. If you look at the performance of bond funds in the long run, the least expensive funds typically do the best.

REMEMBER

Don't pay a lot for a bond fund. You don't need to. The recent advent of exchange-traded funds (ETFs) has brought down fund fees dramatically.

Going through a Broker to Buy Treasurys

TIP

Through the U.S. government's own website — www.treasurydirect.gov — you can buy any and all kinds of Treasury bonds without paying any markup or fees whatsoever. You don't need a broker. The website is easy to navigate, and everything (including the bond holding itself) is electronic.

Beware also of active bond funds that combine Treasurys with corporate bonds. You certainly don't need active management when it comes to investing in U.S. government securities, so why pay a management fee for that part of your bond portfolio? (See Chapter 3 for more on investing in Treasury bonds.)

Counting Too Much on High-Yield Bonds

High-yield (or *junk*) bonds look sweet. Historically, they offer higher returns than other bonds. But the return on high-yield bonds is still much less than the return you can expect on stocks. It may not be worth the added risk of getting an extra couple of percentage points to hold high-yield bonds.

WARNING

The main role of bonds in a portfolio is to provide ballast. That's not to say that the interest payments from bonds aren't important — they certainly are. But, above all, bonds should be there for you if your other investments, including stocks, have a bad year or few years. Unfortunately, junk bonds don't provide that ballast. When the economy sours and stocks sink, junk bonds typically sink right along with all your other investments. Investment-grade bonds, such as Treasurys, agency bonds, most munis, and high-quality corporates, usually hold their own and may even rise in value when the going gets rough.

Paying Too Much Attention to the Yield Curve

At times, short-term bonds, even money-market funds (built on very short-term debt instruments), yield as much as intermediate or long-term bonds. During these times, the yield curve is said to be *flat*. Flatness in the yield curve entices many people to move their money from long-term to short-term bonds. In a way, it makes perfect sense. Why tie up your money and take the greater risk that comes with long-term bonds if you aren't getting compensated for it?

But I'd argue that longer-term bonds still belong in your portfolio, even when the yield curve is flat — heck, even when the yield curve becomes *inverted* (meaning short-term bonds yield more than long-term bonds), as happens on rare occasion. Note that the main point of bonds in your portfolio isn't to provide kick-ass returns. That's the job of stocks. The main job of bonds is to provide your portfolio some lift when most of your holdings are sagging. If the economy hits the skids (hint: an inverted yield curve can be a sign of impending recession) and stocks suddenly plummet, chances are good that a lot of money will be funneled into long-term, high-quality bonds. Interest rates will drop; long-term, investment-grade bonds will soar; and you'll wish you were there.

Conversely, when the yield curve is *steep*, and long-term bonds are yielding much more than short-term bonds, you may be tempted to load up on 20-year bonds. Resist. If interest rates pop, your bonds will be hurt badly. It pays to have a well-diversified bond portfolio, regardless of market conditions.

Buying Bonds That Are Too Complicated

Floating-rate bonds, reverse convertible bonds, catastrophe bonds, leveraged and inverse bond exchange-traded notes. . . . Many bonds and bond by-products promise far more than simple interest. But in the end, many (if not most) investors who get involved wind up disappointed. Or crippled.

Keep it simple. Really. There's no such thing as a free lunch, and any bond or bond package that promises to pay you more than plain-vanilla bonds is doing so for a reason. Some risk is involved that you may not see unless you squint really hard — or until that risk pummels your savings.

Ignoring Inflation and Taxation

If you're making 5 percent on your bonds, and you're losing 3 percent to inflation, you're about 2 percent ahead of the game — for a brief moment. But you'll likely be taxed on the 5 percent.

Inflation and taxation can eat seriously into your bond interest payments. That's no reason to skip bond investing. But when doing any kind of projections, counting your bond returns but ignoring inflation and taxation is like visiting Nome, Alaska, in winter and trying to ignore the snow.

REMEMBER

Make sure to do the math, and invest at least partially in tax-free munis if it makes the most sense. And if you have room in your tax-advantaged individual retirement account (IRA) or 401(k), that's usually a good place to stash away your taxable bonds. Unless you have to, don't put munis in an IRA, and don't put taxable bonds in your regular brokerage account.

Relying Too Heavily on Bonds in Retirement

If this were a chapter on the ten most common mistakes that *stock* investors make, I'd advise readers to invest in bonds as well as stocks. But this is a chapter on the ten most common mistakes that *bond* investors make, so I must caution that an all-bond portfolio rarely, if ever, makes sense.

REMEMBER

Stocks offer a greater potential for long-term return and a better chance of staying ahead of inflation than bonds do. They also tend to move in different cycles than bonds, providing delicious diversification. They help dampen volatility and smooth out a portfolio's long-term returns, thereby potentially boosting long-term returns. Stocks and bonds complement each other like spaghetti and sauce.

Index

National Association of Personal Financial Advisors (NAPFA), 94

Saturna, 82

Treasury website, 55

online savings accounts, 135

online trading, 95–98
  buying, 96–97
  overview, 95–96
  selling, 98

open market operations, 39

P

paper bonds, 56

par value, 8, 28, 31–32

P/E ratio, 151

PEFCO (Private Export Funding Corporation), 67

PIMCO, 71

pool of mortgages, 70–71

portfolios, 12–14, 161–238
  annuities, 203–204
  balancing, 193–199
    assessing time frame, 195
    case studies of, 197–199
    estimating allocation, 195
    maximizing return, 194
    minimizing volatility, 193–194
    rules for, 196
  bond funds, 224–226
    actively managed funds, 225–226
    diversifying away risks, 224
    ease of investing with, 224–225
    index funds, 225–226
    minimizing costs, 226
  bonds
    finding perfect fit, 213–219
    general discussion of, 201
  choosing retirement accounts, 236–238

early-withdrawal penalties, 237–238

for minimal taxation, 237

commodities and real estate, 204–205

diversification, 13–14, 208–213
  complication vs., 211–213
  managerial risk, 210–211
  by maturity, 208
  by risk-and-return potential, 210
  by type of issuer, 209–210

estimating target, 131

finding frugal funds, 222

freedom portfolio, 130

fundamentals of
  investment options, 169–170
  objectives, 162–165
  principles of, 170–174
  savings options, 166–168

individual bonds, 227–231
  debunking myths about, 227–229
  scenarios for, 229–231

rebalancing, 141–146, 205–208
  buying low and selling high, 143–145
  overview, 141–143, 205–207
  rolling bond interest back in, 145–146
  scheduling, 207–208
  variables, 146

returns, 13–14, 184–188
  fixed-income investments, 184–185
  historical, 185–186
  investing in bonds despite, 186–187

risks, 175–184
  default risk, 181–182
  defined, 176
  downgrades, 182
  fear-of-missing-out (FOMO) risk, 183–184

About the Author

Russell Wild is a financial advisor and principal of Global Portfolios, a fee-only investment advisory firm based in Philadelphia. He calls his firm Global Portfolios to reflect his ardent belief in international diversification — using mostly low-cost index funds to build well-diversified, tax-efficient portfolios.

In addition to the fun he has with his financial calculator, Wild is an accomplished writer who helps readers understand and make wise choices about their money. His articles have appeared in many national publications, and he is the author or coauthor of two dozen nonfiction books, including other *For Dummies* titles in addition to this one: *Exchange-Traded Funds For Dummies, Index Investing For Dummies,* and *Bond Investing For Dummies.* No stranger to the mass media, Wild has shared his wit and wisdom on such television shows as *The Oprah Winfrey Show, The View, CBS Mornings,* and *Good Day New York,* as well as in hundreds of radio interviews.

Wild holds a master of business administration (MBA) degree with a concentration in finance from Arizona State University's Thunderbird School of Global Management; a bachelor of science (BS) degree in business/economics magna cum laude from American University in Washington, D.C.; and a graduate certificate in personal financial planning from Moravian College in Bethlehem, Pennsylvania. A member of the National Association of Personal Financial Advisors (NAPFA) since 2002, Wild is also a longtime member and past president of the American Society of Journalists and Authors (ASJA).

Having grown up on Long Island, Wild now lives in Philadelphia but spends considerable time in southern Vermont. His website is www.russellwild.com.

Dedication

To my financial planning clients of the past 20 years — your trust means a lot.

Author's Acknowledgments

This being my latest in a number of *For Dummies* books, I'd like to thank once again all the good people at Wiley for, well, being good people. The production process runs like a well-oiled machine, and the editors are always a delight.

I'm indebted to a good number of my financial planning colleagues for generously sharing their experience and knowledge. They're mentioned by name throughout the pages of this book. I want to thank the folks of the U.S. Treasury, the Financial Industry Regulatory Authority, and the U.S. Securities and Exchange Commission for their very helpful assistance. And I'd like to give my applause to the number crunchers and analysts at Morningstar for their generous sharing of data. Big thanks, too, to Vanguard for providing important data. I appreciate your help, one and all.

Thanks to my literary agent, Marilyn Allen, who has handled the business end of my publishing career for longer than I can remember. And special thanks to a very special person — my beloved daughter, Addie.

Publisher's Acknowledgments

Senior Acquisitions Editor:
Tracy Boggier

Senior Managing Editor:
Kristie Pyles

Compilation Editor:
Georgette Beatty

Editor: Elizabeth Kuball

Production Editor: Pradesh Kumar

Cover Design: Wiley

Cover Images:

Frame: © aleksandarvelasevic/
Getty Images

Paper texture: © Dmitr1ch/
Getty Images

Inset: © 13ree_design/
Adobe Stock

PERSONAL ENRICHMENT

Staying Sharp
9781119187790
USA $26.00
CAN $31.99
UK £19.99

Facebook
9781119179030
USA $21.99
CAN $25.99
UK £16.99

Guitar
9781119293354
USA $24.99
CAN $29.99
UK £17.99

Investing
9781119293347
USA $22.99
CAN $27.99
UK £16.99

Beekeeping
9781119310068
USA $22.99
CAN $27.99
UK £16.99

Digital Photography
9781119235606
USA $24.99
CAN $29.99
UK £17.99

Meditation
9781119251163
USA $24.99
CAN $29.99
UK £17.99

Pregnancy
9781119235491
USA $26.99
CAN $31.99
UK £19.99

Samsung Galaxy S7
9781119279952
USA $24.99
CAN $29.99
UK £17.99

iPhone
9781119283133
USA $24.99
CAN $29.99
UK £17.99

Crocheting
9781119287117
USA $24.99
CAN $29.99
UK £16.99

Nutrition
9781119130246
USA $22.99
CAN $27.99
UK £16.99

PROFESSIONAL DEVELOPMENT

Windows 10
9781119311041
USA $24.99
CAN $29.99
UK £17.99

AutoCAD
9781119255796
USA $39.99
CAN $47.99
UK £27.99

Excel 2016
9781119293439
USA $26.99
CAN $31.99
UK £19.99

QuickBooks 2017
9781119281467
USA $26.99
CAN $31.99
UK £19.99

macOS Sierra
9781119280651
USA $29.99
CAN $35.99
UK £21.99

LinkedIn
9781119251132
USA $24.99
CAN $29.99
UK £17.99

Windows
9781119310
USA $34.00
CAN $41.99
UK £24.99

SharePoint 2016
9781119181705
USA $29.99
CAN $35.99
UK £21.99

Fundamental Analysis
9781119263593
USA $26.99
CAN $31.99
UK £19.99

Networking
9781119257769
USA $29.99
CAN $35.99
UK £21.99

Office 2016
9781119293477
USA $26.99
CAN $31.99
UK £19.99

Office 365
9781119265313
USA $24.99
CAN $29.99
UK £17.99

Salesforce.com
9781119239314
USA $29.99
CAN $35.99
UK £21.99

Coding
9781119293
USA $29.9
CAN $35.9
UK £21.99

dummies.com

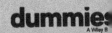